Englisch für berufliche Schulen

2nd edition

Do it!

W0382334

von
Steve Williams

unter Mitarbeit der Verlagsredaktion

Cornelsen

Do it!

Englisch für berufliche Schulen
2nd edition

Verfasser:	Steve Williams, Corio Bay Media, Melbourne
Beraterinnen:	Anne-Marie Basgier, Tübingen; Julia Gieger, Alzey; Beatrix Verheyen, Kevelaer
Projektleitung:	Andreas Goebel
Verlagsredaktion:	Kari-ann Warnakulasuriya
Außenredaktion:	Joanne Popp, editing etc.
Redaktionelle Mitarbeit:	Oliver Busch (Wörterverzeichnisse), Megan Hadgraft, Louise Turner
Layout und technische Umsetzung:	zweiband.media, Berlin
Umschlaggestaltung:	Ungermeyer – grafische Angelegenheiten, Berlin
Titelfoto:	Shutterstock / FS Stock
Illustrationen:	D'Avila Illustration Agency

Erhältlich sind auch:

Schülerbuch – Lehrerfassung mit Lösungen, Audio-CD und Zusatzmaterialien online ISBN 978-3-06-452180-3

www.cornelsen.de

Soweit in diesem Lehrwerk Personen fotografisch abgebildet sind und ihnen von der Redaktion fiktive Namen, Berufe, Dialoge und Ähnliches zugeordnet oder diese Personen in bestimmte Kontexte gesetzt werden, dienen diese Zuordnungen und Darstellungen ausschließlich der Veranschaulichung und dem besseren Verständnis des Inhalts.

1. Auflage, 1. Druck 2020

Alle Drucke dieser Auflage sind inhaltlich unverändert und können im Unterricht nebeneinander verwendet werden.

Druck und Bindung: Mohn Media Mohndruck, Gütersloh

ISBN 978-3-06-450949-8 (Schülerbuch)
ISBN 978-3-06-452244-2 (E-Book)

PEFC
PEFC/04-31-1033

PEFC zertifiziert
Dieses Produkt stammt aus nachhaltig bewirtschafteten Wäldern und kontrollierten Quellen.
www.pefc.de

Contents

Unit	Title/Topics	Working towards work	Skills practice	Project	Grammar	Page
1	**Getting to know you** **A** Small talk **B** Why English?	Telephoning	Telephoning	Introducing me: Social media profile	simple present	5
2	**My life** **A** The story of our lives **B** School and work experience	CVs	Reading	Milestones: Timeline	simple past	15
3	**Me and my community** **A** What's important to you? **B** A training session	Trouble at work	Listening	Cultures in my community: Role play	imperative, *must/ have to*	25
4	**Where I live** **A** It's a big country … **B** Welcome to Melbourne!	Describing workplaces	Writing an opinion	Where we live: Social media information page	*there is / there are, some/any*	35
5	**The things we do** **A** Time thieves! **B** How to …	Describing jobs	Mediation	'How-to' video	present progressive	45
6	**'At work'** **A** Just a job? **B** An ethical employer	Workplaces and vocational training	Reading	Job skills game	modal verbs	55
7	**Plans for the future** **A** Career plans **B** Unexpected career paths	Writing letters/ emails	Managing situations	Vision board	*will* future	65
8	**First steps** **A** Getting ready **B** Job ads	Interviews	Writing a composition	Do it! quiz	present perfect	75
	Video exercises					85
	Pairwork files					89
	Differentiation files					93
	Chronologische Wortliste					101
	Alphabetische Wortliste					129
	Irregular verbs					142

Auf einen Blick

Do it! 2nd edition ist die vollständige Neubearbeitung des bewährten Lehrwerks und eignet sich besonders für den Unterricht im Berufsgrundbildungsjahr, in berufsvorbereitenden Bildungsgängen sowie im ersten Jahr der Berufsfachschule. Es enthält Materialien auf Stufe A1-A2 des Gemeinsamen europäischen Referenzrahmens.

So finden Sie sich im Buch zurecht:

Warm up: Jede Unit beginnt mit einer Einstiegsseite, die kommunikativ in das Thema einführt.

Parts: Auf diesen Doppelseiten werden lebensnahe Inhalte und Themen mit interessanten Texten, abwechslungsreichen Aufgaben und vielen Sprechanlässen behandelt. Eine große Vielfalt an Differenzierungsaufgaben, die mit diesem Symbol ☆ markiert sind und die Sie im Anhang finden, fördern dabei das individualisierte Lernen.

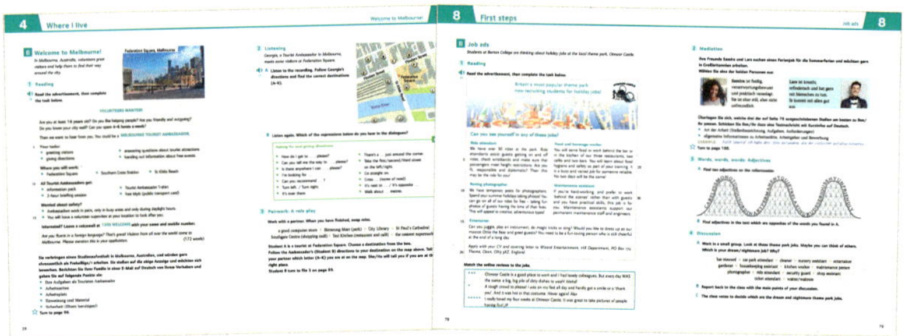

Working towards work: Diese Doppelseite entwickelt ein tieferes Verständnis des englischen Sprachgebrauchs im beruflichen Kontext.

Skills practice: Hier wird die Arbeit an verschiedenen Fertigkeiten explizit geübt und vertieft.

Project: Am Ende einer jeden Unit steht ein handlungsorientiertes Projekt; hier soll mit den erworbenen sprachlichen Fertigkeiten ein haptisches Produkt erstellt werden. Außerdem kann man mit Hilfe des *Snapshot*-Kästchens über das Gelernte selbst reflektieren.

Videos: Kurze Videos beleuchten einzelne Aspekte der Units aus einem anderen Blickwinkel. Übungen dazu sind im Anhang zu finden.

Anhang: Außerdem finden Sie *Partner files*, *Differentiation files* und Wörterverzeichnisse.

Die Symbole 🔊 und ▶ verweisen auf die Audio- und Videomaterialien, die Sie in der Lehrerfassung finden. Die Übungen zu den Videos befinden sich im Anhang.

Lehrerfassung: Die praktische Lehrerfassung des Buches bietet Lösungen direkt auf der Seite und zeigt neue Vokabeln an. Außerdem gibt es viele nützliche Zusatzmaterialien wie Kopiervorlagen und Differenzierungsblätter, die per Webcode abrufbar sind.

Viel Spaß beim Lernen und gutes Gelingen wünschen Ihnen Autor und Verlag!

Getting to know you 1

Warm-up: All about me

A Write notes about yourself:

- a colour that you like
- a drink that you hate
- a film or series that you love
- a sport that you don't like

beige black blue
brown green grey
maroon orange pink
purple red white yellow

Likes and dislikes L

- I love …
- I like …
- I don't mind …
- I don't like …
- I hate … / I can't stand …

B Speed chat: You have <u>two</u> minutes with each partner.
Find people who have the same likes and dislikes as you.
Make notes and write down their names.

Like/Dislike	Name
I love 'Joker'	*Annika*

Agreeing and disagreeing L

So do I!
Me too!
Really? I don't. I …

I hate ...

Really? I don't.

I love ...

Me too!

Great! What's your name?

C Tell the class what you found out.

EXAMPLE:

Selim and I (both) hate the colour blue.

Annika and I (both) love the film 'Joker'.

1 Getting to know you

A Small talk

It is Friday afternoon and the end of the first week of term at Barton College. Two new students, Lisandra and Mo, are at the 'Meet and Greet' session.

1 Before you read

A Decide whether these hints are things you should do or things you should not do when you make small talk.

Get it right: SMALL TALK

- Ask general, 'safe' questions.
- Ask personal questions.
- Give a little information about yourself.
- Introduce yourself.
- Just listen.
- Remember what the person said.
- Start an argument.
- Talk about yourself a lot.

B Compare your answers with a partner.

2 Reading

2 **Read the dialogue, then answer the questions below.**

Lisandra: Hi!
Mo: Hi, how are you?
Lisandra: I'm fine, thanks. What about you?
Mo: Great, thanks … Do I know you from class? I'm Mo, by the way.
Lisandra: Hi, I'm Lisandra. Yes, you're in my maths class, aren't you?
Mo: That's right … Lisa.
Lisandra: Lisandra.
Mo: Yes, that's – that's an unusual name … is it Danish?
Lisandra: No, Estonian. It's a very common name in my country.
Mo: Cool … Do you like coffee?
Lisandra: Yes. What about you?
Mo: Yes, I do. Actually, do you want a coffee now?
Lisandra: Sure, why not?
Mo: Oh, here's my friend Jack … Hi, Jack. This is Lizzy, from Finland.

Lisandra: Err … actually my name is Lisandra, and I'm from Estonia. Hi, Jack, pleased to meet you.
Jack: Hi, Lisandra, nice to meet you too.
Mo: Liz and I are just going for a coffee …
Lisandra: Actually, I need to go to my, err … study group now. Sorry, Mo!
Mo: Oh. Bye.
Lisandra: Bye, guys!
Jack: Nice girl … Are you okay, Mo?
Mo: Sure …

1 Is Mo good at small talk? How do you know? (Tip: look at task 1A again.)
2 Why does Lisandra change her mind about going for a coffee?

3 Pairwork: A role play

Use the role cards to make small talk. Partner A go to file 1 on page 89, partner B go to file 4 on page 90, partner C go to file 8 on page 91, partner D go to file 10 on page 92. When you have finished, swap partners.

G

The simple present

Das *simple present* wird für allgemeingültige Aussagen und regelmäßig wiederkehrende Handlungen verwendet.

to like (mögen)

Aussage	Frage	Verneinung
I/you/we/they like	*What* ***do*** *I/you/we/they like?*	*I/you/we/they* ***don't*** *like*
*he/she/it like****s***	*What* ***does*** *he/she/it like?*	*he/she/it* ***doesn't*** *like*

to be (sein) → Unregelmäßige Verben, S. 142

Aussage	Frage	Verneinung
I ***am/'m***	*What* ***am*** *I?*	*I'****m*** *not*
he/she/it ***is***	*What* ***is*** *he/she/it?*	*he/she/it* ***isn't***
we/you/they ***are***	*What* ***are*** *we/you/they?*	*we/you/they* ***aren't***

4 Practice: Simple present

A **Check it out!** **Suchen Sie folgende Verbformen im Dialog auf Seite 6:**

1 drei Kurzformen von *to be*
2 zwei weitere Verben in der ich-Form
3 drei Fragen mit *do*

B **Complete this summary of the text with verbs from the box. Put them into the correct form.**

be ▪ know ▪ like ▪ meet ▪ remember ▪ want ▪ be

1 Mo and Lisandra ___ at the 'Meet and Greet' session.
2 Mo ___ Lisandra because they ___ in the same class.
3 They both ___ coffee.
4 Mo ___ to have coffee with Lisandra.
5 Unfortunately, Mo ___ bad at small talk.
6 Lisandra suddenly ___ her study group.

☆ **Turn to page 93.**

5 'Fake news'

A **Write three sentences about yourself in the simple present:**

- two true sentences
- one false sentence

☆ **Turn to page 93.**

B **Read your sentences out to the class. Can the class guess which sentence is 'fake news'?**

B Why English?

1 Reading

A Before you read Anja's blog post, make a list of words that are the same in German and English. Compare your lists in class. Who has found the most words?

– Anja's English –

Hi, how's it going? Welcome to my English blog! My name's Anja, I'm German and Tunisian and I learn English at college. It's hard ☹ so I hope that writing a blog will make it easier and more fun.

Did you know that English **isn't** the most spoken language in the world? That's Mandarin Chinese. Still, English is the official language of 53 countries. About 400 million people around the world speak it as their first language. That's a lot of people!
Hmm ... but I don't know any native English speakers, that's too bad! ☺
Luckily, English has other uses! It's the most common **second** language in the world. So, if you want to speak to someone from another country, English is probably the language you share. When I go on holiday to Italy or Greece with my family, I can usually find someone who speaks English. That's useful, because I don't speak Italian or Greek!
English is also the language of the internet. Around 600 million people use the internet every day, and about half of the world's most popular websites are in English. So English is very useful when I go online.
When I finish college, I want to work for a big international company. Many of those companies expect their employees to speak English – even in Germany. So it's sensible to learn English in order to get a good job. It's the language of international business.
Because English is so widely spoken, there are English words in many other languages, for example 'small talk' in German, so learning English is easier than learning Chinese.
Are you learning English? Are you a native English speaker? Then please say hi and leave a comment. ☺
#learningenglish #worldlanguage

(284 words)

B Read the blog and write six more hashtags for Anja's blog.

☆ **Turn to page 93.**

C **Decide whether these statements are true or false. Correct the false statements.**

1 Anja finds English difficult to learn.
2 She knows lots of native speakers of English.
3 She speaks English on holiday in the UK and Ireland.
4 Big companies in Germany want English speakers.

Video 1

Watch the video and look at page 85 for more information about the English-speaking world.

2 Discussion

A **Discuss these questions with a partner. Make notes about your discussion and report back to the class when you have finished.**

- What do you use English for now?
- What about when you leave school?
- Where do you see English words in daily life?

B **Use your notes to write a short comment on Anja's blog post.**
☆ **Turn to page 93.**

3 Words, words, words: Acrostics

A **Complete the acrostic *(Akrostichon)* with more English words from Anja's blog.**

B **Make your own acrostic using one of the ideas below or your own ideas. You can use any English words that you know.**

E	*asier*	*leichter*
N		*Muttersprachler*
G		*global*
L		*Sprache*
I		*international*
S		*vernünftig*
H		*Urlaub*

LANGUAGE ▪ SCHOOL ▪ HOLIDAY ▪ ONLINE

C **Are there any words in your acrostics which are the same in English and German? Underline them in blue.**

D **Are there any false friends? Underline them in red.**

! **False friends – falsche Freunde**

Wörter, die im Deutschen (fast) dieselbe Form wie im Englischen haben, aber unterschiedliche Bedeutungen besitzen, nennt man *false friends*.

Wie lautet die korrekte deutsche Übersetzung für folgende englischen Wörter: handy ▪ sensible ▪ gift ▪ also

C Can I take a message?

1 Listening: Taking a message

Laura is a new apprentice at Ehlers garage. Mr Ehlers asks her to answer the phone while he goes out. A few minutes later, the phone rings and Laura answers it.

4 **Listen to the recording, then complete the tasks below.**

Hörverstehen

Bevor Sie sich den Dialog anhören,
- sehen Sie sich das Foto genau an und
- lesen Sie sich die Aufgabe aufmerksam durch.

So bekommen Sie eine erste Vorstellung davon, worum es in dem Hörtext geht.

A Which of these expressions do you hear?

1 A How can I help you?
  B May I help you?
2 A I'd like to speak to …, please.
  B Can you put me through to …, please?
3 A I'm sorry, … isn't answering his phone.
  B I'm sorry, … isn't here at the moment.
4 A Can I take a message?
  B Can I pass on a message?
5 A Can you spell that for me, please?
  B How do you spell that, please?
6 A Can you let him know …?
  B Please ask him to call me back.
7 A I'll tell him.
  B I'll pass that message on.

B Listen again and make notes in German explaining:

1 Weshalb ist Herr Ehlers telefonisch nicht erreichbar?
2 Wie heißt die Anruferin?
3 Was hat Herr Ehlers zu Hause vergessen?

2 Spelling

A Match the phonetics below to the right cities. The alphabet on page 128 will help you.

1 Berlin	a belˈfɑːst
2 Brighton	b bɜːˈlɪn
3 Belfast	c ˈberɪk
4 Bristol	d ˈbrædfəd
5 Bradford	e ˈbrɪstl
6 Berwick	f ˈbraɪtn

5 **B Listen to the recording and write down the names.**

3 Telephone language

Put the missing parts of the conversation 1–8 in the right places.

A: Guten Morgen/Tag, *(Firmenname)*. Mein Name ist *(Ihr Name)*, wie kann ich Ihnen helfen?
B: EXAMPLE: 3
A: Yes, I do. How can I help you?
B: ___
A: I'm sorry, Ms Schmidt isn't here at the moment. Can I take a message?
B: ___
A: May I have your name, please?
B: ___
A: Can you spell that for me, please?
B: ___
A: *(Wiederholt den Namen der Anruferin / des Anrufers)*.
B: ___
A: What message should I pass on to Ms Schmidt?
B: ___
A: Yes, of course. I'll pass that message on, Ms/ Mr *(Nachname der Anfruferin / des Anrufers)*.
B: ___
A: Goodbye!

1 Can you let her know that her order has arrived, please?
2 Can you put me through to Ms Schmidt, please?
3 I'm sorry, I don't speak German. Do you speak English?
4 It's *(Ihr Name)*.
5 Of course, *(Buchstabieren Sie Ihren Namen)*.
6 Thank you. Bye!
7 That's right.
8 Yes, please.

4 Conversation: Answering the phone

Work with a partner. Use the diagram to practise answering the phone. When you have finished, swap roles.

A: answering	B: calling
📞 *(Melden Sie sich auf Deutsch.)* →	English?
✓ ? →	Mr Jones?
✗ ☹ … ✎ ? →	✓ Can you let him know that *(your message)*?
✓ Name ? →	It's *(your name)*.
✎ abcdefghi … ? →	? A–B–C–D–E–F–G–H–I
A–B–C–D–E–F–G–H–I ? →	✓ / ✗ *(Korrektur falls nötig)*
✉ → Mr Jones. →	☺ ✋
✋	

☆ **Turn to page 94.**

Skills practice: Telephoning

In dieser Übung geht es darum, ein alltägliches Telefongespräch mit einem/r englischen Muttersprachler/in zu führen, um z.B. eine Buchung vorzunehmen, zu stornieren oder zu bestätigen. Bei den Aufgaben sind die vorgegebenen Antworten den entsprechenden Lücken zuzuordnen.

Get it right: *Wie löse ich eine 'Telephoning'-Aufgabe?*

- Lesen Sie sich die Situationsbeschreibung aufmerksam durch. Worum geht es?
- Überfliegen Sie den Dialog, um eine Vorstellung vom Gesprächsablauf zu bekommen (= Grobverständnis).
- Gehen Sie nun den Dialog Zeile für Zeile durch. Finden Sie für jede Lücke (1–5) die passende Äußerung (A–G).
- Achtung: Unter den Äußerungen A–G ist jeweils eine, die nicht passt!
- Wenn Sie glauben, die Aufgabe vollständig gelöst zu haben, lesen Sie sich Ihre Lösung Zeile für Zeile durch. Ergibt die Abfolge der Äußerungen einen Sinn?

A A change of plan

Laura Meyer and her boyfriend Peter want to stay in Ireland for a short holiday, but they have to change their plans. Laura phones the B&B.

Find the responses A–G that fit the gaps 1–5 to complete the dialogue. One response doesn't fit.

Alice: Wicklow House, Alice O'Connell speaking.
EXAMPLE: (0) **D**
Alice: Hello, Ms Meyer. How can I help you?
Laura: (1)
Alice: That's right! I remember now. You're staying with us from 1st to 5th October.
Laura: (2)
Alice: Oh dear! What's the problem?
Laura: (3)
Alice: Oh, no! So, do you want to cancel the booking?
Laura: (4)
Alice: Yes, that's fine. I can easily change the booking for you.
Laura: (5)
Alice: You're welcome. Have a lovely day.
Laura: Thank you, Ms O'Connell. Have a nice day, too! Bye!

A That's right. We have a booking for a double room. We have a small problem.
B Thank you very much!
C No, we don't want to do that. Can we have the room from 2nd October, please?
D Hello, Ms O'Connell. It's Laura Meyer here.
E I'm sorry about the change. I hope it isn't a problem.
F My boyfriend Peter and I have a booking with you.
G We can't come on 1st October. Peter has to work that day.

B An appointment at the doctor's surgery

While Laura and Peter are in Ireland, Peter feels ill and needs to see a doctor. Alice O'Connell gives him the phone number of the local doctor's surgery.

Find the responses A–G that fit the gaps 1–5 to complete the dialogue. One response doesn't fit.

Brendan: Oldbridge Family Clinic, this is Brendan.
EXAMPLE: (0) **F**
Brendan Yes, of course. Do you need an appointment today?
Peter: (1)
Brendan: Let me look. … This afternoon at 3:30 p.m. with Dr Jones?
Peter: (2)
Brendan: Can I have your full name, please?
Peter: (3)
Brendan: Thanks, Mr Weber. Now, what's your address, please?
Peter: (4)
Brendan: No, thanks. Please come to the surgery ten minutes before your appointment.
Peter: (5)
Brendan: You're welcome. We'll see you at 3:20 p.m. this afternoon, then. Goodbye!
Peter: Thank you. Goodbye!

A It's Peter Weber, W-E-B-E-R.
B Yes, please. If that's possible. I'm not feeling well.
C I feel sick and my head hurts.
D I'm staying at Wicklow House B&B. Do you want my home address?
E Okay, I've got that. Thank you very much for your help.
F Hello, my name is Peter Weber. Can I make an appointment to see a doctor, please?
G 3:30 p.m.? That's fine, thank you.

Get it right: *CHECKLISTE*

- ☑ Aufgabe gelesen?
- ☑ Dialoge gelesen?
- ☑ Äußerungen A–G gelesen?
- ☑ Äußerungen den Lücken zugeordnet?
- ☑ Kompletten Dialog gelesen?
- ☑ Alles korrekt?
- ☑ Abgeben!

Project page: Introducing … me!

You are going to create a social media profile for yourself.

A Basic information

Answer the questions.

- What is your name (or nickname)?
- How old are you?

B More about me

Answer four of these questions.

- What is your favourite food?
- What is your favourite animal?
- What sport are you bad at?
- What is always in your fridge?
- What is your dream job

OR

Write down the answers to four of these things:

- why you like the weekend.
- what a perfect Saturday evening looks like.
- something you are.
- something you have.
- something you can do.
- something you love.
- something you want.

What else should we know about you?

C Social media profile

Write your social media profile, using your answers to A and B. Write complete sentences. Start with a greeting.

EXAMPLE: *Hi, I'm (your name). I'm 18 years old and I'm a …*

You can include a photo, drawing or avatar if you like. Present your profile to the class in a gallery walk.

Snapshot

What was your favourite thing in this unit?	What important thing did you learn?	What do you need to work on?

My life 2

Warm-up: Family and friends

A Complete the family tree with the relationship words in the box.

aunt ▪ brother ▪ cousin ▪ father ▪ grandfather
grandmother ▪ mother ▪ nephew ▪ niece
sister ▪ uncle ▪ brother-in-law

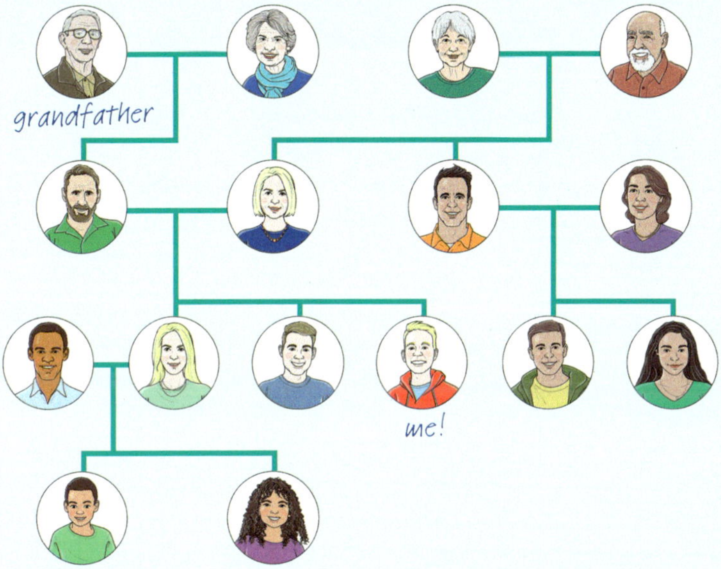

B Work with a partner. What do we need from the people who are close to us? Discuss with your partner and then number <u>your</u> priorities 1 (important) – 6 (not important).

It's important to have someone in your life who …

- gives you good advice.
- listens without criticizing.
- cheers you up when you're down.
- gives practical help when you need it (e.g. money, fixing things, etc.)
- is a good role model.
- (your own ideas)

C Who is an important person in <u>your</u> life? Why?

EXAMPLE: *My Uncle David is an important person in my life. He listens and gives me good advice.*

A The story of our lives

Mo is sitting in the college café, looking at some photos. Lisandra sits down at the next table.

1 Reading

6 **A Read the dialogue. Find the names of the people in Mo's photos and their relationship to Mo.**

B Think of a title for each photo.

1

2

3

4

Mo: Hi, Lizzy!

Lisandra: Mo, my name's Lisandra! Why can't you remember my name?

Mo: I'm sorry, Liz- … Lisandra. It's because I'm dyslexic. I find it difficult to remember names.

Lisandra: Oh, I see. Sorry, I didn't know … Who's that old lady? Nice bike!

Mo: That's my grandmother, Saba. She's 79. She learned to ride a motorbike when she was 67.

Lisandra: Wow! That's great! And who's this little boy, the one climbing?

Mo: That's my nephew, Ali. He started rock climbing lessons two months ago. He's five.

Lisandra: I like family photos, they're so interesting. Any more?

Mo: Yes … these are my uncles, Oz and Simon. Oz, is my real uncle, and Simon is his husband. They started a business last year.

Lisandra: Cool … so, do you have any brothers and sisters?

Mo: Yes, a brother and a sister. My sister, Maya, is a nurse, and my brother, Imran, is a car mechanic. This is him, he finished his apprenticeship two years ago.

Lisandra: So, you're the youngest?

Mo: That's right.

Lisandra: What about your parents?

Mo: I live with my mum and her boyfriend, Paul. My dad left when I was ten. He lives in Perth, in Australia.

Lisandra: When did you last see him?

Mo: Last year, it was great!

Lisandra: You have an interesting family, Mo.

Mo: Yes … I'm the only boring one.

Lisandra: Why did you say that?

Mo: I can't do anything special. I didn't even learn to read and write until I was ten years old.

Lisandra: But that's because of your learning difficulty, and you can write now. Better than me!

Mo: Not much better, and English isn't even your first language.

Lisandra: No, but I learned English in Germany before I came to England.

Mo: But you're from Estonia …

Lisandra: Yes, but my family didn't come straight here from Estonia. We lived in Germany for a few years. That's another story. We're late for class!

Mo: Oh, no! Not again!

C **Copy this table and complete it using information from the dialogue on page 16.**

Name	Relationship to Mo	What they achieved	When
Saba	*grandmother*	*learned to ride a motorbike*	*when she was 67*
Ali			
Oz + Simon			
Imran			

G

The simple past

Das *simple past* wird verwendet, wenn man ausdrücken will, dass etwas zu einem bestimmten Zeitpunkt in der Vergangenheit geschehen ist.

Regelmäßige Verben, z. B.: ***to learn* (lernen)**

Aussage	Frage	Verneinung
*I/you/he/she/it/we/ they learn**ed***	*What **did** I/you/he/she/it/ we/ they learn?*	*I/you/he/she/it/we/they **didn't** learn*

Unregelmäßige Verben, z. B.: ***to be* (sein)** → Unregelmäßige Verben, S. 142

Aussage	Frage	Verneinung
*I/he/she/it **was*** *we/you/they **were***	*What **was** I/he/she/it?* *What **were** we/you/they?*	*I/he/she/it **wasn't*** *we/you/they **weren't***

2 Practice: Simple past

A **Check it out! Suchen Sie folgende Verbformen im Dialog auf Seite 16:**

1 drei Aussagen im *simple past*
2 drei Verneinungen im *simple past*
3 zwei Fragen im *simple past*

B **Complete these sentences about Mo's family with verbs from the box (you need some of them more than once). Put them into the correct form.**

begin ▪ be ▪ fall ▪ do ▪ learn ▪ have ▪ see ▪ start

1 Mo's grandmother ___ 67 when she ___ to ride a motorbike.
2 Ali ___ climbing lessons last year.
3 Oz and Simon ___ in love and ___ a business.
4 Imran ___ an apprenticeship two years ago.
5 Mo ___ his dad much when he ___ young.
6 Mo ___ to read and write about eight years ago.

☆ **Turn to page 94.**

B School and work experience

1 Reading

7 **Read Anja's blog post, then complete the tasks below.**

– Anja's English –

Hello again! How's it going?
I came to Dublin on a working holiday – just for the summer. I did an intensive English course and I'm working in a sandwich bar. Now I want to stay here to do an apprenticeship as a pastry chef. That's two years!

Why? Well, I love Ireland. At first I didn't know anyone, but I soon made friends. Dublin is a friendly, interesting city – big enough but not too big.

I also love cooking. My grandmother taught me to cook traditional Tunisian food and I learned German cooking from my mother. Two years ago I started an apprenticeship as a baker, but I decided that it wasn't quite right for me. I got bored with all that bread! So I left the apprenticeship. My parents were worried.

At the weekend I phoned Mum and Dad and discussed my new plans. Mum liked the idea, but Dad was worried about his 'little girl' alone in a foreign country – he's a typical Tunisian dad! Eventually I persuaded him.

I need to write a CV to apply for apprenticeships. It's difficult to write about yourself and your life in a professional way. Luckily all young people are in the same situation. My friend Callum works as a chef, so he can help me, I hope.

I plan to start with a personal timeline: important events in my life, how I felt about them and what I learned from them.

#dublinworklife #apprenticeships

(240 words)

A Work with a partner. What do you know about Anja? Tell each other facts.

EXAMPLE: *Anja lives in Dublin.*
That's right! She works in a sandwich bar ...
Yes, and then she ...

B Complete the sentences.

1 Anja came to Dublin and she wanted ___
2 Anja's mother and grandmother both enjoy cooking, so ___
3 She didn't finish her apprenticeship, because ___
4 Anja's father was worried about her, but ___

☆ **Turn to page 94.**

C Write four more hashtags for Anja's blog.

2 Listening: Personal timeline

8 Listen to Anja telling her friend Callum about her life. Find the right place for each comment (1–11) on the timeline.

When I was …	What I did	Comments
6	primary school in Tunisia	🙂 This was my happy time.
11	left Tunisia → Germany	☹️
	secondary school in Stuttgart	☹️
12	joined soccer team	🙂
	repeated year 7	🙂
14	changed schools	🙂
	coached under-14s soccer team	🙂
16	apprenticeship (baker)	🙂
18	voluntary work	🙂
19	Ireland!	🙂

1 I was bored. 🙂
2 I got bored with my job. 🙂
3 It was cold! I missed my grandparents. ☹️
4 It was fun, I met new people. 🙂
5 German was difficult. ☹️
6 I loved work at first. 🙂
7 I made friends, got fit. 🙂
8 I made friends, improved my English. 🙂
9 I studied practical subjects, felt motivated. 🙂
10 This was my happy time. 🙂 ✔
11 I had new responsibilities. 🙂

3 More practice: Simple past

A Use the simple past to complete the sentences about Anja's life.

1 Anja ___ unhappy in Stuttgart. (be)
2 She ___ friends at the soccer club. (make)
3 She ___ happier in her new school. (feel)
4 Her role as soccer coach ___ her new responsibilities. (give)
5 She ___ bored with her apprenticeship. (get)
6 She ___ an English course in Dublin. (do)

B Now write three sentences about your life.

1 I was excited when ___
2 I was sad when ___
3 I was proud when ___

C CV (= Curriculum Vitae)

1 Anja's CV

Complete Anja's CV using the information on the next page. There is one item that you do not need.

Video 2
Watch the video and look at page 85 and 86 for more information about CVs.

Personal information

Name	Anja Schuster Habib	Telephone	01 836 254
Address	12 Amiens Street Dublin D01 X6P6	Email	anja.schabib@coolmail.nex
Nationality	(1)		

Professional summary
I am a reliable, hard-working person. I have experience in commercial baking and serving customers. **(2)**

Work experience

July 202_ – present	(3)
Sept 202_ – Aug 202_	**Bakery apprenticeship**, Bäckerei Müller, Stuttgart, Germany
Sept 202_ – March 202_	**Assistant Team Leader**, Free Food Café, Stuttgart, Germany (voluntary position)

Education and Training

July – Aug 202_	**English Academy**, Dublin, Ireland. Intensive English course
201_ – 202_	**Vocational College**, Stuttgart, Germany. Apprenticeship in bakery, first two years of a three-year course
201_ – 201_	**Secondary school**, Stuttgart, Germany
200_ – 201_	**Primary school**, Tunis, Tunisia

Qualifications

English	Cambridge First Certificate in English
Secondary School	Secondary school leaving certificate (grade average 3.0)

Personal skills

Languages

Native	German, Arabic, French
Foreign	(4)

Organizational and Teamwork

– (5)

– I coached an under-14s soccer team for two years.

Digital and Creative

(6)

a I would like an apprenticeship as a chef.
b **Food Server,** Tessa's Sandwich Bar, Liffey Street, Dublin
c German and Tunisian
d I can create documents and spreadsheets in MS Office and I write a blog in WordPress.
e I organized fundraising events for a food charity and raised €400.
f I enjoy TV, music and social media.
g English (B1 speaking/understanding, A2 writing)

Lebenslauf auf Englisch

In englischsprachigen Ländern gelten folgende Richtlinien:

- Das Geburtsdatum *(date of birth)* muss nicht angegeben werden (wegen Altersdiskriminierung).
- Es ist nicht üblich, ein Foto beizufügen.
- Referenzen werden nicht beigefügt; sie werden nur auf Anfrage vorgelegt.

2 Reading

Read the CV on page 20 again. Write questions for these answers.

1 It's anja.schabib@coolmail.net.
2 She's reliable and hard-working.
3 She worked in the Free Food Café.
4 No, she only did two years of the course.
5 She has a Cambridge First Certificate.
6 She has three different kinds of skills.

3 Words, words, words: Job skills

A **Your teacher will give you skills cards and a set of instructions. Play the skills game.**

B **Write a professional summary, like the one in Anja's CV, for the cards that you have at the end of the game.**

EXAMPLE: *I'm hard-working, able to work under pressure and I'm friendly and polite. I would like a position as a car mechanic.*

C **Now write a professional summary using your skills and a job you would like to do.**
☆ **Turn to page 95.**

Berufsbezeichnungen immer mit *a/an!*

I would like a position as **a** car mechanic.
I worked as **an** assistant for six months.

4 Talking about a cartoon

Is the person suitable for the job? Give reasons for your answer.

Skills practice: Reading

Bei dieser Übung geht es darum, einen ausführlichen Text (z.B. einen Zeitungsartikel oder einen Blogeintrag) zu lesen und anschließend Aufgaben zum Leseverständnis zu lösen.

Get it right: *Wie löse ich eine 'Reading'-Aufgabe?*

1. Orientieren Sie sich vor dem Lesen. Worum geht es? (Bilder? Überschrift? Anleitung? Aufgaben? Alles hilft!)
2. Überfliegen Sie den Artikel, um einen ersten Eindruck vom Inhalt zu gewinnen (= Grobverständnis).
3. Lesen Sie die erste Aufgabe aufmerksam durch: Welche Informationen aus dem Text benötigen Sie?
4. Lesen Sie den Text genau durch, um diese Informationen zu finden (= Detailverständnis).
5. Lösen Sie die Aufgabe anhand dieser Informationen.
6. Lesen Sie den ganzen Text noch einmal durch und vergleichen Sie Ihre Lösungen mit dem Text.
7. Korrigieren oder ergänzen Sie, soweit nötig, Ihre Lösungen.
8. Bei den weiteren Aufgaben wiederholen Sie die Schritte 3–7.

The Boomerang Family

I'm Joanna O'Donohue, I'm 17 and I'm at high school. My family lives in New York State, in a little town called Greenport. We call ourselves 'The Boomerang Family'. Let me tell you why.

When my older sisters grew up, they left home and went out into the world. Our big, old house was empty and sad without them. But then, just like boomerangs, they started to come back.

My sister Lucy was the first one. When her husband Roy lost his job, they didn't have much money, so Mom said, "Move back in with us, it's the sensible thing to do." Lucy and Roy and their daughters Destiny and Autumn came to live with us. That was two years ago.

Then last year my sister Emily Rose and her girlfriend Ella moved from Seattle back home to New York. They wanted to start a business, but needed to save money first, so Dad said, "Hey, why don't you move in here for a while?" So, they did.

Earlier this year my grandpa died. Grandma was alone. "That won't do, Ma," said Mom, "Move in with us!" Grandma wasn't sure at first, she's an independent old lady, but now she lives with us.

So now there are four generations under one roof. It works well, because we all help. We eat most meals together, around the big dining table. I love playing with my young nieces and chatting with Grandma.

In my family, we look after each other. Grandma says that most families used to be this way, in the old days. (265 words)

Get it right: *Wie löse ich eine 'Aussagen über den Text'-Aufgabe?*

- Lesen Sie sich die Aussagen genau durch.
- Achten Sie besonders auf die Verben und ihre Verneinungen.

A Aussagen über den Text

Entscheiden Sie, ob die Aussagen richtig *(true)* oder falsch *(false)* sind.

1 Joanna wohnt in New York City.
2 Ihr Familienname ist Boomerang.
3 Ihre Schwester Lucy ist verheiratet und hat zwei Kinder.
4 Emily Rose möchte sich mit ihrer Partnerin selbstständig machen.
5 Ihr Großvater ist neulich gestorben.
6 Emily Rose and Ella needed money for a new flat.
7 At first, Grandma didn't want to move in with the family.
8 Joanna finds the house too noisy and full of people now.
9 The table isn't big enough for everyone to eat together.
10 It was normal for family members to help each other in the past.

Get it right: *Wie löse ich eine 'Finish the sentences'-Aufgabe?*

Achten Sie darauf, dass Ihre Lösungen …
- … dem Textinhalt entsprechen.
- … sinnvolle Sätze ergeben.

B Finish the sentences

Use only information from the text.

1 Greenport is ___ .
2 Joanna felt sad when ___ .
3 Grandma was alone in her home after ___ .
4 Everything works because ___ .

Get it right: *Wie löse eine 'Matching'-Aufgabe?*

Achten Sie darauf, dass Ihre Lösungen …
- … dem Textinhalt entsprechen.
- … vollständige Sätze ergeben.

C Matching

Match the beginnings 1–5 to the endings A–E.

1 The O'Donohues call themselves 'The Boomerang Family' because …
2 Emily Rose and Ella didn't have enough money to …
3 Mealtimes in the O'Donohue family …
4 Joanna likes to …
5 Grandma moved in earlier this year because …

A spend time with the oldest and youngest family members.
B the daughters left home, then came back.
C grandpa died.
D are an important part of family life.
E start a business.

Project page: Milestones

Work in a small group.

A Brainstorm important milestones in the life of a young person.

EXAMPLE: *learned to spell my name ... started to help at home ... got my first phone ... posted my first video online ... moved to Germany*

B Ask and answer questions about your partner's and your milestones.

EXAMPLE:

What did you do for the first time when you were ...?

When I was *(one)* I *(spoke)* for the first time.

When did you learn to ...?

I learned to *(ride a bike)* when I was *(about five)*.

When did you start to ...?

I started to *(help at home)* before I was *(ten)*.

I haven't done that yet!

! ~~'What did you when you were ...?'~~

C Draw a timeline, like the one on page 19, on a sheet of paper. Write important milestones in your life on it. You don't need to find a milestone for every age.

EXAMPLE: *6: I left my home in Tunisia and moved to Germany with my family.*

D In small groups (5 or 6 students) draw a timeline for your group's life milestones. You can include photos or drawings.

Snapshot

What was your favourite thing in this unit?

What important thing did you learn?

What do you need to work on?

Me and my community 3

Warm-up: Feelings

A **Match the emojis to the feelings in the box.**

angry ▪ bored ▪ excited ▪ happy ▪ in love ▪ nervous ▪ sad ▪ scared ▪ surprised

B **Now match the emojis to the situations below. Some emojis might match more than one situation. Discuss your answers with a partner.**

She probably feels happy.

I think she feels excited.

C **Discuss with a partner. Which emojis do you use most often? When do you use them?**

D **When are you … ? When were you … ? Write two sentences in the present and two sentences in the past.**

EXAMPLES: *I'm happy when my football team wins.*
I was sad when I lost my phone.

A What's important to you?

It's the end of the day at Barton College and Mo is looking at his phone while he is waiting for Jack.

1 Before you read

If Lisandra sent you the 16:15 emoji, what would you think?

Mo | **Lisandra**

Mo: Maths test tomorrow! 16:10

Lisandra: Mm, I know. 16:11

Mo: See you there. 🥰 16:12

Lisandra: 😨 16:15

> **!**
> bor**ed** – *gelangweilt*
> bor**ing** – *langweilig*
>
> interest**ed** – *interessiert*
> interest**ing** – *interessant*
>
> excit**ed** – *aufgeregt*
> excit**ing** – *spannend*

2 Reading

9 **A Read the dialogue, then answer the questions below.**

Jack: Hey, Mo! What's up?
Mo: Hi, Jack …
Jack: Something important on your phone?
Mo: No, just a bit strange. I don't understand this …
Jack: What?
Mo: I just got a message from Lisandra. I don't know what it means.
Jack: Let me have a look … Okay, she's scared because there's a maths test tomorrow. That's what it means.
Mo: No, I think she's scared because I sent her those hearts.
Jack: Hmm, I didn't see it that way … No, I think you're wrong. You're good friends, aren't you?
Mo: Yes, but maybe she doesn't like me, you know, that way. As a boyfriend.
Jack: Hey! Mo's in love! You really like her a lot, don't you?
Mo: Yes, I do.
Jack: She isn't your usual type of girl. She's quite … serious, I think.
Mo: So? I'm serious, too. Sometimes.
Jack: You're not serious at all, Mo! You're … chatty and lazy. Lisandra is hard-working and quiet.
Mo: I'm not chatty when I'm around her. I'm very quiet, because I can't think of anything interesting to say.
Jack: Ah … Well, do you have anything in common? You could talk about that.
Mo: I don't know … We both like gaming and chilling out.
Jack: Yes, and you also like parties.
Mo: Lisandra doesn't like parties. She gets bored at parties.
Jack: Really? I think you need a girlfriend who loves parties. One who's loud …
Mo: Loud? Are you sure?
Jack: Well, we're friends, aren't we?
Mo: True …
Jack: Come on, let's go to the skatepark!

1 What does Jack think Lisandra's emoji means?
2 Does it match your ideas in task 1?

B Which is the best summary of the dialogue – a, b or c?

a Mo got a strange text message from Lisandra. Now he is worried: maybe she doesn't like him. Jack thinks that Lisandra isn't a good girlfriend for Mo.

b Mo sent an 'in love' emoji to Lisandra by mistake. Now he's worried that Lisandra is in love with him. He prefers girls who aren't hard-working and quiet.

c Mo got a strange text message from Lisandra. Jack thinks that it means that Lisandra likes him. Mo is worried because he isn't in love with Lisandra.

3 Words, words, words: Descriptions

A Write short descriptions of Mo and Lisandra. Use words from the box.

chatty ▪ clever ▪ confident ▪ cool ▪ funny ▪ hard-working ▪ honest
lazy ▪ loud ▪ quiet ▪ sensitive ▪ serious ▪ sporty ▪ strong ▪ wild

EXAMPLE: *Mo isn't serious. He's ...*

B Now describe yourself, using words from above and your own words. You can also use 'quite', 'very' and 'not very' to make your description more precise.

EXAMPLE: *I'm quite lazy and very chatty.*

C Your teacher will now read out some of the sentences from B. Guess which of your classmates he/she is describing. Add one more sentence to the description.

EXAMPLE:

I'm lazy and very chatty.

That's Samira. She's also sporty.

4 Likes and dislikes

A Which of these things describe what you like 👍? Which things don't you like 👎?

arguments and discussions ▪ chilling out ▪ spending time online ▪ crowds
exercise ▪ loud music ▪ nature ▪ parties ▪ practical tasks ▪ films

B Speed chat: Find someone in the class who has different preferences to you.

EXAMPLE:

I like chilling out and spending time online. I don't like exercise or parties.

Really? I love parties, and I like exercise. I don't like nature at all!

5 Friends

What makes a good friend? Write a profile for your 'ideal' friend.

EXAMPLE: *My ideal friend is quiet and sensitive, but he's/she's also cool and funny. She/He likes nature, but she/he also likes loud music and parties. She/He doesn't like arguments and discussions.*

☆ Turn to page 95.

B A training session

Lisandra has started a martial arts course at Micky Matsuhara's Martial Arts Academy.

1 Before you read

What rules are there for the sports or activities that you do? Think of at least two rules.

2 Reading

10 **Read the rules of the academy, then complete the tasks below.**

Micky Matsuhara's Martial Arts Academy – Rules

1
- Treat other students with respect.
- Don't talk loudly in the dojo.
- Don't take photos or shoot videos in the dojo.

2
- Listen carefully to the sensei or sempai.
- If you aren't sure what to do: ask!

3
- Leave your mobile phone (and other valuables) in a locker.
- Do not use your phone during class.
- Leave the dojo if you need to make an urgent phone call.

dojo = training room
sensei = instructor
sempai = senior student
gi = uniform

4
- Stay at home if you are unwell.
- Tell the sensei or sempai if you have an injury.

5
- Take off your shoes and leave them at the entrance to the dojo.
- Make sure that your gi is clean and tidy.

6

Before the session:
- Sweep the floor.
- Bring out the equipment.
- Warm up.

After the session:
- Tidy up.
- Sweep the floor.
- Take all of your possessions home!

A Choose the best heading for each set of rules (1–6). There are two that you do not need.

Cleaning ▪ Clothing ▪ Communication ▪ Health and Hygiene ▪ Injuries ▪ Phones ▪ Respect ▪ Routine tasks

B Design a poster with signs explaining the rules of the academy.

3 Listening

Micky talks to the students at the beginning of every class.

11 **A Listen to the recording. Which rules does Micky remind the students about? Find them in the list on page 28.**

B Listen again.

1 Explain which rule Micky agrees to change, and why.

2 Describe Luke's responsibilities as sempai.

C Which of the expressions from the green box were used? Listen back to check.

L

Being polite in English

Attracting attention
- Excuse me, …
- Sorry, …

Apologizing
- Sorry!
- I'm really sorry! *(something more serious)*

Asking someone to do something
- Please could you … ?
- Please (don't) … !

Asking for permission
- Can/May I … ?
- Is it okay to … ?

Please … ▪ Thank you. ▪ Thanks. ▪ You're welcome.

'Danke' und 'bitte' werden im Englischen wesentlich häufiger gebraucht als im Deutschen:

Teacher: *Please shut the door.*
Student: *No problem.*
Teacher: *Thanks.*
Student: *You're welcome.*

G

The imperative

Listen! ***Don't*** *talk!*
Don't ist die Kurzform von *do not:*
Do not *talk!*
(formal/schriftlich)

4 Practice: Imperative

Write instructions to go with these signs. Where might you see the signs?

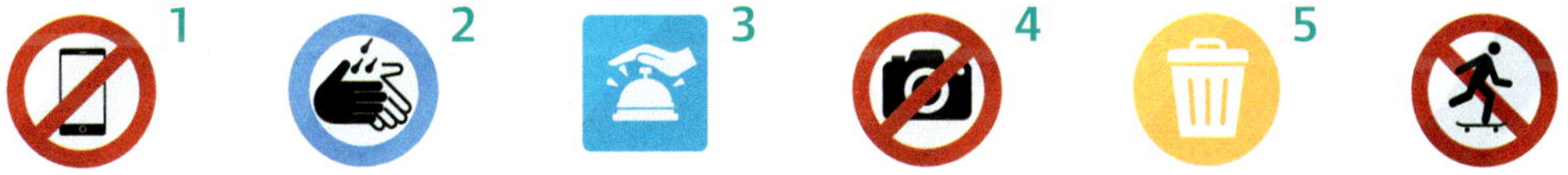

1 2 3 4 5 6

☆ **Turn to page 95.**

5 Pairwork: A role play

Act a dialogue for one of these situations. Use polite expressions from the box in 3C.
- you can't find something in a new supermarket
- it's your first day at a new school
- you're on the bus in a new town

C Trouble at work

1 Reading

12 **Read the text, then complete the tasks below.**

– Anja's English –

I had a problem with a colleague the other day at the sandwich bar. I always try to get along with people, so it made me sad.

One colleague, let's call him 'Pat', always gets to work late. It makes me angry, because the start of the day is always busy: it's the time when we make all the sandwich fillings, put out the bread and so on. The rest of us have to do his work.

So the other day, I was tired and a bit grumpy, and I made a comment when Pat came in late, as usual. I said something like, "You must try harder to get here on time, Pat!"

Pat became very quiet. He's normally chatty and friendly, but that morning he didn't say much at all. Later in the day, another colleague, let's call her 'Sarah', said to me, "You mustn't criticize other workers, Anja. You're not the boss! You hurt Pat. He's very upset."

I said sorry to Pat (even though I was right and he was wrong). But the situation confused me: in the sandwich bar, we are often rude to each other – in a friendly way. So why was I wrong to criticize Pat?

#troubleatwork #cultureclash

(194 words)

A What was the problem?

a Anja's colleague was rude to her.
b Anja criticized a colleague.
c Anja's colleague did not do enough work.

B Work with a partner. Tell each other what you think about Anja's comment.

- I think Anja was right to say something.
- Everyone else had to work harder.
- It wasn't fair.
- Pat was always late.
- I don't think what Anja said was right.
- Anja made a rude comment.
- It was more difficult to work together.
- It wasn't helpful.

C **Now read Darren's comment. Do you agree with him? Give reasons.**

Comments:
Anja, I hope it's okay to say this: sometimes you're very German! In German culture, it's okay to criticize people. It's normal behaviour. In other cultures, it may seem rude or arrogant.
In Irish culture, we're informal and often not serious. We are often rude to each other – but usually only to our friends! It's strange, I know: if someone is rude to you, it might mean that they like you! Serious criticism is different. Irish people criticize themselves all the time, but we don't like criticism from other people. Also, we have a different attitude to time …
I can say this because I'm half German and half Irish. 😁
Darren

2 Words, words, words: Interacting with other people

A **Decide if these verbs are positive or negative phrases.**

annoy ▪ be nice to ▪ be rude to ▪ confuse ▪ criticize ▪ disagree with ▪ get along with ▪ hurt

B **Use your answers to A to make three 'rules' for a happy workplace.**

G

***must* (müssen)**
- *I/you/he/she/it/we/they* ***must*** *(talk)*
- *I/you/he/she/it/we/they* ***mustn't*** *(talk)*

mustn't ist die Kurzform von ***must not*** (formal, schriftlich)

***have to* (müssen)**
- *I/you/we/they* ***have to*** *(talk)*
- *he/she/it* ***has to*** *(talk)*

!
mustn't = **darf** nicht
not have to = **muss** nicht

3 Practice: must/mustn't/have to …

A **Check it out!** **Suchen Sie folgende Ausdrücke im Blog auf Seite 30:**
1 einmal mit *must*
2 einmal mit *mustn't*
3 einmal mit *have to*

B **Decide whether these actions are things you must, mustn't, have to or don't have to do in the classroom. Write instructions for a new student.**
1 use your phone
2 agree with the teacher's opinion
3 listen to the teacher
4 be polite to everyone
5 be rude to other students
6 be friendly with other students

4 Writing

Write your own comment on Anja's blog post. Try to use must/mustn't/don't have to.
- Who was right, Darren or Anja? Why?
- What is important to remember when you work with people from other cultures?

☆ **Turn to page 95.**

Skills practice: Listening

Bei 'Listening' geht es darum, einem kurzen Gespräch auf Englisch zuzuhören und Hörverständnisaufgaben dazu auf Deutsch zu lösen.

Get it right: *Wie löse ich eine 'Listening'-Aufgabe?*

- Orientieren Sie sich vor dem Hören. Worum geht es?
- Erstes Zuhören: Hören Sie genau zu und notieren Sie allenfalls kurze Stichwörter – alles andere lenkt ab!
- Lösen Sie die Aufgabe.
- Zweites Zuhören: Überprüfen und korrigieren Sie beim Zuhören Ihre Lösungen.
- Überprüfen Sie Ihre Lösungen ein letztes Mal.

A In the souvenir shop

13

Laura und Peter sind in Dublin am Ende ihres Kurzurlaubs. Laura will Peter mit einem Geschenk überraschen.

a) Hören Sie sich den Dialog ein erstes Mal an. Was kauft Laura?

b) Hören Sie sich den Dialog ein zweites Mal an und beantworten Sie die folgenden Fragen auf Deutsch. Stichwörter genügen.

1 In welchen Farben gibt es das Irland-Sweatshirt?
2 Welche Größe möchte Laura?
3 Welche Farbe wählt sie schließlich?
4 Was kostet das Sweatshirt?
5 Bezahlt sie bar oder mit Karte?

B Talking about apps

14

Mo und Lisandra vergleichen die Apps auf ihren Handys. Hören Sie sich den Dialog zweimal an.

a) Ordnen Sie die Apps entsprechend zu.

	Blue Sky	Transmit	BeatPro	InTouch	Burn!
Fitness					
Messaging					
Music					
News					
Weather					

b) Vervollständigen Sie die folgenden Sätze:

1 Lisandras Lieblingsapp ist ___ .

2 Sie kostet ___ alle ___ .

Get it right: *CHECKLISTE*

- ☑ Aufgabe gelesen?
- ☑ Hörtext genau angehört?
- ☑ Aufgabe gelöst?
- ☑ Hörtext nochmals angehört?
- ☑ Aufgabe überprüft und ergänzt?
- ☑ Abgeben!

Project page: Cultures in my community

Mo, Jack and Lisandra attended an intercultural awareness workshop at Barton Business Centre. This is a handout from the workshop.

Video 3

Watch the video and look at page 86 for more information about how to get along with Brits.

DID YOU KNOW?

We have the following ethnic minorities in our community – and probably several more!

CHINESE
VIETNAMESE
KOREAN
PAKISTANI
BANGLADESHI
INDIAN
MIDDLE EASTERN AND NORTH AFRICAN
NORTH AMERICAN
POLISH
ITALIAN
OTHER EUROPEAN

FIND OUT ABOUT

Greetings

- Handshake/Bow/Namaste
- Use of first and surname

Small talk

- 'Safe' subjects
- Subjects to avoid

Body language

- Eye contact
- Physical contact/distance

Every family or group has its own culture! There are variations and exceptions to these 'rules'. Tell us if you disagree with our advice and what we got wrong. ☺

A **You are going to do a role play making small talk with people from different cultures. In a group, think of the following things before you start.**

1 three greetings
2 two small talk topics
3 two things to remember about your body language

B **Speed chat: Work in groups. Partner A go to file 5 on page 90, partner B go to file 6 on 90, partner C go to file 9 on page 92, partner D go to file 11 on page 92.**

- Introduce yourself to your partner *(Ihr Name und Herkunft)*.
- Greet each other.
- Make small talk about 'safe' subjects.
- If your partner tries to do or say something that isn't 'polite' in your culture, say 'Please don't …'.

At the end of the chat, swap role cards with your partner, then find another partner.

C **Find out about cultures in your community. Write role cards for them like the ones in B.**

Snapshot

What was your favourite thing in this unit?

What important thing did you learn?

What do you need to work on?

Where I live 4

Warm-up: Buildings around town

A **Match the names in the box to the places 1–12 in the picture. There are two names that you do not need.**

bakery ▪ bus stop ▪ café ▪ gym ▪ information centre
library ▪ park ▪ public toilets ▪ railway station
school/college ▪ shopping mall /centre ▪ supermarket
swimming pool ▪ taxi rank

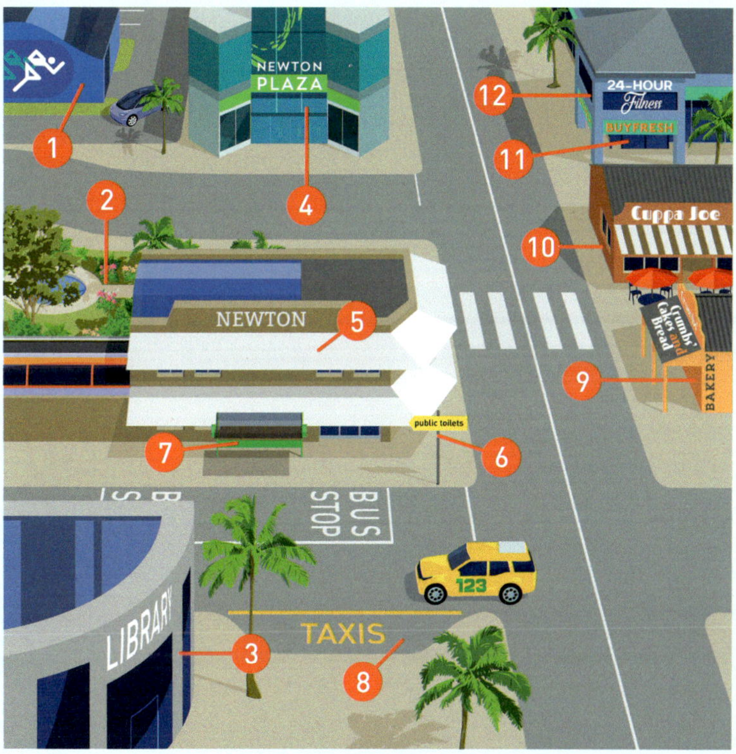

B **Brainstorm. What places are there in your area?**

C **Class survey. What places do people go to in your area? How often? Do a survey.**

EXAMPLE:

	every day	often	sometimes	never
library	I	II	III	II
...				

A It's a big country ...

Mo gets an interesting email from his uncles, Oz and Simon.

Video 4

Watch the video and look at page 87 for more information about Australia.

1 Before you read

What do you know about Australia? Think about these things.

- Cities
- Animals and nature
- Climate/weather
- Sights and things to do

2 Reading

15

A Read the dialogue, then find the underlined places on the map above or on page 144.

Lisandra: Hi, Mo! What's up?

Mo: Oh, hi, Lisandra ... My uncles sent me an interesting email.

Lisandra: Your uncles?

Mo: Yes, Oz and Simon. I told you about them. They want me to come and stay with them in Melbourne after I finish college.

Lisandra: Wow! A holiday in Australia ...

Mo: More than a holiday. They suggested coming for a year, maybe two.

Lisandra: Oh! That's a long time.

Mo: I know. I've been to Perth, where my Dad lives. Perth is in the west and Melbourne's in the southeast. Australia's a very big country.

Lisandra: How big?

Mo: As big as Europe.

Lisandra: I see. What's Melbourne like, then?

Mo: I haven't been there yet, but Oz says it's a really nice city. It's lively, and there is a lot to do. Oz and Simon live near the beach.

Lisandra: So it's on the coast?

Mo: That's right. There are great beaches. You can swim, sunbathe and windsurf, right in the city.

Lisandra: Cool! I don't know anything about Australia. I know it's famous for the Outback – and kangaroos.

Mo: The Outback is a long way from Melbourne. There aren't many people there. It's very hot and dry. And mostly flat. There are some big hills, and there's Uluru. There are some rivers and lakes, but they're dry most of the time.

Lisandra: So it's hot and there isn't any water? It sounds horrible!

Mo: No, it's awesome! There is so much space.

Lisandra: So, is all of Australia hot and dry?

Mo: No, there are mountains in the east. The ones near Melbourne are called the Australian Alps. There are forests, rivers and lakes – and snow. Aussies go skiing there in the winter.

Lisandra: Skiing in Australia? You're joking!

Mo: No, really. Oz and Simon go every year. There are lots of ski resorts.

Lisandra: Mo. I think you should go to Australia. It's a great opportunity!

Mo: Hmm. I don't know. I'll think about it.

B Decide whether these statements are true or false. Correct the false ones.

1. Oz and Simon invited Mo to come to Melbourne for a short holiday.
2. Melbourne is great if you like watersports.
3. Mo doesn't like the Outback.
4. There aren't any mountains in Australia.

G

There is/are

*There **is** so much space.*
*There **are** great beaches.*

There isn't/aren't

*There **isn't** any water.*
*There **aren't** many people there.*

!

***Some* in bejahenden Aussagen,**
***any* in Verneinungen und Fragen.**

There are **some** lakes near here.
Are there **any** lakes near here?
There aren't **any** lakes near here.

3 Practice: There is/are, some/any

A Check it out! Suchen Sie folgende Sätze im Dialog auf Seite 36:

1. zwei Sätze mit *there is*
2. ein Satz mit *there isn't*
3. zwei Sätze mit *there are*
4. ein Satz mit *there aren't*

B Which is the correct form?

1. There are any/some strange animals in Australia.
2. There isn't/aren't any snow in the mountains in summer.
3. Are there any/some ski resorts near Melbourne?
4. Any/Some Australians love to go skiing.

4 Quiz

A Think of a country that you know (not Germany). Make notes about it. Think about:

- Is it cold or warm there?
- What sights are there?
- What do they eat there?
- What is it famous for?

B Write a short description of the country. Don't write the name of the country.
☆ **Turn to page 96.**

C Read out your description to the class. Who can guess the name of the country? The person who guesses right reads out their description next.

4 Where I live

B Welcome to Melbourne!

In Melbourne, Australia, volunteers greet visitors and help them to find their way around the city.

Federation Square, Melbourne

1 Reading

16 **Read the advertisement, then complete the task below.**

VOLUNTEERS WANTED!

Are you at least **16 years** old? Do you like helping people? Are you friendly and outgoing? Do you know your city well? Can you spare **4–6 hours a week**?

Then we want to hear from you. You could be a **MELBOURNE TOURIST AMBASSADOR**.

Your tasks:

- greeting visitors
- giving directions
- answering questions about tourist attractions
- handing out information about free events

Where you will work:

- Federation Square
- Southern Cross Station
- St Kilda Beach

All Tourist Ambassadors get:

- information pack
- 2-hour briefing session
- Tourist Ambassador T-shirt
- free Myki (public transport card)

Worried about safety?

- Ambassadors work in pairs, only in busy areas and only during daylight hours.
- You will have a volunteer supervisor at your location to look after you.

Interested? Leave a voicemail at 1300 WELCOME with your name and mobile number.

Are you fluent in a foreign language? That's great! Visitors from all over the world come to Melbourne. Please mention this in your application. (172 words)

Sie verbringen einen Studienaufenthalt in Melbourne, Australien, und würden gern ehrenamtlich als Freiwillige/r arbeiten. Sie stoßen auf die obige Anzeige und möchten sich bewerben. Berichten Sie Ihrer Familie in einer E-Mail auf Deutsch von Ihrem Vorhaben und gehen Sie auf folgende Punkte ein:

- Ihre Aufgaben als Touristen Ambassador
- Arbeitszeiten
- Arbeitsplatz
- Einweisung und Material
- Sicherheit (Eltern beruhigen!)

☆ **Turn to page 96.**

2 Listening

Georgia, a Tourist Ambassador in Melbourne, meets some visitors at Federation Square.

17 **A Listen to the recording. Follow Georgia's directions and find the correct destinations (A–K).**

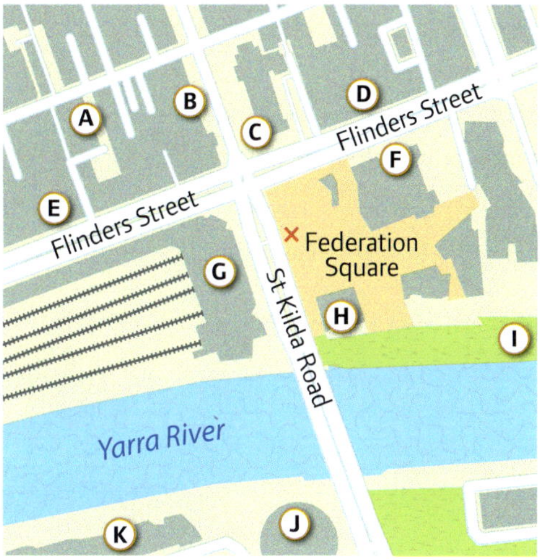

B Listen again. Which of the expressions below do you hear in the dialogues?

L

Asking for and giving directions

- How do I get to … , please?
- Can you tell me the way to … , please?
- Is there anywhere I can … , please?
- I'm looking for …
- Can you recommend … ?
- Turn left. / Turn right.
- It's over there.
- There's a … just around the corner.
- Take the first/second/third street on the left/right.
- Go straight on.
- Cross … *(name of road)*.
- It's next to … / It's opposite …
- Walk about … metres.

3 Pairwork: A role play

Work with a partner. When you have finished, swap roles.

a good computer store ▪ Birrarung Marr (park) ▪ City Library ▪ St Paul's Cathedral
Southgate Centre (shopping mall) ▪ Taxi Kitchen (restaurant and café) ▪ the nearest supermarket

Student A is a tourist at Federation Square. Choose a destination from the box.
Follow the Ambassador's (Student B) directions to your destination on the map above. Tell your partner which letter (A–K) you are at on the map. She/He will tell you if you are at the right place.
Student B turn to file 3 on page 89.

C Working at the railway station

Georgia is thinking about working at a train station when she finishes college. She finds out about jobs from her neighbour, Bob, who is a railway worker.

1 Listening

A Before you listen: match the descriptions to the jobs. One job has two descriptions.

1	cleaner	**a**	serves food e.g. in the station café or on a train
2	food server	**b**	sells tickets and gives travel information
3	porter	**c**	helps passengers with their luggage
4	sales assistant	**d**	responsible for train safety
5	signaller	**e**	responsible for the people who work at the station
6	station manager	**f**	makes sure that the toilets, platforms, concourse, etc. are clean
7	ticket clerk	**g**	controls the movement of trains
8	train guard	**h**	assists passengers on the platform
		i	sells goods to customers

18 **B Now listen and check your answers.**

C Listen again. Decide which job would involve these tasks.

1 check tickets
2 do administrative tasks
3 help to load and unload luggage
4 in charge of day-to-day operations
5 make announcements
6 often work for a contractor
7 operate the train doors
8 work on the train with the driver

D Describe a job at the station to your partner. Can she/he guess the job? Swap roles.

EXAMPLE:

This person assists passengers.

Is it a ticket clerk?

!
I work as **a** ticket clerk.
I'm **an** apprentice train guard.

2 Reading

Read the article. Which of these jobs would you like to do? Why?

19

Cool working-holiday jobs in Australia

Park ranger

Park rangers look after national parks and other beautiful wild parts of Australia. They help visitors to enjoy the parks and keep to the rules. There are lots of maintenance jobs to do around the park, looking after buildings, roads, walking trails and bathroom facilities. A driving licence is essential, and you need to work hard and use your initiative. If you love koalas and snakes, this is the job for you!

Island caretaker

Does living on a tropical island for free sound like your dream job? Maybe you should be an island caretaker. There are thousands of islands around Australia. But this isn't a paid holiday! It's hard work and you may not have much fresh water or electricity. You may have to paint buildings and clean toilets. The best part? After work, you can relax on the beach or go for a swim!

Station hand

Station hands work on Outback stations (large Australian farm). They do a range of different things, assisting the farmer with their daily tasks. You might fly in a helicopter, ride a horse, ride a quad bike, ride a dirt bike or drive a tractor. You need to be confident around big animals. Don't worry about being lonely: stations are small, but close communities. You'll meet lots of interesting people!

(225 words)

3 Words, words, words: The right meaning

A Find the English words in the texts for these German ones.

1 Instandhaltung	**4** bezahlter Urlaub	**7** Reihe
2 Sanitäranlagen	**5** Strom	**8** selbstbewusst
3 Führerschein	**6** Gebäude streichen	**9** Gemeinden

☆ **Turn to page 97.**

B What is the right German meaning for the marked words: *Arbeit* or *arbeiten*?

1 … to work hard …

2 It's hard work and …

3 After work, you can …

4 Station hands work on …

Skills practice: Writing an opinion

Bei 'Writing an opinion' geht es darum, in einem kurzen Text auf eine Behauptung zu reagieren.

Get it right: *Wie löse ich eine 'Writing an opinion'-Aufgabe?*

- Lesen Sie sich die Aufgabenstellung genau durch: Worum geht es?
- Notieren Sie sich ein paar Ideen: Was fällt Ihnen spontan zum Thema ein?
- Schreiben Sie einen kompakten Text, in dem Sie wie folgt argumentieren:
  - Was halten Sie von der aufgestellten Behauptung? (Reaktion)
  - Weshalb sind Sie dieser Ansicht? (Begründung)
  - Nennen Sie drei Beispiele, die Ihre Ansicht stützen. (Beispiele)
- Lesen Sie Ihren Text durch:
  - Sind Ihre Argumente logisch?
  - Ist die Rechtschreibung korrekt?
  - Ist die Grammatik korrekt?
  - Sind die Sätze vollständig?
  - Ist die verlangte Wortanzahl erreicht? (Schreiben Sie lieber ein paar Wörter zu viel als zu wenig, aber übertreiben Sie es nicht!)
- Lesen Sie sich Ihren Text nochmals durch und korrigieren Sie, wo nötig.

A The importance of English

Do you think learning English is important? Why? Why not? Give three examples. Write 30 words in complete English sentences.
Ihre Notizen könnten z. B. so aussehen:

English – important? yes!
useful → communication, entertainment
e.g. on holiday   web pages in English
songs in English

! e.g. = for example (z. B. zum Beispiel)

B The importance of exercise

Do you think it's important to exercise every day? Why? Why not? Give three examples. Write 30 words in complete English sentences.

> **Richtig oder falsch?**
>
> Es gibt keine 'richtigen' und 'falschen' Meinungen. Jedoch müssen Begründungen schlüssig und Beispiele treffend sein.

C The importance of travel

Do you think it is important to travel? Why? Why not? Give three examples. Write 30 words in complete English sentences.

D The importance of social media

Do you think social media is important? Why? Why not? Give three examples. Write 30 words in complete English sentences.

Get it right: *CHECKLISTE*

- ☑ Aufgabe gelesen?
- ☑ Notizen gemacht?
- ☑ Text geschrieben?
- ☑ Text überprüft?
- ☑ Text ggf. korrigiert?
- ☑ Abgeben!

Project page: Where we live

Your English-speaking friend comes to visit you. What will you do with him or her? What can you show them in your town or in another town or area you know?

Work in a small group. Sit around a large sheet of paper. In the centre of the paper, write the name of your town, city or region.

A **Make notes in your corner of the placemat. Write down three important things in your area that you want to see or do with your friend.**
EXAMPLE: *swimming lake – escape room – rock climbing wall*

B **Discuss your ideas with the rest of the group. Agree on 5–8 things and write them in the centre of the sheet around the title.**
EXAMPLE:

She/He mustn't miss the swimming lake ...

Maybe it's too cold for swimming .... What about the escape room?

No, the escape room is boring. Let's take her/him to ...

C **Use your ideas to design a social media page to show your friend (and other visitors) what there is to see and do.**
Tips:
- Start with a friendly welcome to your area.
- Describe the good things about each place.
- Use simple, short sentences and bullet points.
- Use photos and maybe a map.

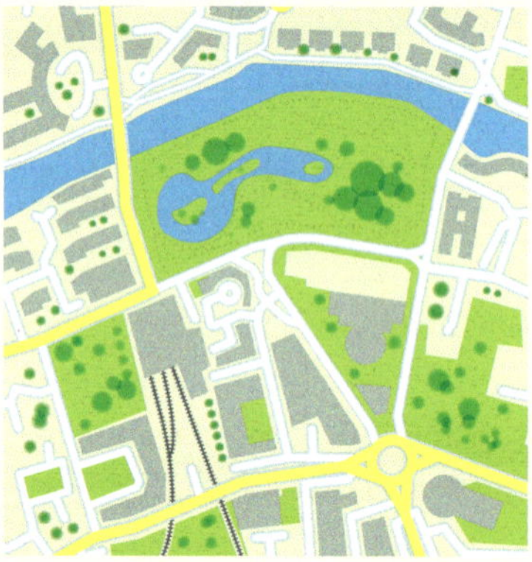

D **Do a gallery walk. Give feedback to the other groups about their pages. Which page is best?**

Snapshot

What was your favourite thing in this unit?

What important thing did you learn?

What do you need to work on?

The things we do 5

Warm-up: Free-time activities

A Put the free-time activities into groups. Some activities might fit in more than one group.

chat online ▪ ride a bike ▪ go out with friends
work out ▪ listen to music ▪ play games
take photos ▪ volunteer ▪ stream movies
surf the internet for information ▪ make videos

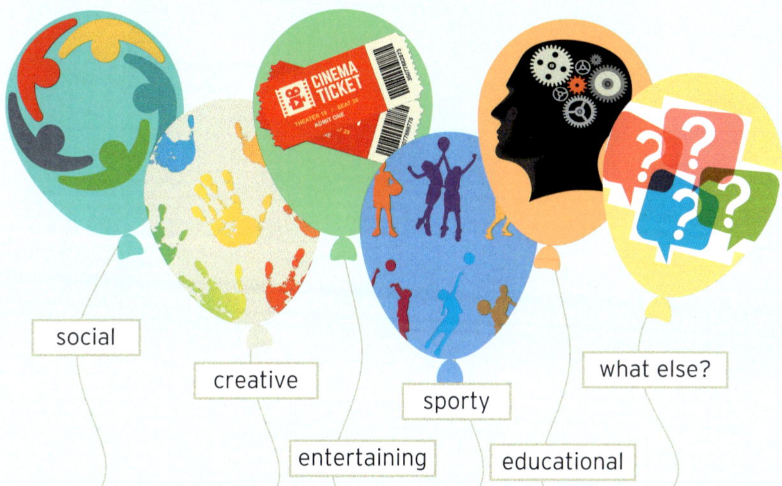

B Add your own favourite activities to the groups.

C How much of your spare time do you spend on each type of activity? Draw a pie chart.

My free time

- social
- creative
- entertaining
- sporty
- educational
- what else?

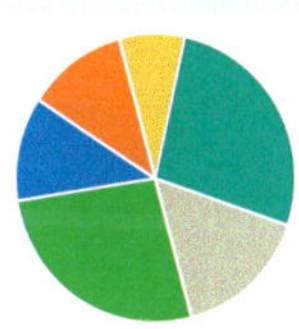

D Speed chat: Find someone whose pie chart looks different to yours. Talk about how your interests are different.

EXAMPLE:

I love playing online games and streaming movies.

I like movies too, but I'm in a football team. We have lots of training and matches on Saturdays.

5 The things we do

A Time thieves!

It's Friday evening. Mo, Jack, Lisandra and Jack's friend Ruby are going to the cinema.

1 Before you read

What might the dialogue 'Time thieves!' be about? Discuss your ideas with a partner.

2 Reading

20 **Read the dialogue, then complete the tasks below.**

Outside the cinema, Lisandra and Jack are waiting for Mo. Ruby is buying the tickets.

Lisandra: There you are! You're late!

Mo: Sorry!

Lisandra: Well, you're here now, anyway. Ruby is getting impatient.

Ruby: Come on! The film starts in five minutes. Everyone else is going in.

Jack: Mo's just parking his scooter.

Ruby: At last! … Look, I'm going in. Here are your tickets.

Jack: I'm coming with you, Ruby.

Lisandra: We won't be long.

Mo parks his scooter then walks to the cinema with Lisandra.

Lisandra: You're looking tired …

Mo: I'm not feeling very relaxed at the moment. I never have enough time.

Lisandra: You are trying to do too much, Mo.

Mo: How do you mean?

Lisandra: You're studying hard at school, you're working part-time … and you are still doing all your other activities, like football.

Mo: Sure, but I need to save up for Australia. And I don't want to lose my place on the football team. And I don't want to fail my exams.

Lisandra: Hmm, but then you stay up half the night, on your phone!

Mo: I love streaming films, it helps me relax.

Lisandra: I understand … but sometimes we have to make choices.

Mo: Yes, I know. I know. You're beginning to sound like my mum!

Lisandra: Well, maybe she's right. Phones are real 'time thieves'.

Mo: Time thieves?

Lisandra: Things that steal your time. Come on … I'll buy you an ice cream.

Mo: There isn't time! The film's about to start.

Lisandra: There's lots of time. There are always lots of adverts before the film starts ... remember?

A **Think about your ideas in task 1 again. Were you right or wrong about the dialogue?**

B **Complete the sentences.**

1 Ruby is impatient because …
2 Mo is tired because …
3 Although Mo finds his phone a good way to relax, …

☆ **Turn to page 97.**

3 Discussion

A Make sentences with the parts below and write them down.

Mo should	give up football sell his scooter to pay for the trip spend less time with his friends stop playing games work fewer hours at his job	because	he doesn't need it in Australia. it's a waste of time. it's important to pass your exams. it's not necessary. it's too tiring.

B What do you think Mo should do? Why? Use your sentences from A or your own ideas.

C Discuss with a partner. What are your 'time thieves'? Give your partner advice about his/her time thieves.

EXAMPLE: *One of my time thieves is ...* *You could spend less time ...*

The present progressive

G

Das *present progressive* wird für vorübergehende oder im Moment des Sprechens ablaufende Handlungen verwendet.

! run → run**n**ing begin → begin**n**ing

to play (spielen)

Aussage	**Frage**	**Verneinung**
I'm / *he/she/it* ***is*** / *you/we/they* ***are*** } *play**ing***	***Am** I* / ***Is** he/she/it* / ***Are** you/we/they* } *play**ing**?*	*I'**m not*** / *he/she/it* ***isn't*** / *you/we/they* ***aren't*** } *play**ing***

4 Practice: Present progressive

A Check it out! Suchen Sie folgende Verbformen im Dialog auf Seite 46:

1 drei Aussagen im *present progressive* (mit Kurzformen)
2 eine Verneinung im *present progressive*

B Look at these sentences. When do you use present progressive? When do you use simple present?

Mo often feels stressed, but this morning he's feeling relaxed.
Usually Mo and Jack do some sport after school, and right now they're playing football.

C Complete these sentences with verbs from the box. Put them into the correct form.

buy ■ help ■ do ■ try ■ go ■ wait

1 The friends ___ to the cinema.
2 Ruby ___ the tickets.
3 Mo ___ too many things.
4 Ruby and Jack ___ for the others.
5 Lisandra ___ Mo feel better.
6 "I ___ my best," says Mo.

☆ **Turn to page 97.**

B How to …

In Ireland, Anja is moving into a new flat. She is having a few problems.

1 Reading

Read Anja's blog and complete the task below. 21

– Anja's English –

DIY skills needed!

Hello there! Just a short post from me today. I'm just moving into a lovely shared flat in Dublin. My room doesn't have much furniture, though – just a bed. So, I'm buying some flat-pack furniture (a bookshelf and a desk). Flat-pack furniture is easier to move house with! But it doesn't always turn out the way it's supposed to. I usually break or lose something, or there is something important missing. I haven't even got an electric drill here. What can I do? I've just opened the box with the bookshelf in. There are no instructions, only drawings. They are easier to understand than complicated explanations – I hope.

Now I need to roll up my sleeves and grab a screwdriver and a hammer – for the nails, not to smash it up!

#loveDIY #flatpacksrule (134 words)

1 Explain why Anja needs DIY skills.
2 Describe the problem Anja has today.
3 Suggest a solution.

2 How to use an electric drill

Read the instructions for using an electric drill. Put the steps in the correct order.

How to use an electric drill

You need the following things:

electric drill ■ drill bits ■ ear + eye protection

Steps

a Wear safe clothing, ear and eye protection.
b Test that the drill bit turns correctly.
c Adjust the force on the drill so you can drill easily.
d Fit the drill bit firmly into the chuck (the mouth in the drill for the drill bit).
e Remove the drill bit from the hole and check it is the right depth.
f Choose the correct drill bit for the hole you want to drill.
g Don't overheat the drill bit – don't drill for too long.
h Hold the drill steady and push it gently into the material you are drilling.

☆ **Turn to page 97.**

3 A 'how-to' video

A **Have you ever done any DIY at home? Did you have any problems that you needed help with?**

B **Find the correct captions for the video frames. There are more captions than you need.**

I'm checking I have all the components. ■ I'm finished and I'm checking it looks like the picture. ■ I'm following the steps closely, and looking carefully at the pictures, too. I'm getting the tools I need. ■ Something doesn't fit, I'm checking the instructions again. I'm opening the box carefully (I'm not using a knife). ■ I'm tightening all the screws.

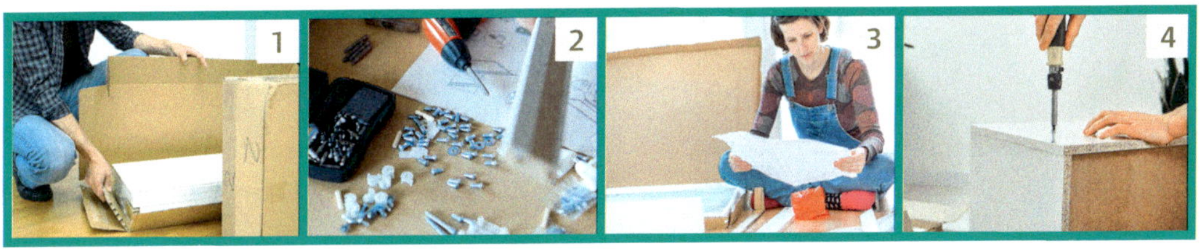

C **Put all the captions in B into the correct order to describe building a piece of furniture.**

4 Pairwork: A role play

A **Work with a partner. When you have finished, swap roles.**

Student A: **Demonstrate one of the tasks below.**
Student B: **Explain what your partner is doing.**
EXAMPLE: *Lukas is showing us how to paint a wall.*
He's covering the floor with newspaper. Now he's …

Painting a wall
- move the furniture
- cover the floor
- paint the wall
- wait until dry
- paint second coat

Planting herbs in a pot
- fill pot with compost
- make some small holes
- plant seeds
- fill holes with compost
- water

Dyeing your hair
- read instructions
- put on gloves
- apply dye to hair
- set timer, wait
- wash your hair

Making a burger
- cook burgers
- slice burger bap and toast it
- wash salad ingredients
- slice tomatoes, onions and cheese
- assemble your burger, don't forget some sauce

B **Here are some how-to ideas that you can explain to the class. Use a dictionary to help you.**

- Hang a picture on the wall.
- Mend a flat tyre on your bike.
- Put on makeup.
- Load the dishwasher.

C On the job

It's Saturday morning and Mo is starting a new part-time job with Matt Green, a landscape gardener. Green Landscapes is working at Barton Park, an outdoor music venue.

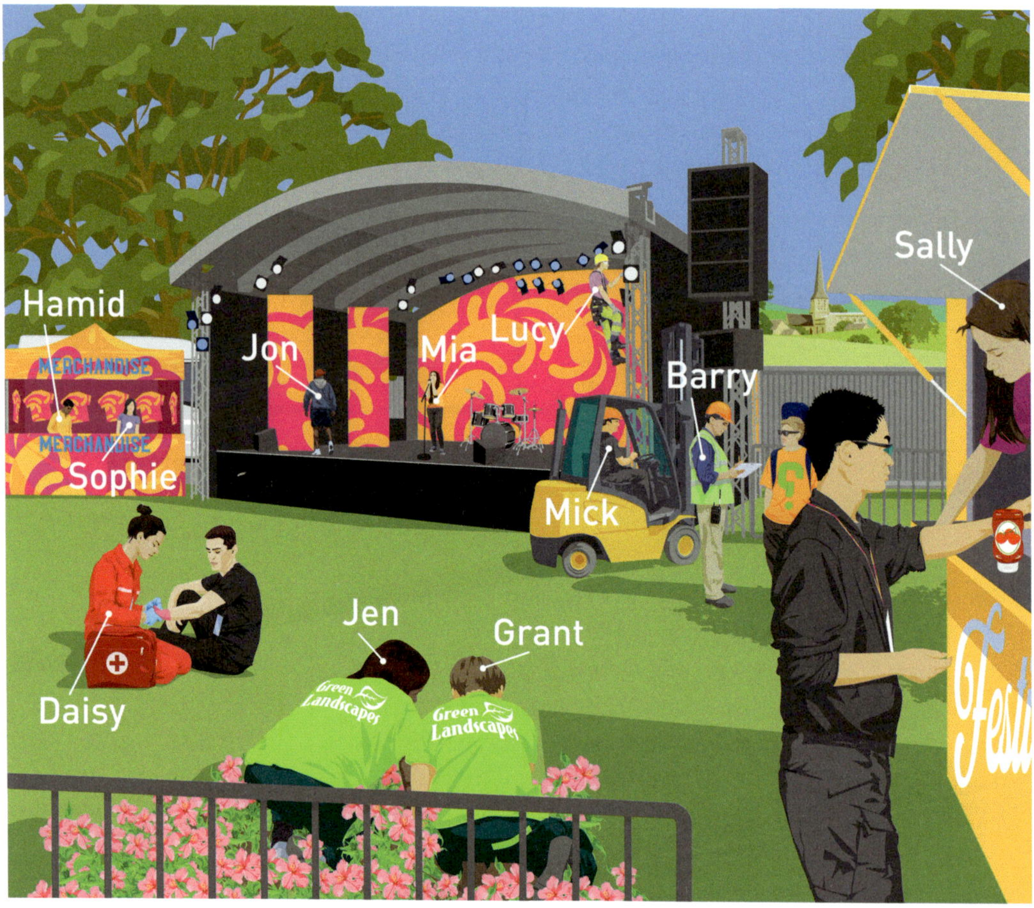

1 Words, words, words: Jobs

A **Match the jobs in the box to the people in the picture. There are two jobs that you do not need.**

EXAMPLE: *Jen and Grant are gardeners.*

builder ▪ delivery driver ▪ electrician ▪ event security officer ▪ food server ▪ forklift operator ▪ gardener ▪ paramedic ▪ sales assistant ▪ sound engineer

B **Describe the tasks the people are doing. Use verbs from the box on the left and nouns from the box on the right. Put the verbs in the correct form.**

EXAMPLE: *Jen and Grant are planting flowers.*

arrange ▪ help ▪ check ▪ install ▪ move ▪ plant ▪ serve ▪ test

customer ▪ equipment ▪ flowers ▪ goods for sale ▪ lighting ▪ patient ▪ security pass ▪ sound equipment

☆ **Turn to page 98.**

2 Listening

Listen to the recording, then complete the job description for Mo's new job.
22

Job Description

Assistant landscape gardener

- (1) out with general duties.
- (2) gardeners with planting trees and smaller plants.
- (3) a lawnmower.
- (4) heavy loads.
- (5) outdoors in any (6).

Must be (7) and (8) and a hard worker. No (9) licence required.

3 What's the job?

A Read the job descriptions below. What jobs are they for? (The jobs are all in task 1.)

(1)
- Serve food
- Keep truck clean
- Take orders and add up bills
- Flexible hours
- Be organized and work fast

(3)
- Check tickets, IDs, wristbands
- Communicate politely and effectively
- Identify security risks
- Use security equipment (CCTV)
- Work with police officers

(2)
- Communicate easily with patients
- Evaluate medical problems
- Give injections and medicine
- Stay calm in an emergency
- Use medical equipment

(4)
- Set up, test and adjust audio equipment
- Repair and maintain audio equipment
- Mix sound at live music events
- Work with musicians and event managers
- Pack up audio equipment after events

B Discuss with a partner. Which of these jobs do you find most interesting? Explain why (in German).

4 It's your turn

A Write a job description for another job from the picture or a job that you know about.

B Read out your description to your partner. Don't say the name of the job. Can they guess what it is?

Part-time work for teenagers – the law

In the UK (and other English-speaking countries), many teenagers have part-time jobs when they are at school.

Term time

From 13 years old, teenagers can work a maximum of 12 hours a week. They can work 2 hours on school days and Sundays and 5 hours (aged 13–14) or 8 hours (aged 15–16) on Saturdays.

School holidays

aged 13–14: maximum 25 hours a week
aged 15–16: maximum 35 hours a week

Skills practice: Mediation

Mediation bedeutet, jemandem, der kein Englisch kann, den Inhalt eines englischen Texts zu vermitteln. Es sollen jedoch nur die wesentlichen Informationen auf Deutsch zusammengefasst werden – Sie brauchen nicht den ganzen Text ins Deutsche zu übersetzen!

Vermeiden Sie es, Ihre persönliche Meinung oder eigenes Wissen in die Mediation einzubringen. Geben Sie den Inhalt neutral wieder!

Get it right: *Wie löse ich eine 'Mediation'-Aufgabe?*

- Orientieren Sie sich vor dem Lesen. Worum geht es? (Bilder? Überschrift? Anleitung? Aufgaben? Alles hilft!
- Überfliegen Sie den Artikel, um einen ersten Eindruck vom Inhalt zu gewinnen (= Grobverständnis).
- Lesen Sie sich die Aufgabe genau durch: Für wen schreiben Sie? Welche Art Text sollen Sie schreiben? Welche Infos aus dem Text sind hierfür wesentlich?
- Suchen Sie im Text die Angaben, die Sie benötigen. (= Detailverständnis)
- Notieren Sie sich diese Infos auf Deutsch.
- Nutzen Sie Ihre Notizen, um einen kurzen zusammenhängenden Text auf Deutsch zu schreiben.
- Lesen Sie Ihren Mediationstext kritisch durch. (Infos korrekt? Rechtschreibung und Grammatik in Ordnung?)
- Nehmen Sie nötige Korrekturen vor.

Smartphones – part of the festival fun?

If you go to a music festival or other live event, your phone is part of the experience. You arrive, check in on social media and even read your friends' messages while you are waiting for the show to start. While the music is on, you take photos and make videos. Then you share your photos, videos or comments on social media.

It can be annoying, though. Look out across the audience and you see bright smartphone screens everywhere. Some people hold their phones high above their heads to get a good shot – right in front of your face.

Smartphones and tablets in the audience can also be a problem for performers and organizers. A lot of the photos and recordings are uploaded onto social media. However, those images and recordings belong to the performer, not to the person who uploads them.

You aren't allowed to take photos and videos at some live events. Some events have phone-free zones. You can bring your phone to the show – but it goes in a magnetic bag, which a member of staff locks. You can't use your phone until you leave the event. (196 words)

A **Ihre Gemeinde plant ein Musikfestival. Einige der gebuchten Bands möchten die Nutzung von Smartphones auf dem Konzertgelände verbieten. Sie stoßen auf den Artikel auf** **Seite 52** **und möchten die anderen Mitglieder des Organisationsteams darüber informieren.**

Schreiben Sie einen zusammenhängenden Text auf Deutsch in ganzen Sätzen. Erwähnen Sie folgende Punkte:

- Warum ist die Nutzung von Smartphones bei Konzerten so beliebt?
- Welche Nachteile hat die Smartphone-Nutzung für andere Konzertbesucher?
- Warum finden Organisatoren und Künstler die Smartphone-Nutzung problematisch?
- Wie kann man mit magnetisch abgeschirmten Taschen Smartphone-freie Konzerte veranstalten?

B **Ihr/e Freund/in hat möchte Influencer werden. Sie finden diesen Artikel zum Thema und möchten sie/ihn darüber informieren.**

So you want to be an influencer?

Being an influencer seems like a great job. You don't need money or qualifications to start your business. You just make fun, informative videos and posts, upload them onto social media and then wait for followers. Money comes from advertising and sponsorship.

Sadly, it isn't quite that simple. A good influencer may seem like your online friend, but in reality, he or she is a talented, hard-working media professional. Those useful tips are the result of hours of research, and that five-minute video was the best out of 20 attempts. If you have the talent, it really can be a great job. You set your own schedule. You choose interesting, exciting topics and brands to work on. People are truly interested in what you have to say.

On the other hand, getting the balance right is difficult – are you only enthusiastic about this brand because the company paid you? After all, influencers only have influence because they seem authentic. Followers' trust is hard to gain and easy to lose. Furthermore, an influencer has no job security. One bad post or video and you can say goodbye to all of your sponsors!

(198 words)

Schreiben Sie einen zusammenhängenden Text auf Deutsch in ganzen Sätzen. Erwähnen Sie folgende Punkte:

- Warum erscheint eine Arbeit als Influencer so locker und mühelos?
- Welche Voraussetzungen braucht man?
- Welche Vorteile hat diese Arbeit tatsächlich?
- Was muss man dabei unbedingt vermeiden?

Get it right: *CHECKLISTE*

- ☑ Text gelesen?
- ☑ Aufgabe gelesen?
- ☑ Wesentliche Punkte notiert?
- ☑ Mit der Aufgabe verglichen?
- ☑ Text geschrieben?
- ☑ Korrektur gelesen?
- ☑ Abgeben!

Project page: Making a "how-to …" video

Work in a small group.

A Each person thinks of at least one skill they can demonstrate to others (see task 4 on page 49 for ideas). One person writes down all the ideas.

B Discuss the skills ideas from A. Which are practical for a two-minute 'how-to' video? They must be …

- **simple** enough to describe in about 5 steps.
- **visual** and easy to show on a video.
- **safe** for viewers to try themselves after watching the video.

Video 5

Watch the video and look at page 87 for more information about how to make a video.

C Choose the best idea.

D Decide who will take on each role.

Producer	Checks the script, selects the location.
Director	Runs the shoot, tells everyone what to do.
Camera operator	Operates the camera.
Props manager	Finds and takes care of all the objects that need to be in the video.
Lighting engineer	Places and operates lights to get a good-quality video.
Actor(s)	Appear(s) and speak(s) in the video.

Working together L

Deciding roles

- I'd like to be responsible for …
- Sophie is good at …
- She should be the …
- Would you like to … ?

Asking for / Offering help

- I need some help with …
- Would you like some help with … ?

Reaching agreement

- Do we all agree that … ?
- I'm (not) happy with …

E Separate the script into sections like this:

Introduction	Actors introduce themselves, explain the skill, what things are needed, etc.
Step 1	Actors demonstrate and explain step 1.
…	
Summary	Actors describe what they did, say goodbye.

F Shoot! Make the video.

Snapshot

What was your favourite thing in this unit?

What important thing did you learn?

What do you need to work on?

At work 6

Warm-up: The world of work

A What do people want from work? Label the pictures with words from the box.

friendly colleagues ▪ interesting tasks
lots of money ▪ respect and status ▪ to be useful

1

2

3

4

5

B Work with a partner. What do <u>you</u> want from work? Draw a mind map in your exercise book.

C Pick <u>five</u> statements a–h that you strongly agree with.

Self-starter **a** I prefer to work things out myself. **b** I want to try new things.	**Team player** **e** Teams are more effective than individuals. **f** It's important that everyone does his/her share.
Breadwinner **c** I want to do my job, get paid and then go home. **d** I like to do things that I know about.	**Influencer** **g** I want to be involved in making decisions. **h** My status in the team is important to me.

D Which type are you, according to your results? Do you agree? Discuss with your partner.

6 At work

A Just a job?

Ruby finished college last year and works in a care home. She is talking about her job with her friends.

1 Before you read

A Which of these pictures do you think shows Ruby's work situation?

1

2

B Skim the text. Did you guess correctly?

2 Reading

Read the dialogue, then complete the tasks opposite.

23

Mo: How's your job going, Ruby? Are you still enjoying it?

Ruby: Hmm … there are things that I like about it, and things that I'm not happy with. The residents – the old people – are great, mostly. Some of their stories are really interesting.

Mo: But … ?

Ruby: I don't like the company that I work for. I think that our working conditions aren't good enough. I also don't think that we provide a good service to the residents.

Lisandra: Oh? How do you mean?

Ruby: We don't have time to do our jobs properly. We just can't do everything. In my opinion, we need at least ten more carers. Some of the old people sit in their rooms all day, with nobody to talk to.

Mo: Wow! That sounds really bad …

Ruby: Yes, it is. The manager says that he can't afford more staff.

Jack: The care home should get some volunteers, if you ask me.

Mo: Good idea!

Ruby: I disagree. I don't think that's a good idea. This isn't a job that anyone can do, without training.

Jack: Sorry, I didn't mean to suggest that.

Ruby: It's okay. Actually, I think that volunteers can help. They can spend time with the residents and listen to them. Volunteers need someone to supervise them though.

Lisandra: I see. What can you do about it?

Ruby: I can't do much. I can leave and try to find another job.

Mo: Complain to the manager.

Ruby: I'm just a new trainee, Mo. Nobody listens to my opinion!

Lisandra: I agree with Mo. You mustn't just give up, in my opinion.

Jack: I disagree. Ruby shouldn't have to solve everybody's problems. I think that you should stay for a while, get more experience, then leave and get a better job.

Ruby: I don't know …

What problems are there in the care home? What solutions do Ruby's friends have? Make a list.

☆ Turn to page 98.

Video 6

Watch the video and look at page 88 for more information about drawing a sketchnote.

3 Ruby's complaints

Work with a partner. Choose a problem from task 2 on page 56. Draw a sketchnote to look at the problem and possible solutions.

4 Words, words, words: Opinions

A Find expressions in the dialogue to complete the lists.

Giving an opinion	Agreeing and disagreeing with an opinion
■ I think that …	■ I agree (with sb)

B Put the letters in the right order to make 'opinion' words.

1 aeeidgrs
2 euggsst
3 iooulnst
4 oodg aeid
5 aeegr
6 iionnp

G

Modal verbs

Aussage	Verneinung
I/you/he/she/it/we/they	*I/you/he/she/it/we/they*
can/should/must *(do something about it).*	***can't/couldn't/mustn't*** *(do anything about it).*

! *mustn't* = nicht dürfen

5 Practice: Modal verbs

A **Check it out!** Suchen Sie drei Sätze im Dialog auf Seite 56 mit unterschiedlichen Modalverben.

B Complete the sentences with a modal verb and the ideas in the box.

spend some money ■ do things themselves ■ talk to the manager
help in the care home

1 Ruby and her colleagues …
2 Volunteers …
3 The company which runs the home …
4 The residents at the home …

6 Staff meeting

Hold a staff meeting in groups of four. One person takes notes. Decide what you can/should/must do to improve the situation at the care home. Use expressions from task 4. Report back to the class with your decisions.

B An ethical employer

Mo's uncles, Oz and Simon, have written a crowdfunding page for their new painting and decorating business.

1 Mediation

24 **Read Oz and Simon's crowdfunding page, then complete the tasks opposite.**

Ethical Painting and Decorating

Our experience so far: "We have worked in many painting and decorating businesses. The pay was low, and the hours were long. As trainees, we were given the worst tasks. The paint and tools we used contained chemicals and other damaging materials and they gave us headaches and skin problems. They also weren't environmentally friendly. Our protective equipment was also old and faulty, so our workplace was unsafe."

Our idea: "We know that we can do better …

so we are starting the Ethical Painting and Decorating Company."

Oz Hussain & Simon Brown

Our vision:

Non-toxic paints: Our paints only use natural raw materials. They last just as long as other paints and the colours are more beautiful. They don't contain toxic chemicals.
The result: safe working conditions for us and a healthy, beautiful home for our customers!

Social and environmental responsibility: A Fairtrade company makes our tools – paint brushes and rollers – in Sri Lanka. We pay a fair price to the suppliers and they pay a fair wage to their employees. Everything we use is eco-friendly – even our new electric van will be.

Community projects: We financially support the Homeless Youth Action project and we want to employ one trainee per year who is either homeless or in insecure housing.

Equal opportunities employer: We do not discriminate because of gender, sexual orientation, age, ethnic background or physical ability of our employees.

Target funding: $45,000
to buy an electric van and other equipment

A **Arbeiten Sie in einer kleinen Gruppe. Jede Person liest einen Teil des Textes und berichtet der Gruppe auf Deutsch, worum es in ihrem Teil geht.**

B **Sie finden Oz und Simons Idee gut und fragen sich, ob man ein ähnliches Start-up-Unternehmen auch in Ihrer Stadt gründen könnte. Sie schreiben einen Text für diejenigen Ihrer Freundinnen/Freunde, die vielleicht auch Interesse daran hätten.**

Schreiben Sie einen zusammenhängenden Text auf Deutsch in ganzen Sätzen. Erwähnen Sie folgende Punkte aus dem Text gegenüber:

- Welche Probleme kann es bei Betrieben geben, die nicht auf die Herkunft und Qualität ihrer Rohstoffe und Materialien achten?
- Welche Vorteile haben die Materialien, die Oz und Simons ethischen Malerbetrieb verwenden will?
- Wie will sich die Firma gemeinnützig engagieren?
- Wie will die Firma mit ihren Arbeitskräften umgehen?

☆ **Turn to page 98.**

2 Words, words, words: Jobs and working conditions

A **Look at the text and find the English for these German words.**

1 Bezahlung
2 Azubi
3 Aufgabe
4 Werkzeug
5 Schutzausrüstung
6 giftig
7 Chancengleichheit
8 Arbeitgeber/in
9 Arbeitnehmer/in
10 diskriminieren

B **Complete the sentences. All the words are in the text on page 58.**

1 'Is your company a good ___?' – 'Yes, it treats us well and the ___ is good.'
2 ___ have less responsibility than qualified ___ because they aren't experienced in the job yet.
3 If you are using ___ materials, it's very important to wear ___ equipment.
4 You must use the right ___ for the ___ that you're doing, or you might hurt yourself.
5 It's unfair to ___ against people from particular groups: everyone should get ___ treatment.

3 A company of our own

Work in a small group around a big sheet of paper. Work out a 'vision' for your own start-up company.

- What product/service does it provide? Write it in the centre of the paper. Find a good name.
- Each person chooses one of the topics below and writes notes on his/her corner of the paper.

Working conditions	How do you treat your employees? Are there benefits for your employees?
Product/service	What is the best thing about your product/service? Why should customers buy it?
Tools and equipment	What things do you need for your business?
Workplace	Where do you run your business from? Where is it?

When you have finished, do a gallery walk and look at the other groups' business ideas.

C All in a day's work

What is the difference between apprenticeships in Germany and in English-speaking countries?

1 Before you listen

Discuss with a partner. Which of the workplaces in the photos would be the most interesting to work in? Why?

1

2

3

2 Listening

25 **A Listen to the recording. Say which workplaces in task 1 the speakers work in.**

1 Emily

2 Amira

3 Luke

B What are the jobs called in German? Find out about them on the internet.

event technician ▪ barista ▪ upcycler / furniture maker

C Listen to each person again, then complete the table.

Job	Good points	Bad points
Event technician	variety,	stress,
Barista		
Upcycler / Furniture maker		

☆ Turn to page 99.

3 Discussion

26 **Work with a partner. Read the email from your friend Lex, who lives in Australia, then complete the task below.**

Vocational training in Germany and Australia

Hi!

How are you? Things are busy here. I finished my plumbing course last month and I'm applying for jobs now.

I read online that the apprenticeship system in Germany is very good – but very strict. There are lots of jobs that you need to do an apprenticeship for! I remember reading that there are apprenticeships that take three years, but you can also do some that only take two years. You can then work in the same area, but the job you do isn't so skilled. I think that is a really good idea if you aren't so good at exams. It's interesting that the different jobs and apprenticeships have special names.

Over here in Australia (and also in the UK and the USA, I think), apprenticeships are less important. I mean, there are apprenticeships – for lots of different jobs – but an apprenticeship isn't usually compulsory. You can work as a baker or a joiner or manage a shop without any formal qualifications. Companies take on unskilled trainees and train them 'on the job'.

For jobs where safety and quality are very important, qualifications are necessary, of course. You can't just call yourself an electrician or a paramedic or a bank clerk without the correct qualification!

All the same, it seems to me that our system is more flexible than the German system. If I don't like what I'm doing, I can change careers – even 'reinvent myself' – quite easily.

What do you think about it all?

Lex (270 words)

- Compare the German and the Australian training system. What is different?
- What advantages could the Australian system have for young people?
- What disadvantages can you think of?
- Which system do you prefer? Why?

Report back to the class with the main points of your discussion.

4 Writing

You want to thank Lex for his email and tell him which system you prefer and why. Write your email to Lex. You can start like this:

Hi Lex!

Thanks for your email. It was nice to hear from you.

…

Skills practice: Reading

Bei dieser Übung geht es darum, einen längeren Text (z.B. einen Zeitungsartikel oder einen Blogeintrag) aufmerksam und sorgfältig zu lesen, um anschließend Fragen zum Leseverständnis zu beantworten.

Get it right: *Leseverständnis*

1. Orientieren Sie sich vor dem Lesen: Worum geht es?
2. Überfliegen Sie den Artikel, um einen ersten Eindruck vom Inhalt zu gewinnen (= Grobverständnis).
3. Lesen Sie sich die Aufgabe genau durch: Welche Informationen aus dem Text benötigen Sie?
4. Suchen Sie die entsprechenden Informationen im Text und lesen Sie sich die jeweiligen Passagen aufmerksam durch (= Detailverständnis).
5. Beantworten Sie die Aufgabe.
6. Lesen Sie sich den gesamten Text nochmals durch und vergleichen Sie Ihre Lösungen mit dem Text.
7. Korrigieren Sie oder ergänzen Sie soweit nötig Ihre Lösungen.
8. Bei weiteren Aufgaben wiederholen Sie die Schritte 3–7.

Surprising benefits of team sport

We all know that sport and exercise are good for our physical and mental health. However, it seems that sports, particularly team sports, have other benefits at school. An American survey of high-school students found that students who play a team sport generally get better grades.

The researchers looked at information from 9,700 students. The students came from schools in inner-city, suburban and rural areas. They all did after-school activities of some kind. Some did dance or drama classes. Some played music, and some took part in clubs which prepared them for the world of work. Others did team sports.

The researchers found that the students who did team sports did best in class. They learned better in the classroom and they had stronger motivation. They had a more positive opinion of school.

This fits in with more recent research in Australia and the Netherlands about teenagers and younger children. All kinds of sport and physical activity improve students' learning. However, it seems that team sports are particularly important.

So why is the average amount of time spent on sport and exercise in schools sinking? In some schools, students spend less than 10 minutes a day doing exercise: that isn't much. Outside school, organized community sport is being offered less.

Why do team sports have this positive effect on learning? Educational experts think that playing sport in a team improves people's concentration, ability to plan and ability to work with others. It also improves self-confidence and social skills.

(253 words)

A Aussagen über den Text

Entscheiden Sie, ob die Aussagen richtig *(true)* oder falsch *(false)* sind.

1 Der Text handelt nur von den USA.
2 Die Studie betraf ausschließlich Schulen in den Innenstädten.
3 Alle Schüler/innen in der Studie nahmen an außerschulischen Aktivitäten teil.
4 Nicht alle Schüler/innen in der Studie trieben Sport.
5 Die Mannschaftssportler/innen zeigen die besten schulischen Leistungen.
6 Research in Australia and Europe had similar results to the US study.
7 All kinds of exercise are equally good for school performance.
8 Young people have fewer opportunities to do sport than before.
9 Ten minutes of sport a day is enough.
10 Experts are worried that team sports distract students from their schoolwork.

B Finish the sentences

Use only information from the text.

1 Nearly 10,000 students
2 In class, students who did team sports
3 Although team sports have the most benefits,
4 Unfortunately, young people
5 Experts believe

C Matching

Match the beginnings 1–5 to the endings A–E according to the text.

1 The study looked at …
2 Team sport leads to …
3 Other after-school classes don't give students …
4 Community groups organize fewer …
5 Team sports probably improve …

A students' planning and group work.
B the same learning benefits.
C team sport and school grades.
D sports teams and team sport events.
E more motivation in school.

Get it right: *CHECKLISTE*

- ☑ Text gelesen?
- ☑ Aufgabe genau gelesen?
- ☑ Wichtige Punkte im Text markiert?
- ☑ Aufgabe gelöst?
- ☑ Aufgabe gecheckt?
- ☑ Abgeben!

Project page: Job skills game

Work in a small group. Make a job skills card game for jobs that you know.

A Brainstorm jobs that you can do an apprenticeship for. You need <u>five</u> different jobs per person. Here are some jobs to start with:

baker ■ care assistant ■ chimney sweep ■ cook ■ courier ■ fire officer ■ tailor
emergency paramedic ■ make-up and hair artist ■ market researcher ■ media designer
motorcycle mechanic ■ personal trainer ■ sales assistant ■ veterinary assistant

B Make a card, like this one, for each job. Think about the job and guess the skill level (1–5).

job side:

COOK

skill side:

SKILL LEVEL

Creative:	3
Manual:	5
Numerical:	2
Social:	3
Technical:	1

C Put all of the cards in one pile. You can see the job side of the top card.

D Play the game. When you have finished, swap cards with another group and play again.

1 Mix the cards and deal them – **job side up**. Leave your cards on the table.
2 The youngest player chooses a skill. For example: 'Creative'.
3 This player picks up the **top card**, turns it over and reads out the skill level. For example: 'Creative – three'.
4 The other players read out the level for the same skill from their **top card**. For example: 'Creative – five'.
5 The player with the highest skill level wins the round. The winner collects **the top cards** from the other players.
6 The winner chooses a skill from her/his next card. Repeat the game from step 3.
7 The player with the most cards wins the game.
! If two or more players have the highest level, the player who started the round chooses another skill.

Snapshot

What was your favourite thing in this unit?

What important thing did you learn?

What do you need to work on?

Plans for the future 7

Warm-up: Life goals, life skills

A **What do you want to achieve in the next few years? Make your own 'my life' poster like the example below. Add the phrases from the box or use your own ideas.**

do part-time jobs ■ explore the world ■ find a partner ■ get qualifications ■ learn to drive ■ make a home ■ meet new people ■ save up ■ start a family

B **Look at your partner's poster.**

- What do you think is missing? Tell them.
- What do you think isn't important? Explain why.

C **Predict what will happen in your 'life story'. Draw a path through the life events on your poster.**

D **Use your poster to tell your partner your life story. You can either be looking forward to what 'will' happen or looking back at what 'happened'.**

EXAMPLE: *After I leave school, I will do casual jobs for a few months. I will save some money and then I ...*

or *After I left school, I did casual jobs for a few months. I saved up, and then I ...*

A Career plans

Lisandra discusses a career idea with her friends. Not everyone is convinced.

1 Before you read

Look at the picture. What do you think Lisandra's career idea is? What do you think of it?

2 Reading

Read the dialogue, then complete the tasks on the next page.

27

Ruby: Lisandra, what will you do when you leave school? Do you have any career plans?

Lisandra: I have an idea. It isn't really a plan yet. But … you'll laugh at me.

Ruby: No, of course we won't laugh at you. Come on, tell us!

Lisandra: Okay, … well you know that I'm fit and energetic.

Mo: You're the fittest person I know.

Lisandra: And you know that I'm good with people – "good interpersonal skills", the careers adviser calls it.

Ruby: Definitely. You can talk to anyone – and get them to talk to you.

Lisandra: Right. And I love animals …

Mo: Yes, you're definitely an animal lover. You love your dog, Titan.

Jack: He may be the smallest, ugliest dog I know, with a bad temper … but …

Mo: Titan's cute! What you mean is, he doesn't like you, Jack.

Ruby: Shh, you two! Lisandra's trying to tell us about her career plans.

Mo: Sorry. Go on, Lisandra.

Lisandra: Well, I put all of those things together and I thought: I'll be a personal trainer … for pets!

Jack: Hahaha!

Lisandra: See! I knew it! You're laughing!

Mo: Stop it, Jack! … I think that it's a great idea … but … is it a real job? I mean, is it something that people do – as a career?

Lisandra: I don't know. Maybe I'll be the first one – in Barton. Think about it: there are lots of people with dogs that never get a proper walk. The dogs get fat and lazy because they don't get any exercise. Then there are people who work all day. Their dogs stay at home, lonely and bored, and they bark and bark. So, the neighbours get angry.

Jack: Yes! There's a dog on our street that barks all day. My dad says he'll …

Ruby: I don't want to seem negative, but isn't that just a dog walker?

Lisandra: No, because I'll work out a proper fitness plan – like a personal trainer does for people.

Jack: Why do you need interpersonal skills? Your customers will be animals!

Lisandra: The animals have owners, Jack – people. And the owners will only trust me if they like and respect me.

Mo: How will you find your customers?

Lisandra: Well, I'll put an ad up at the vet's. I'll also use social media, and …

A **What is this dog thinking? Use information from the text.**

B **Beurteilen Sie Lisandras Berufsdiee anhand bestimmter Kriterien. Übertragen Sie die Tabelle in Ihr Heft und füllen Sie sie aus.**

	Berufsidee ‚Privattrainerin für Haustiere'
Interessen und Vorlieben	*Tiere, ...*
Fertigkeiten und Eignung	
Praktische Erfahrung (Beruf/Hobby)	
Recherche, konkrete Pläne	

3 Discussion

Read the comments from Lisandra's friends and family. Which do you agree /disagree with?

1 Wow! Unusual ideas often turn out to be the best.
2 You won't succeed without vocational qualifications. Are there courses for this?
3 You won't earn enough to live on. You should get a proper job.
4 You'll need a lot of money to start a business. I'm not gonna pay!
5 OMG! You want to do what? It's a crazy idea, but it might work.
6 What about some work experience at an animal shelter? That'll really help you!

G

The will future

Das *will-Futur* wird verwendet, wenn man ausdrücken möchte, dass etwas in der Zukunft geschehen wird.

! won't = will not

to work (arbeiten)

Aussage	Frage	Verneinung
*I/you/he/she/it/we/they **will** work.*	***Will** I/you/he/she/it/we/they work?*	*I/you/he/she/it/we/they **won't** work.*

4 Practice: Will future

A **Check it out!** **Suchen Sie drei Beispiele der *will future* im Dialog auf Seite 66.**

B **Complete these sentences with verbs from the box. Make three of them positive (will) and three of them negative (won't).**

go ▪ laugh ▪ advise ▪ offer ▪ finish ▪ tell

1 I ___ school this summer.
2 I ___ on holiday with my family.
3 Lisandra ___ her parents about her idea.
4 They ___ at her idea.
5 Her dad ___ her about what to do.
6 Her mum ___ lots of advice.

☆ **Turn to page 99.**

B Unexpected career paths

Not everything runs smoothly in our lives. Sometimes there are unexpected changes which can turn into (positive) opportunities.

1 Reading

A Arbeiten Sie mit einer Partnerin / einem Partner zusammen.
Partner/in A: Lesen Sie die Texte unten. Haben Sie die Hauptpunkte verstanden?
Partner/in B: Schlagen Sie Seite 91 auf.

Befragen Sie jetzt Ihre/n Partner/in nach ihrer/seiner Hälfte der Geschichte: Wie ging die Geschichte zu Ende, bzw. wie hatte sie begonnen? Machen Sie sich Notizen auf Deutsch.

Lily's story, part 1 **A**

Lily was 16. She enjoyed school and was a popular student. Then she realized that she was pregnant. Lily and her boyfriend decided to keep the baby, although their parents were against it. The young couple had a lot of stress. Perhaps that is why their relationship ended soon after the baby was born. Lily left school to look after the baby. She had no qualifications, no job and no plans for the future. She lived at home with her parents.

Charlie's story, part 1 **B**

Charlie's parents had a difficult relationship and argued all the time. Finally, when Charlie was 15, they split up. Neither Charlie's mum nor his dad had a real home – or anywhere for Charlie to sleep. As a result, Charlie became homeless and dropped out of school. At first, his friends and family let him 'couch surf', but it became harder and harder to find somewhere to stay. That's when he started to sleep on the streets.

Sameen's story, part 2 **C**

Sameen was at home without a job and didn't know what to do next. Bored and depressed, she played video games with her brother and his friends. Sameen became good at the games because of her fast reactions and good strategy. She was also entertaining to watch – making up funny commentaries while she beat player after player. She streamed her games online. Soon she started to get advertising and sponsorship deals. Her hobby became a business.

Dylan's story, part 2 **D**

One day, Dylan walked past his old workplace. He stopped to chat with Mr Chan, the owner of the café next door. Mr Chan complained about all the waste that his café had to throw away. He mentioned that old coffee waste made good compost. It was great to grow mushrooms in. Dylan did some online research about growing mushrooms. With free coffee waste from cafés, it was easy and cheap – but gourmet mushrooms were expensive! Dylan decided to set up a business growing mushrooms in compost made from coffee waste. This was good for the environment and he made lots of money selling mushrooms to local restaurants.

B The class separates into four groups. Which is your favourite story? Discuss in your group. Use your notes from A.

2 Listening

Lily, Charlie, Sameen and Dylan talk about their stories in a podcast.

28

A Listen to the recording. Who is described in each sentence below: Lily, Charlie, Sameen or Dylan?

1 ___ never thought about life goals before things went wrong.
2 ___ was certain about the right thing to do.
3 ___ believes that we all have lots of paths to choose from.
4 ___ found it difficult to ask for help.

B Listen again. What did they say? Match two pieces of advice to each person.

Lily

Charlie

Sameen

Dylan

1 Be flexible.
2 Look for opportunities around you.
3 Talk to people.
4 Find out what your talents and interests are.
5 Don't give up.
6 Be kind to yourself and others.
7 Don't be afraid to ask for help.
8 Find someone to be your mentor.

☆ **Turn to page 99.**

Video 7

Watch the video and look at page 88 for more information about how to generate ideas.

3 Discussion

A Read Oliver's story.

Oliver's story

'You're one of life's underdogs.' Oliver hears that a lot. Things just go wrong for him. He was about to start an apprenticeship as a motorbike mechanic. Everything was arranged, but then it fell apart. Oliver got into a fight and got into trouble with the police. His future employer found out about it. Suddenly, there was no place for an apprentice. Now Oliver's father says that he can't afford to look after him, so he has to move out.

B Work with a partner. What advice would you give Oliver? Make notes.
Think about: Who could Oliver talk to? What could he do to make his 'future employer' change his mind? How could he pay his father so he could stay living at home?

C When you have finished, report back to the class with the main points of your discussion.

C I'm writing to …

Lisandra and Ruby decide to make some videos together – for fun. They upload the videos about animal training and sports fashion onto social media as 'Andi & Ruby's Pet Bootcamp' and get a lot of likes and follows. They see a business opportunity.

1 Reading

29 **A Read the advertisement, then complete the task below.**

Seeking social media reviewers*

Are you a social media reviewer, tester or influencer?
Do you like sport? Are you interested in sports equipment and sports fashion?
Then we are interested in hearing from you.

Treebird Sports Fashion is an ethical, cruelty-free, carbon neutral sports fashion company. No sweatshops, no animal products. Just natural fibres that look great and are great to wear. We have some exciting new product lines and we want to create a buzz on social media.

Interested?
Please write to our PR Manager, Jason Kyte (jason.kyte@treebird-sportsfashion.nex) with the subject line 'Social Media Review Application'.
Explain what you do and why your personality and interests fit with our brand.
Include some links to show us your work.
Tell us which product lines you wish to review:
women's sport, women's leisure, men's sport, men's leisure

TREEBIRD · Sports Fashion · Naturally

*Reviewers receive free samples of the chosen product line for their review only. There is no payment for reviews. Reviewers are free to provide an unbiased, honest review. (178 words)

Make notes about the following:

1 the company's name
2 who they are looking for
3 reasons for the advertisement
4 important information that should be included in your application
5 payment

B Lisandra replies to the advertisement. Compare her reply with your notes. Does she include all the information the company needs?

Social Media Review Application

Dear Mr Kyte,

My name is Lisandra Tamm. I am writing to offer my services as a social media reviewer for your products.

My business partner Ruby McColl and I run the video channel 'Andi & Ruby's Pet Bootcamp'. We are fit, energetic young animal lovers who have great interpersonal skills too! Because you are an ethical, cruelty-free brand, your products suit our show very well.

You can see examples of our work on our video channel here. Our short videos feature sports fashion and animal training advice.

I look forward to hearing from you.

Yours sincerely,

Lisandra Tamm

2 Words, words, words: Writing an email

Read Lisandra's email again, then complete the language box below (1–6).

L

Writing a formal email

Greeting

(1) Mr/Mrs …

(2) Sir/Madam (*Name der Empfängerin / des Empfängers ist unbekannt*)

Introduction

(3) (offer / ask about / apply for) …

Polite ending

(4) hearing from you.

(5) for your help.

Close

(6) (*Name der Empfängerin / des Empfängers ist bekannt*)

Yours faithfully, (*Name der Empfängerin / des Empfängers ist unbekannt*)

3 Over to you

You want to be a social media reviewer for Treebird. Write your reply to the advertisement. Think of the following information:

- Why you would be good in this role
- The content that you produce (videos, blog, etc.)
- URLs/hashtags for your work
- Which products you want to review

☆ **Turn to page 99.**

Skills practice: Managing situations

Bei dieser Übung geht es darum, eine Alltagssituation mit einem/r englischen Muttersprachler/in sprachlich zu bewältigen. Sie sollen auf dessen/deren Fragen, Bitten oder Vorschläge reagieren und die auf Deutsch vorgegebenen Informationen auf Englisch ausdrücken.

Get it right: *Wie löse ich eine 'Managing situations'-Aufgabe?*

- Folgende Themen treten häufig auf:
  - Wegbeschreibungen
  - Small Talk
  - Einkauf z. B. von Souvenirs
  - sich mit einer Freundin / einem Freund verabreden
- Sie sollten folgende sprachliche Gepflogenheiten beherrschen:
  - höfliches Bitten und Danken: *please* und *thank you, you're welcome*
  - sich freundlich begrüßen und verabschieden
  - nach dem Befinden fragen und darauf antworten
  - Hilfe anbieten und annehmen

Achten Sie bei Verben darauf, dass Sie für die jeweilige Situation die passende Zeitform benutzen!

A **Sie sind in der Stadt unterwegs und werden von einer irischen Touristin angesprochen. Die junge Frau bittet Sie um Hilfe, spricht aber kein Deutsch. Was würden Sie im folgenden Dialog auf Englisch sagen?**

Ava: *Excuse me! Are you from around here?*
You: (0) Ja. Wie kann ich dir helfen?
EXAMPLE: *Yes. How can I help you?*
Ava: *I'm meeting my friends at the cinema. We want to watch an English film and I can't find the cinema on the map on my phone!*
You: (1) Das Kino ist gar nicht weit von hier, vielleicht fünf Minuten zu Fuß.
...
Ava: *Oh, good! How do I get there?*
You: (2) Geh geradeaus, nimm die zweite Straße links, dann die erste Straße rechts. Dann ist das Kino auf der rechten Seite.
...
Ava: *I go left, then right, then ... Oh, dear! I'm hopeless with directions! I hope I'll find it ...*
You: (3) Ich komme mit dir. Ich muss sowieso in diese Richtung.
...
Ava: *Thanks!*
...

Five minutes later ...

You: (4) So, hier das Kino.
...
Ava: *And here are my friends. Thanks for your help!*
You: (5) Tschüss! Viel Spaß bei dem Film!
...
Ava: *Thanks! Bye!*

B **Sie sind zu Besuch in Edinburgh, Schottland, und Sie gehen mit ihren Freunden in ein Café. Auf dem Weg zurück in die Jugendherberge stellen Sie fest, dass Sie Ihre Tasche im Café vergessen haben. Sie eilen zurück und sprechen den Kellner an.**
Was würden Sie im folgenden Dialog auf Englisch sagen?

You: (1) Entschuldigung! Können Sie mir bitte helfen?
...
Waiter: *Certainly! Is there a problem?*
You: (2) Ja! Ich war vor einer Viertelstunde mit meinen beiden Freunden hier und habe meine Tasche liegen lassen.
...
Waiter: *Ah, okay. I'll see if I can find it for you. What does it look like?*
You: (3) Sie ist klein und schwarz.
...
Waiter: *Where were you sitting?*
You: (4) Wir waren da drüben, am zweiten Tisch links neben der Tür.
...
Waiter: *Let me have a look for you. I'll be right back.*
You: (5) Hoffentlich finden Sie sie ...
...
Waiter: *Don't worry. I expect it will still be where you left it.*

Two minutes later ...

Waiter: *Is this it?*
You: (6) Ja, das ist sie! Vielen Dank!
...
Waiter: *No problem. I'm glad I could help. Enjoy the rest of your day!*
You: (7) Sie auch! Auf Wiedersehen!
...
Waiter: *Goodbye! And keep hold of that bag!*

Get it right: *CHECKLISTE*

- ☑ Aufgabe genau gelesen?
- ☑ Dialog durchgelesen?
- ☑ Lückenangaben gelesen?
- ☑ Deutsch ungefähr ins Englische übersetzt?
- ☑ Den kompletten Dialog gelesen?
- ☑ Alles korrekt?
- ☑ Abgeben!

Project page: My vision

A **Skills and talents. What are you good at? Make your own word cloud.**

EXAMPLE:

listening
online research
problem solving
creative projects
video games

B **What do you want from life? Find images which show your goals and dreams. Use them to make a 'vision board' with your word cloud.**

C **Present your vision board to the class. Do a gallery walk.**

Snapshot

What was your favourite thing in this unit?

What important thing did you learn?

What do you need to work on?

Warm-up: My summer job

Read the comic strip and then complete the tasks below.

1 Which summer jobs are mentioned above? Think of two pros and two cons of each job.
2 What job skills would you get from the summer jobs?
3 Which one of the summer jobs would you most like to do? Why?

8 First steps

A Getting ready

Jack is looking for a summer job. He gets some good news.

1 Before you read

Work with a partner. Copy the mind map into your exercise book. Add the ideas from the box, then some of your own ideas.

ask friends and relatives about vacancies ▪ search for jobs online ▪ contact local businesses directly ▪ fill out application forms ▪ identify my skills ▪ send emails ▪ write my CV

GET "JOB FIT" — **SUMMER HOLIDAY JOB** — *GET THE JOB*

FIND JOBS

2 Reading

30 **Jack phones Ruby to tell her his news. Read the dialogue, then complete the tasks on the next page.**

Jack: Hi, Ruby! I've got an interview for a summer job!

Ruby: Cool! What's the job?

Jack:: Charity fundraiser. They said there's a lot of work outdoors.

Ruby: Sounds good. How did you find it?

Jack:: On a website for summer jobs. I filled out lots of application forms and this is my first interview.

Ruby: That's okay. You only need one job …

Jack: I haven't got the job yet. I'm a bit nervous. I don't know what to expect.

Ruby: Have you ever applied for a job before?

Jack: No, I haven't. I've done some work experience for school, but I haven't had a proper job.

Ruby: Here are a few things that helped me. Choose smart clothes for the interview.

Jack: I'll be outside. It's not an office job.

Ruby: You'll still need to look smart for the interview, though. Good trousers and a proper shirt.

Jack: Right … What else?

Ruby: Have you thought of any questions?

Jack: Questions? No, I haven't. They'll ask me the questions!

Ruby: You'll get a chance to ask questions too. It's important to show that you're interested. Research the employer. Anything you can't find online – ask. You can even say 'I didn't find anything on your website about …'.

Jack: Nice! … Anything else?

Ruby: Review your application, so that you can predict some of the interviewer's questions and prepare your answers.

Jack: How do I do that?

Ruby: Didn't you fill out an application form?

Jack: Yes. And I uploaded my CV, too.

Ruby: Have you told them about your skills, interests and so on?

Jack: Yes, of course.

Ruby: Well, the interviewer will want to know more about them. You need to be ready to answer questions about them, give them more details, and also examples to show that you really have the skills.

Jack: Ah …

Ruby: Jack, you didn't tell them about skills you haven't actually got, did you?

Jack: Err, no. Not really …

Ruby: Jack!

A **Which photo shows the sort of job that Jack has applied for?**

1

2

3

B **Write Jack's job interview checklist. All the information you need is in the text on page 76.**

1 *Choose smart clothes.*
2 ___

C **Class brainstorm. Think of more ideas how to prepare for a job interview.**

G

The present perfect

Das *present perfect* wird verwendet, wenn man sagen will, dass (nicht wann!) etwas geschehen ist. Mit dem *present perfect* drückt man auch aus, seit wann oder wie lange ein Zustand schon andauert.

to work (arbeiten) → Unregelmäßige Verben, S. 142

Aussage	Frage	Verneinung
I/you/we/they ***have*** *work****ed***	***Have*** *I/you/we/they work****ed****?*	*I/you/we/they* ***haven't*** *work****ed***
he/she/it ***has*** *work****ed***	***Has*** *he/she/it work****ed****?*	*he/she/it* ***hasn't*** *work****ed***

3 Practice: Present perfect

A **Check it out!** **Suchen Sie drei Beispiele der *present perfect* im Dialog auf Seite 76.**

B **Complete these sentences with verbs from the box. Put them into the correct form.**

(not) work ▪ walk ▪ (not) fill out ▪ apply for ▪ (not) speak ▪ live

1 I ___ here since I was ten.
2 He ___ up this mountain before.
3 They ___ jobs in Spain.
4 They ___ to each other for years.
5 She ___ in a café before.
6 I ___ the application form yet.

☆ **Turn to page 100.**

C **Work with a partner.**

Partner A: **You have a job interview next week. Your partner helps you prepare.**
Partner B: **Ask your partner questions in the present perfect to prepare them for their interview.**
EXAMPLE: *Have you chosen smart clothes for the interview? – Yes, I have. / No, I haven't done that yet.*

When you have finished, swap roles.

B Job ads

Students at Barton College are thinking about holiday jobs at the local theme park, Otmoor Castle.

1 Reading

Read the advertisement, then complete the task below.

31

Britain's most popular theme park
now recruiting students for holiday jobs!

OTMOOR CASTLE

Can you see yourself in any of these jobs?

Ride attendant
We have over 50 rides at the park. Ride attendants assist guests getting on and off rides, check wristbands and make sure that passengers meet height restrictions. Are you fit, responsible and diplomatic? Then this may be the role for you!

Roving photographer
We have temporary posts for photographers. Spend your summer holidays taking photos! You can go on all of our rides for free – taking fun photos of guests having the time of their lives. This will appeal to creative, adventurous types!

Food and beverage worker
You will serve food or work behind the bar or in the kitchen of our three restaurants, two cafés and two bars. You will learn about food hygiene and safety as part of your training. It is a busy and varied job for someone reliable. No two days will be the same!

Maintenance assistant
If you're hard-working, and prefer to work 'behind the scenes' rather than with guests and you have practical skills, this job is for you. Maintenance assistants support our permanent maintenance staff and engineers.

Entertainer
Can you juggle, play an instrument, do magic tricks or sing? Would you like to dress up as our mascot Ottie the Bear and greet guests? You need to be a fun-loving person who is still cheerful at the end of a long day.

Apply with your CV and covering letter to Wizard Entertainment, HR Department, PO Box 172, Thame, Oxon, OX9 3XZ, England.

Match the online reviews to the jobs.

★★★	Otmoor Castle is a good place to work and I had lovely colleagues. But every day WAS the same: a big, big pile of dirty dishes to wash! *Mahdi*
★	A tough crowd to please! I was on my feet all day and hardly got a smile or a 'thank you'. And it was hot in that costume. Never again! *Alex*
★★★★★	I really loved my four weeks at Otmoor Castle. It was great to take pictures of people having fun! *JP*

2 Mediation

Ihre Freunde Samira und Lars suchen einen Ferienjob für die Sommerferien und möchten gern in Großbritannien arbeiten.
Wählen Sie eine der beiden Personen aus:

Samira ist fleißig, verantwortungsbewusst und praktisch veranlagt. Sie ist eher still, aber nicht unfreundlich.

Lars ist kreativ, erfinderisch und hat gern mit Menschen zu tun. Er kommt mit allen gut aus.

Überlegen Sie sich, welche drei der auf Seite 78 ausgeschriebenen Stellen am besten zu ihm/ihr passen. Schicken Sie ihm/ihr dazu eine Textnachricht mit Kurzinfos auf Deutsch.

- Art der Arbeit (Stellenbezeichnung, Aufgaben, Anforderungen)
- allgemeine Informationen zu Arbeitsstätte, Arbeitgeber und Bewerbung

EXAMPLE: *Hallo Samira! Ich habe drei Jobs gefunden, die dir vielleicht gefallen könnten …*

☆ **Turn to page 100.**

3 Words, words, words: Adjectives

A **Find ten adjectives on the rollercoaster.**

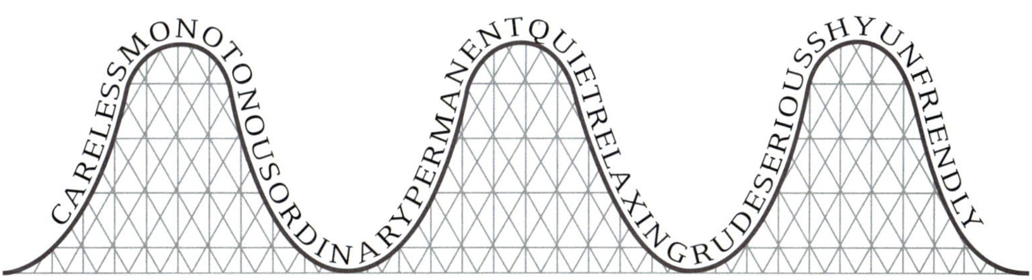

B **Find adjectives in the text which are opposites of the words you found in A.**

4 Discussion

A **Work in a small group. Look at these theme park jobs. Maybe you can think of others. Which is your dream/nightmare job? Why?**

bar steward ▪ car park attendant ▪ cleaner ▪ nursery assistant ▪ entertainer
gardener ▪ housekeeping assistant ▪ kitchen worker ▪ maintenance person
photographer ▪ ride attendant ▪ security guard ▪ shop assistant
ticket attendant ▪ waiter/waitress

B **Report back to the class with the main points of your discussion.**

C **The class votes to decide which are the dream and nightmare theme park jobs.**

C Interviews

Rita, Oliver and Sarah, students at Barton College, have got interviews as ride attendants at Otmoor Castle.

Video 8
Watch the video and look at page 88 for more information about how to ace a job interview.

1 Listening

32 **Listen to the three interviews with Rita, Oliver and Sarah.**

A Match the interviewer's notes to the three candidates. Who are they about?

a *Well prepared but too confident.*
b *Confident and honest.*
c *Nervous and gives unclear answers.*

B Listen again to the three candidates. Stop the recording after each candidate and complete the table.

	Strengths	Weaknesses
Rita	*hard-working,*	*weak motivation,*
Oliver		
Sarah		

☆ Turn to page 100.

C Look at the table in B. Who would you choose for the job as the ride attendant? Say why.

2 Placemat: The interview panel

Work in a small group around a large sheet of paper. You are the members of the interview panel at Otmoor Castle.

1 Write 'ride attendant' and the job requirements (see page 78) in the middle of the piece of paper.
2 Each student thinks about one candidate: Rita, Oliver or Sarah.
3 Write points for your candidate in your corner of the placemat.
4 Discuss the candidates. Try hard to make everyone vote for your candidate!

Write the name of the successful candidate in the middle of the placemat.

3 Words, words, words: Personal qualities

Without using a dictionary write down the English words for as many of the German words in the box below as possible. Compare with your partner and fill in any gaps. If your list still isn't full, look up any words in a dictionary.

kreativ ▪ verantwortungsbewusst ▪ abenteuerlustig ▪ praktisch
voller Energie ▪ diplomatisch ▪ kontaktfreudig ▪ zuverlässig ▪ selbstbewusst ▪ ehrlich

4 A job interview role play

A Read the interviewer's questions and decide which three answers match each question.

Interviewer's questions:

1 Why did you apply for this job?
2 Can you tell me about yourself, please?
3 What do you see as your biggest challenge in this job?
4 Can you tell me about any teamwork experience you have?

Interviewee's answers:

a Making sure everyone is safe.
b I started a drama group at school with other students.
c I play in the school football team.
d I like helping people.
e Working effectively in a team.
f I enjoy meeting new people.
g I think it will be good work experience.
h I'm 18 and I go to Barton College.
i The job sounds perfect for me.
j I'm a sociable person and like adventures.
k I like working on my own.
l Helping the guests have a fun day out.

B Think of some phrases you can use as the interviewer and interviewee to start and finish a job interview. Write them down.

C With a partner act out an interview for one of the jobs on page 78.
Student A: You are the interviewer. Think of a nice way to start the interview. Then ask the questions in part A.
Student B: You are the interviewee. Think of your answers to the questions in A. You can use the suggestions given or your own ideas. Think of one question to ask the interviewer at the end of the interview.
When you have finished, swap roles.

Skills practice: Writing a composition

Als 'composition' bezeichnet man einen kurzen Text, der ein in sich geschlossenes Ganzes ergibt, z.B. einen Bericht, einen Aufsatz oder wie hier eine E-Mail.

Get it right: *Wie löse ich eine 'Writing a composition'-Aufgabe?*

- Lesen Sie sich die Aufgabe aufmerksam durch: Wem sollen Sie schreiben? Worüber sollen Sie im Einzelnen berichten?
- Notieren Sie sich zu jedem Punkt ein paar Stichwörter.
- Überlegen Sie sich, wie Sie den Text aufbauen wollen.
- Schreiben Sie Ihren Text. Beginnen Sie z.B. mit *Dear …, I'd like to …*
- Wenn Sie fertig sind, überprüfen Sie:
  - Gedankenfolge logisch?
  - Rechtschreibung und Grammatik korrekt?
  - Geforderte Wortanzahl erreicht? (Lieber etwas zu viel als zu wenig …)
- Falls nötig, korrigieren Sie noch einmal.

A A trip to the UK

You have finished school and have a summer job at a sports camp in Wales. The job starts in four weeks. On your way to Wales, you want to visit Mo in Barton, England.

Write him an email.
Write about 40 words in complete English sentences.

Tell him:

- about the job
  - how you found it
  - what you will be doing
- what you did this spring
  - prepared for school tests
  - shopping trip / bike ride with friends

Make a suggestion about what you want to do in Barton.

- visit Otmoor Castle

Hier schreiben Sie am besten eine informelle E-Mail. Verwenden Sie passende Anrede- und Schlussformeln:

Hi Mo! / Hello Mo!
…
…
See you soon! / All the best,
(Ihr Name)

B Your summer job

It's after the summer holidays and you have finished your summer job. You want to tell your cousin Spike in Scotland about it.

Write him an email.
Write about 40 words in complete English sentences.

Tell him:

- about your summer job
  - where you worked
  - what you did
  - what you thought of it
- what you are going to do now
  - apprenticeship
  - holiday

C Making plans for a visitor

Your friend (Goldie/Barack) from the USA wants to visit you. She/He will arrive in two weeks.

Write her/him an email.
Write about 40 words in complete English sentences.

Tell her/him:

- what there is to do and visit in your local area
  - sights
  - activities
- what you did last week
  - school-leavers' party
  - exams

Ask about:

- her/his plans in Germany
- how long she/he can stay

Get it right: *CHECKLISTE*

☑ Aufgabe genau durchgelesen?
☑ Inhaltliche Stichpunkte für den Text gemacht?
☑ Struktur klar?
☑ Text geschrieben?
☑ Korrektur gelesen?
☑ Alles korrekt?
☑ Abgeben!

Project page: Do it! quiz

Work with a partner. Write a quiz about what you have learned during this course. Write eight questions (one question per unit). You can use the ideas below or your own ideas. When you have finished, give your quiz to another pair to answer.

Your quiz questions can be about people and places in the units or about language (e.g. meanings of words, grammar).

Unit 1
- A question about Lisandra

- 'False friends'

Unit 2
- A question about Mo's family

- Headings in a CV

Unit 3
- A question about Anja's blog

- Emotions and emojis

Unit 4
- A question about Australia

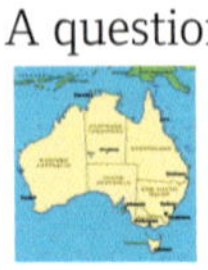

- Places around town

Unit 5
- A question about Mo's new job

- Jobs at an outdoor music festival

Unit 6
- A question about this workplace

- Giving an opinion

Unit 7
- A question about this company

TREEBIRD

- Writing an email

Unit 8
- A question about Otmoor Castle

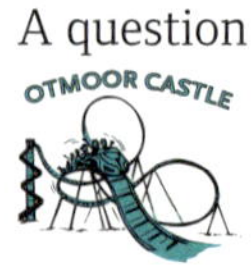

- Present perfect

Snapshot

What was your favourite thing in this unit?

What important thing did you learn?

What do you need to work on?

Video tasks

1 The English-speaking world

1

A While you watch

Match the informal greetings to the T-shirts. There is one T-shirt that you do not need.

1 Aussie 2 Brit 3 Canadian 4 Kiwi 5 South African 6 American

a G'day!

b Gooday, eh?

c Howdy!

d Howzit!

e Kia ora!

B What can you remember?

True or false? Correct the three false statements.

1 The United Kingdom is four countries.
2 Most US Americans are native speakers of Spanish.
3 Most Canadians are native English or French speakers.
4 There are 15 native Australian languages.
5 'Kia ora' has two meanings.
6 English is the main language in South Africa.

2 How to write your CV

2

A While you watch

1 Write down examples of 'work-relevant experience' from the box.

charity fundraising ▪ community projects ▪ playing video games
sports teams ▪ voluntary jobs ▪ working hard at school

2 Write down which important skills from the box are mentioned.

circus skills ▪ communication and social media skills ▪ IT skills
organizing people ▪ languages ▪ practical skills

B What can you remember?

Write down the right headings you need for a CV.

P(1) I(2) Information about you
P(3) S(4) Statement about you
W(5) E(6) Information about jobs you have had
E(7) and T(8) Information about the schools you have been to
Q(9) Information about exams you have passed
P(10) S(11) Information about other things you can do

3

3 How to get along with Brits

A While you watch

Write down the main topics in the video from the box.

Begrüßung ▪ Einkauf ▪ Höflichkeit und Manieren ▪ Humor
Schlange stehen ▪ Small-Talk und Kennenlernen

B What can you remember?

Are you ready for a trip to Britain? Do the quiz to find out. Choose the best answer, a, b, c or d.

1 If you 'jump the queue' *(sich vordrängeln)*, British people will …
- **a** think you are cool.
- **b** think you are rude.
- **c** not mind because you are foreign.
- **d** not give you any attention.

2 People in Britain shake hands …
- **a** all the time.
- **b** whenever they meet their friends.
- **c** only on a few specific occasions.
- **d** never.

3 Which of these is not a normal way to greet a friend?
- **a** 'How do you do?'
- **b** 'All right?'
- **c** 'How's it going?'
- **d** 'How are you?'

4 British people say 'sorry' when Germans say …
- **a** Sorry!
- **b** Wie bitte?
- **c** Sie spinnen wohl?!
- **d** All of the above.

4 Deadly Australia

4

A While you watch

Match the names of these dangerous Australians with the photos. There are two names you don't need.

billabong ▪ crocodile ▪ drop bear ▪ shark ▪ snake ▪ spider ▪ wombat ▪ kangaroo

1

2

3

4

5

6

B What can you remember?

1 One of the animals in A is not really dangerous. Which one? Why?

2 What other Australian sights and tourist attractions are mentioned in the video?

5 How to plan a video

5

A While you watch

Copy the mind map and then label the different parts.

B What can you remember?

Match these parts of Alice's video brief to the right places on your mind map from A.

a Live action

b It's easy to grow herbs at home in your kitchen.

c Pot, compost, seeds, water, gardening tools

d Alice and Tim (actors) and Daisy (camera person)

e First-time gardeners

f Smartphone

g Alice shows Tim some nice herbs in a pot …

Video tasks

6

6 How to sketchnote

A While you watch

True or false? Write down the numbers of the five true statements.

1 There are many ways to sketchnote.
2 You have to follow the rules.
3 Your sketchnote must be easy for other people to understand.
4 You do not need to be good at drawing to sketchnote.
5 You usually start with a heading.
6 You can add any ideas, facts or thoughts you want.
7 You must use lines, symbols and drawings.
8 You can go back and change things at any time.

B What can you remember?

1 **Correct the false statements in A.**
2 **Use your answers from 1 to make your own sketchnote about 'How to sketchnote'.**

7

7 How to generate ideas

A While you watch

Write down the things in the box which the video recommends you do if you need an idea.

Brainstorm. ▪ Get some exercise. ▪ Make sure you understand the task.
Sit and think until you have an idea. ▪ Surf the internet.

B What can you remember?

Answer the questions in German.

1 Was muss man als Erstes herausfinden? Warum?

2 Auf welche Weise hilft Bewegeung beim Nachdenken?

3 Wie macht man ein Brainstorming?

8

8 How to 'ace' a job interview

A While you watch

Make a list of the things in the box that will make you fail an interview.

Act cool in the interview. ▪ Arrive late for the interview. ▪ Be over-confident.
Be sensible and polite. ▪ Don't say anything. ▪ Put on your coolest 'going out' clothes.
Stop talking when you have answered the question. ▪ Talk without stopping.
Try to make the interviewer laugh. ▪ Wear comfortable but smart clothes.

B What can you remember?

Use your answers to A and your own ideas to make a checklist for a successful interview.

Pairwork files

File 1 Unit 1, Part A, Exercise 3

Emma ♀ Liam ♂ from Wales	
😊	Chinese food, tennis
😐	football, learning German
☹️	maths, Italian food

File 2 Unit 3, Project page

Su Hu ♂ Chen Luli ♀	
Culture	Chinese
Greetings	Say 'Hi!' or 'Hello!', shake hands gently (optional) or nod your head.
Small talk	😊 Ask about family: brothers? sisters? married? children? 'Have you eaten?' is a normal way of starting a conversation. How much things cost is interesting to you.
	☹️ Don't criticize a person, say 'no' to a request or give a strong opinion about anything.
Body language	😊 Smile. Modest and quite formal behaviour.
	☹️ Touching (other than handshake). Waving arms around or other big gestures.

File 3 Unit 4, Part B, Exercise 3

You are a Tourist Ambassador at Federation Square. Greet your partner and find out where she/he wants to go. Find the right letter (A–K) on the map and give your partner directions. (Don't tell them the letter.) Did they go to the right place?

A City Library
B souvenir shops
C St Paul's Cathedral
D a good computer store
E a supermarket
F ACMI (Australian Centre for the Moving Image)
G Flinders Street Station
H Taxi Kitchen (restaurant and café)
I Princes Gardens (park)
J Arts Centre
K Southgate Centre (shopping mall)

File 4 Unit 1, Part A, Exercise 3

Abbie ♀ Harry ♂ from England	
🙂	football, Italian food
😐	maths, tennis
🙁	Chinese food, learning German

File 5 Unit 3, Project page

Ashvik ♂ Shakti ♀	
Culture	Indian
Greetings	Put hands together in front of chest, bow your head and say 'Namaste'.
Small talk	🙂 Detailed personal questions: family? names? jobs? Celebrities. Travel and holiday plans.
	🙁 Personal criticism. Situations where you have to say 'no'. Say 'maybe' instead.
Body language	🙂 Stand close and nod your head while your partner is speaking. Look down. Touching (♂♂ or ♀♀) is okay.
	🙁 Touching (♂♀). Too much eye contact. Pointing with finger (= aggressive, negative). Smiling a lot for no reason.

File 6 Unit 3, Project page

David ♂ Lisa ♀	
Culture	US American
Greetings	Say 'Hi!' or 'Hello!'. Shake hands strongly (optional) with a big smile.
Small talk	🙂 Travel and holiday plans. Sport or showbiz celebrities. Work. Offer opinions freely, react strongly to what your partner says.
	🙁 Personal questions. How much you earn, or paid for things.
Body language	🙂 Smile. Laugh. Hold eye contact. You can be lively and wave your hands or arms around while you talk.
	🙁 Standing too close. Touching too much. Behaviour which seems 'cold' or unfriendly (e.g. no smile, no eye contact).

File 7 Unit 7, Part B, Exercise 1

Lesen Sie die Texte unten. Haben Sie die Hauptpunkte verstanden?

Nach dem Lesen: Fragen Sie Ihre Partnerin / Ihren Partner aus. Was war die ganze Geschichte? Wie kam es dazu bzw. was wurde daraus? Machen Sie Notizen auf Deutsch.

A

Lily's story, part 2

When Lily was 19, her little son Noah started to go to kindergarten. Lily now had time to study at a local community college. She found that she had a talent for maths and financial software. Lily completed college with good qualifications and found a job as a financial adviser. She now helps young adults who are in financial difficulties. She is friends with her ex-boyfriend, and both pairs of grandparents love little Noah.

B

Charlie's story, part 2

Charlie made friends with Hasan, 24, who let Charlie 'couch surf' at his place. Hasan's father, Arif, often came to visit. He liked Charlie and helped him to get his life back together. After a few months and a lot of discussion, Charlie moved in with Arif's family and went back to school. After finishing school, Charlie got an apprenticeship as a hairdresser and now runs his own salon.

C

Sameen's story, part 1

Sameen was 19 and worked in a clothes shop. She was a popular, hard-working employee. Her boss, Annie, liked her and everyone expected Sameen to become assistant manager. Then things started to go wrong. Annie became ill and had to leave her job. The new manager didn't like Sameen: she criticized her work all the time. Sameen started to come to work late. The manager told Sameen that she wasn't needed in the shop any more.

D

Dylan's story, part 1

Dylan was in the second year of his apprenticeship as a plumber. The work was interesting and there was a good atmosphere in the company – it felt like one big family. Unfortunately, times were hard and the company didn't have enough customers. One day Dylan's boss told all the employees that it was time to close the company. Dylan tried hard to find another plumbing company that wanted an apprentice – but had no success.

File 8 Unit 1, Part A, Exercise 3

Ava ♀ Lewis ♂ from Scotland	
😊	Italian food, learning German
😐	football, Chinese food
☹️	maths, tennis

File 9 Unit 3, Project page

Faisal ♂ Farida ♀	
Culture	Pakistani
Greetings	'Salaam' or 'Hello'. Shake hands (optional), then put your right hand on your heart.
Small talk	😊 Detailed personal questions: family? names? jobs? Sport or showbiz celebrities. Make positive comments about your partner's appearance.
	☹ Dating. Personal criticism. Situations where you have to say 'no'. Say 'maybe' instead.
Body language	😊 Stand close to your partner. Listen with a serious expression. Look down. Touching (♂♂ or ♀♀) is okay.
	☹ Touching (♂♀). Too much eye contact. Smiling a lot for no reason. Loud behaviour.

File 10 Unit 1, Part A, Exercise 3

Megan ♀ Adam ♂ from Northern Ireland	
😊	Chinese food, Italian food
😐	maths, learning German
☹	football, tennis

File 11 Unit 3, Project page

Ben ♂ Amy ♀	
Culture	English
Greetings	'Hi' or 'Hello' or 'How are you?' Shake hands (optional), with a little smile.
Small talk	😊 Travel and holiday plans. The weather. Sport or showbiz celebrities. Hobbies and interests. Make small jokes.
	☹ Personal questions. How much you earn, or paid for things. Personal criticism. Negative opinions about things that you like.
Body language	😊 Smile. Make eye contact. Keep far apart from your partner.
	☹ Standing too close. Touching too much. Behaviour which is 'fake' (laughing too much, etc.). No eye contact.

Differentiaton files

Unit 1, Part A, Exercise 4B

Complete this summary of the text with the verbs from the box.

meet ▪ knows ▪ are ▪ like ▪ wants ▪ is ▪ remembers

1 Mo and Lisandra ▢ at the 'Meet and Greet' session.
2 Mo ▢ Lisandra because they ▢ in the same class.
3 They both ▢ coffee.
4 Mo ▢ to have coffee with Lisandra.
5 Unfortunately, Mo ▢ bad at small talk.
6 Lisandra suddenly ▢ her study group.

Unit 1, Part A, Exercise 5A

Here are some ideas for you to use. Choose three of the sentence beginnings. End the sentences with your own ideas but remember to write two true sentences and one false sentence.

I'm from *(Land, Region, Stadt usw.)*
I like *(Sportart, z.B. tennis, football,)*
I love *(Schulfach, z.B. maths, English, German)*
I hate *(Getränk oder Speise, z.B. coffee, chocolate)*

Unit 1, Part B, Exercise 1B

Choose six of these hashtags which match the text. Two do not match the text.

#apps4english
#businessenglish
#deutschenglisch
#english4gamers
#englishatwork
#englishonline
#holidayenglish
#jobtips

Unit 1, Part B, Exercise 2B

Copy the comment and complete it with your own ideas.

Hi, Anja!
I love your blog! I use English *(wo Sie Englisch sprechen, z.B. in der Schule)*. When I leave school I want to *(Berufswunsch)*. English is useful for *(wozu man im Beruf Englisch braucht, z. B. Telefonieren)*. I see a lot of English words *(wo Sie im Alltag Englisch begegnen, z. B. im Internet)*.
(Ihr Name)

Unit 1, Part C, Exercise 4

Use this dialogue to practise the dialogue with your partner.

A: Guten Morgen/Tag. *(Firmenname)*. Mein Name ist *(Ihr Name)*. Wie kann ich Ihnen helfen?
B: Do you speak English?
A: Yes, I do. How can I help you?
B: Can you put me through to Mr Jones, please?
A: I'm sorry, Mr Jones isn't here at the moment. Can I take a message?
B: Can you let him know that my train is late.
A: OK. May I have your name, please?
B: It's *(Ihr Name)*.
A: Can you spell that for me, please?
B: It's *(Name buchstabieren)*.
A: *(Buchstaben wiederholen)*.
B: That's right.
A: I'll pass your message on.
B: Thank you. Bye!

Unit 2, Part A, Exercise 2B

Complete these sentences about Mo's family with the verbs from the box.

was ▪ began ▪ didn't have ▪ fell ▪ started ▪ did ▪ didn't see ▪ was ▪ learned

1 Mo's grandmother ___ 67 when she ___ to ride a motorbike.
2 Ali ___ climbing lessons last year.
3 Oz and Simon ___ in love and ___ a business.
4 Imran ___ an apprenticeship two years ago.
5 Mo ___ his dad much when he ___ young.
6 Mo ___ to read and write about eight years ago.

Unit 2, Part B, Exercise 1B

Match the sentence endings to the beginnings. Two endings do not match. Write out the complete sentences.

1 Anja came to Dublin and she wanted
2 Anja's mother and grandmother both love cooking, so
3 She didn't finish her apprenticeship, because
4 Anja's father was worried about her, but

a he accepted her plans.
b she found it boring.
c the work was too hard.
d they taught her to cook.
e to get a job as a baker.
f to stay just for the summer.

Unit 2, Part C, Exercise 3C

Copy the text and complete it with ideas from boxes 1, 2 and 3 or your own ideas.
I'm a good (1), I'm (2) and I'm (3). I would like a position as a/an *(Ihr Berufswunsch)*.

communicator ▪ listener ▪ problem solver ▪ team player 1

able to take criticism ▪ able to work under pressure
attentive to detail ▪ caring and empathetic ▪ technically-minded 2

creative ▪ friendly and polite ▪ hard-working ▪ practical ▪ responsible
self-confident 3

Unit 3, Part A, Exercise 5

Copy the friend profile and complete it with your own ideas.

My ideal friend is *(1. Eigenschaft, z. B. chatty)*, but she's/he's also *(2. Eigenschaft, z.B. serious)*.
She/He likes *(1. Interesse/Aktivität, z. B. parties)*, but she/he also likes *(2. Interesse/Aktivität, z. B. chilling out)*.
She/He doesn't like *(3. Interesse/Aktivität, z.B. exercise)*.

Unit 3, Part B, Exercise 4

Match the sentence endings to the beginnings. Write out the complete sentences.

1	Please do not use	**a**	photos.
2	Please wash	**b**	skateboards here.
3	Please ring	**c**	the bell.
4	Please do not take	**d**	your hands.
5	Please put	**e**	your mobile phone.
6	Please do not ride	**f**	your rubbish in the bin.

Unit 3, Part C, Exercise 4

Start your comment like this: *Hello Anja, I agree with you. / I think Darren was right.*
Continue with three of these comments or your own ideas.

- Grumpy comments make it more difficult to work together.
- It was right to say something.
- It wasn't helpful to criticize Pat.
- It's important for everyone to share the work.
- It's important to respect different attitudes.
- Pat's behaviour wasn't fair.

End your comment with your name.

Unit 4, Part A, Exercise 4B

Use the information to write a description of Ireland, Canada or India.

Climate

mild ▪ very cold ▪ very hot

Sights

Niagara Falls and the Northern Lights *(Nordlicht)* ▪ the Taj Mahal and the River Ganges
the Wild Atlantic Way

Food

bagels, fries *(Pommes frites)* and maple syrup
meat stew *(Fleischeintopf)* and potatoes *(Kartoffeln)* ▪ spicy food and rice

Famous for …

Bollywood and colourful festivals ▪ polar bears *(Eisbären)* and ice hockey
traditional music and Guinness

Unit 4, Part B, Exercise 1

A Wählen Sie nur diejenigen Einzelheiten aus, die in der Anzeige erwähnt werden.

Aufgaben

Erste Hilfe leisten ▪ Fragen zu Sehenswürdigkeiten beantworten ▪ Stadtführungen leiten
Infos verteilen ▪ Touristen begrüßen ▪ Wege beschreiben

Stunden

vier bis sechs Stunden am Tag ▪ vier bis sechs Stunden in der Woche

Arbeitsplatz

am Federation Square ▪ an verschiedenen Standorten in Melbourne

Vorbereitung und Material

App, Videolernkurs, T-Shirt u. Fahrplan ▪ Info-Paket, Einweisung, T-Shirt u. Fahrausweis

Sicherheit

gruppenweise arbeiten ▪ nur abends ▪ nur tagsüber ▪ paarweise arbeiten

B Verwenden Sie Ihre Lösungen von Aufgabe 1A, um Ihrer Familie eine E-Mail zu schreiben.

Unit 4, Part C, Exercise 3A

Find the English words in the box. There are more words than you need.

bathroom facilities ▪ communities ▪ confident ▪ driving licence ▪ electricity
helicopter ▪ island ▪ maintenance ▪ paid holiday ▪ paint buildings ▪ range ▪ trails

1 Instandhaltung
2 Sanitäranlagen
3 Führerschein
4 bezahlter Urlaub
5 Strom
6 Gebäude streichen
7 Reihe
8 selbstbewusst
9 Gemeinden

Unit 5, Part A, Exercise 2B

Choose the correct answer, a, b or c.

1 Ruby is impatient because …
 a she has to wait for tickets.
 b Mo is late.
 c the cinema is almost full.

2 Mo is tired because …
 a he's doing too many things.
 b he plays too much football.
 c he works long hours at his job.

3 Although Mo finds his phone a good way to relax, …
 a it stops him sleeping.
 b streaming films isn't easy.
 c his mother wants him to stop using it.

Unit 5, Part A, Exercise 4C

Complete the sentences with the present progressive of the verbs in brackets.

1 The friends *are going* to the cinema. (go)
2 Ruby *is* ___ the tickets. (buy)
3 Mo ___ too many things. (do)
4 Ruby and Jack ___ for the others. (not wait)
5 Lisandra ___ Mo feel better. (help)
6 "I ___ my best," says Mo. (try)

Unit 5, Part B, Exercise 2

Put the sentences in the box in the right places below to complete the instructions.

- Test that the drill bit turns correctly.
- Remove the drill bit from the hole and check it is the right depth.
- Adjust the force on the drill so you can drill easily.
- Choose the correct drill bit for the hole you want to drill.

1 Wear safe clothing, ear and eye protection.
2 ___
3 Fit the drill bit firmly into the chuck (the mouth in the drill for the drill bit).
4 ___
5 Hold the drill steady and push it gently into the material you are drilling.
6 ___
7 Don't overheat the drill bit – don't drill for too long.
8 ___

Unit 5, Part C, Exercise 1B

Write sentences in the present progressive in your exercise book. Use the key words.

1 Jen and Grant / plant / flowers
EXAMPLE:
Jen and Grant are planting flowers.
2 Daisy / help / a patient
3 Barry / check / a security pass
4 Hamid and Sophie / arrange / goods for sale
5 Jon and Mia / test / the sound equipment
6 Sally / serve / a customer
7 Mick / move / some equipment
8 Lucy / install / the lighting

Unit 6, Part A, Exercise 2

Decide which of these things are problems in the care home and which ones are solutions that Ruby's friends have suggested. There are five problems and five solutions.

1 Complain to the manager.
2 The working conditions are not good enough.
3 Don't give up.
4 We don't provide a good service to the residents.
5 We don't have time to do a good job.
6 The care home should get some volunteers.
7 Ruby shouldn't try to solve all the problems for everybody else.
8 The manager can't afford more staff.
9 The company doesn't listen to my opinion.
10 Stay for a while, get more experience, then leave and get a better job.

Unit 6, Part B, Exercise 1B

Verwenden Sie dieses Muster für Ihren Text. Entnehmen Sie dem Text auf Seite 58 alle Informationen, die Sie benötigen.

Hallo *(Namen Ihrer Freunde / Freundinnen)* !

Wie geht's euch? Ich habe neulich ein interessantes Start-up-Unternehmen in Melbourne, Australien, kennengelernt. Vielleicht habt ihr ja Lust, etwas Ähnliches zu machen!

Bei vielen Malerei- und Dekorateurbetrieben gibt es folgende Probleme: ...

Diese Firma verwendet Materialien, die ...

Die Firma unterstützt ... und will ...

Das Unternehmen ist gegen Diskriminierung aufgrund von ...

Was meint ihr?

Liebe Grüße,
(Ihr Name)

Unit 6, Part C, Exercise 2C

Listen to each person again, then complete the grid with the information from the box.

chat with customers ■ hours ■ bad pay ■ creative ■ lonely ■ interesting people
no proper meals ■ noisy workplace ■ pay ■ good for the environment
buzz/excitement ■ get to know regulars

Job	Good points	Bad points
Event technician	variety,	stress,
Barista		
Upcycler / Furniture maker		

Unit 7, Part A, Exercise 4B

Complete these sentences with the will future of the verbs in brackets. Make three of them positive (will) and three of them negative (won't).

1 I … school this summer. (finish)
2 I … on holiday with my family. (not go)
3 Lisandra … her parents about her idea. (tell)
4 They … laugh at her idea. (not laugh)
5 Her dad … her about what to do. (not advise)
6 Her mum … lots of advice. (offer)

Unit 7, Part B, Exercise 2B

Listen again. What did they say? Match one piece of advice to each person.

Be flexible. | Don't give up. | Find someone to be your mentor. | Talk to people.

Lily:
Be kind to yourself and others.

Sameen:
Find out what your talents and interests are.

Charlie:
Don't be afraid to ask for help.

Dylan:
Look for opportunities around you.

Unit 7, Part C, Exercise 3

Copy and complete this email.

Dear Mr Kyte,

My name is **(1)**. I am writing to offer my services as **(2)**.
I am **(3)**, so I would be a great reviewer for your products.
I make videos / write a blog / post photos about **(4)**. You can see examples of my work here:
(5) *(fiktive Hashtags, URLs, usw.)*
I am interested in reviewing your **(6)** product line(s).
I look forward to hearing from you.
Yours sincerely,
(Ihr Name)

Unit 8, Part A, Exercise 3B

Complete the sentences with the present perfect of the verbs in brackets.

1 I ___ here since I was ten. (live)
2 He ___ up this mountain before. (walk)
3 They ___ jobs in Spain. (apply for)
4 They ___ to each other for years. (not speak)
5 She ___ in a café before. (not work)
6 I ___ the application form yet. (not fill out)

Unit 8, Part B, Exercise 2

Hier sind einige Stichpunkte für Ihren Text. Vergessen Sie nicht: Sie sollen für Samira oder Lars nur drei der insgesamt fünf ausgeschriebenen Jobs aussuchen!

Ride attendant (Fahrgeschäftsbetreuer/in)
Fahrgäste betreuen u. kontrollieren – sportlich, verantwortungsbewusst, taktvoll

Photographer (mobile/r Fotograf/in)
auf den Fahrgeschäften mitfahren und Gäste fotografieren / filmen – kreativ, abenteuerlustig

Food and beverage worker (Gastronomie-Mitarbeiter/in)
kellnern, an der Theke / in der Küche arbeiten (erhält Ausbildung/Einweisung in Lebensmittelsicherheit u. Hygiene) – zuverlässig

Maintenance assistant (Wartungsassistent/in)
unterstützt Wartungspersonal hinter den Kulissen – praktisch u. fleißig

Entertainer (Unterhaltungskünstler/in)
Jonglieren, Musikinstrumente spielen, Kunststücke zeigen, singen bzw. sich als Maskottchen verkleiden –lebenslustig u. gut gelaunt

Unit 8, Part C, Exercise 1B

Match these strengths and weaknesses to the candidate(s).

Strengths

energetic ▪ good at organizing ▪ good student ▪ ~~hard-working~~ ▪ has done a lot of research ▪ responsible ▪ sociable ▪ ~~strong motivation~~ ▪ honest

Weaknesses

may not follow instructions ▪ doesn't enjoy teamwork ▪ quiet ▪ takes risks ▪ too confident ▪ ~~weak motivation~~

	Strengths	Weaknesses
Rita	*hard-working*	*weak motivation*
Oliver	*strong motivation*	___
Sarah	*strong motivation*	___

Chronologische Wortliste

Wörter aus den Audiotexten sind mit einem gelben Balken, Wörter aus den Differentiation files mit einem grauen Balken und Wörter aus den Pairwork files mit einem türkisenen Balken gekennzeichnet.

AE = American English	*n* = noun *(Substantiv)*	*adv* = adverb	*pl* = plural
BE = British English	*v* = verb	*phr* = phrase *(feststehende Wendung)*	<> = opposite *(Gegensatz)*
AusE = Australian English	*adj* = adjective		

UNIT 1

5	to **get to know sb**	[ˌget tə ˈnəʊ]	to find out what sb is like by spending time with them	jdn kennenlernen
	to **warm up**	[ˌwɔːm ˈʌp]	to prepare to do sth	sich aufwärmen
	beige	[beɪʒ]	a light brown colour	beige
	maroon	[məˈruːn]	a dark red colour	kastanienbraun
	purple	[ˈpɜːpl]	e.g. If you mix red and blue, you get purple.	violett, lila, purpur
	series	[ˈsɪəriːz]	e.g. My favourite TV series is 'Suits'.	Serie
	likes and dislikes *pl*	[ˌlaɪks ən ˈdɪslaɪks]	e.g. My likes include playing football, and my dislikes include going to the dentist.	Vorlieben und Abneigungen
	to **mind sth**	[maɪnd]	e.g. I don't mind hamsters, but they are not my favourite animal.	etw gegen etw haben
	to **stand sth**	[stænd]	e.g. I can't stand getting up early.	etw ertragen, etw aushalten
	chat	[tʃæt]	a conversation with sb	Unterhaltung, Gespräch
	to **agree with sb**	[əˈgriː wɪð]	to have the same opinion as sb	jdm zustimmen, der gleichen Meinung wie jd sein
	to **disagree (with sb)**	[ˌdɪsəˈgriː]	<> to agree (with sb)	anderer Meinung (als jd) sein
6	**term**	[tɜːm]	part of the school year, e.g. from September to December	Trimester
	to **greet sb**	[griːt]	e.g. The teacher greeted the new student.	jdn begrüßen
	session	[ˈseʃn]	a period of time for a special activity	Veranstaltung
	whether	[ˈweðə]	e.g. I always walk the dog, whether it is raining or sunny.	ob
	hint	[hɪnt]	information or advice on how to do sth	Hinweis, Tipp
	to **get sth right**	[ˌget ˈraɪt]	to do sth correctly	etw richtig machen, etw hinbekommen
	general	[ˈdʒenrəl]	normal or usual	allgemein
	safe(ly)	[seɪf]	<> dangerous(ly)	sicher
	personal	[ˈpɜːsənl]	<> public	privat, persönlich
	to **introduce sb/oneself to sb**	[ˌɪntrəˈdjuːs tə]	e.g. Let me introduce myself – my name is Sascha, and I am a teacher.'	jdn/sich jdm vorstellen
	to **remember (sth)**	[rɪˈmembə]	<> forget sth	sich (an etw) erinnern
	argument	[ˈɑːgjumənt]	*v* to argue	Diskussion, Streit
	below	[bɪˈləʊ]	<> above	unten, untenstehend
	by the way	[ˌbaɪ ðə ˈweɪ]	a way to introduce a new topic	übrigens
	maths	[mæθs]	a school subject about numbers	Mathe(matik)
	unusual	[ʌnˈjuːʒʊəl]	<> usual	ungewöhnlich, außergewöhnlich
	common	[ˈkɒmən]	normal or usual	üblich, verbreitet
	actually	[ˈæktʃuəli]	really, in fact	übrigens, wirklich, eigentlich, tatsächlich
	Pleased/Nice to meet you.	[ˌpliːzd/ˌnʌɪs tə ˈmiːt ju]	e.g. Hello, my name is Alex. Nice to meet you.	Schön, dich/Sie/euch kennenzulernen.
	study group	[ˈstʌdi gruːp]	people who meet to learn together	Arbeitsgruppe
	guys *pl*	[gaɪz]	e.g. Hi guys! Did you have a good summer?	Leute
	to change one's mind	[ˌtʃeɪndʒ wʌnz ˈmaɪnd]	e.g. I decided to have coffee, then changed my mind and had tea.	es sich anders überlegen, seine Meinung ändern
7	**in pairs**	[ɪn ˈpeəz]	together with one other person	paarweise
	role card	[ˈrəʊl kɑːd]	a card which tells sb which identity they will take in a role play	Rollenkarte, Rollenkärtchen
	to **check sth out**	[ˌtʃek ˈaʊt]	to get information about sth	sich etw (genau) ansehen
	unfortunately	[ʌnˈfɔːtʃənətli]	e.g. Unfortunately it's raining and we can't have a picnic.	leider, unglücklicherweise
	to **be bad at sth**	[bi ˈbæd ət]	e.g. I'm bad at playing cards and lose every game.	etw nicht gut können, in etw nicht gut sein
	suddenly	[ˈsʌdnli]	quickly, with no warning	plötzlich

	fake news	[ˈfeɪk njuːz]	false information which seems correct	Falschmeldungen, verdrehte Fakten
	true	[truː]	<> false	wahr, zutreffend, richtig
	false	[fɔːls]	<> true	falsch, unzutreffend
	to **compare sth**	[kəmˈpeə]	to look at things and see what is different or the same between them	etw vergleichen
	welcome to ...	[ˈwelkəm tə]	a friendly, polite greeting	willkommen bei/ im/in/zu ...
8	to **hope**	[həʊp]	*n* hope	hoffen
	still	[stɪl]	e.g. I ordered a coffee half an hour ago and I am still waiting for it.	nach wie vor, immer noch
	official language	[əˌfɪʃl ˈlæŋgwɪdʒ]	e.g. The official language of Spain is Spanish.	Amtssprache
	around the world	[əˌraʊnd ðə ˈwɜːld]	e.g. We can communicate with people around the world.	auf der ganzen Welt
	native speaker	[ˌneɪtɪv ˈspiːkə]	sb who speaks the language of the country where they were born	Muttersprachler/in
	That's too bad!	[ðəts ˌtuː ˈbæd]	what you say when sth bad but small happens	Das ist schade! Zu dumm!
	luckily	[ˈlʌkɪli]	*n* luck	glücklicherweise, zum Glück
	use	[juːs]	e.g. I use a bicycle to get to school.	Verwendung, Gebrauch, Nutzen
	probably	[ˈprɒbəbli]	e.g. There are lots of clouds – it's probably going to rain.	wahrscheinlich
	to **share sth**	[ʃeə]	e.g. We share the same interest in fashion.	etw gemeinsam haben
	useful	[ˈjuːsfl]	<> useless	nützlich
	around	[əˈraʊnd]	e.g. There are ca. 7.8 billion people in the world.	ungefähr
	popular	[ˈpɒpjələ]	when a lot of people like sth	beliebt
	company	[ˈkʌmpəni]	e.g. My parents work for a big company.	Unternehmen, Firma
	to **expect sb to do sth**	[ɪkˈspekt]	e.g. Our teacher expects us to do our homework.	von jdm erwarten, etw zu tun; erwarten, dass jd etw tut
	even	[ˈiːvn]	e.g. I love playing football, even if it's raining.	sogar
	sensible	[ˈsensəbl]	*adv* sensibly	vernünftig
	in order to	[ɪn ˈɔːdə tə]	e.g. You need qualifications in order to get a job.	um ... zu
	business	[ˈbɪznəs]	e.g. Frankfurt is the business centre of Germany.	Wirtschaft
	widely spoken	[ˌwaɪdli ˈspəʊkən]	e.g. Spanish is widely spoken in South America.	(Sprache:) weit verbreitet
	for example	[fər ɪgˈzɑːmpl]	e.g.	zum Beispiel
	to **leave sth**	[liːv]	e.g. It's nice to leave a message on sb's blog.	etw hinterlassen
	comment	[ˈkɒment]	*v* to comment	Bemerkung, Kommentar
9	**statement**	[ˈsteɪtmənt]	sth that sb says or writes officially	Aussage
	difficult	[ˈdɪfɪkəlt]	<> easy	schwierig, schwer
	English speaker	[ˈɪŋglɪʃ spiːkə]	sb who can speak English	Englischsprachige/r
	to **discuss sth**	[dɪˈskʌs]	*n* discussion	etw besprechen, etw diskutieren
	to **report back to sb**	[rɪˌpɔːt ˈbæk tə]	to give information to sb after doing research	jdm berichten, jdm Bericht erstatten
	to **have finished**	[həv ˈfɪnɪʃt]	e.g. I have finished work and am going home.	fertig sein
	to **leave school**	[liːv ˈskuːl]	e.g. After I leave school I want to go to university.	von der Schule abgehen, mit der Schule fertig sein, den Schulabschluss machen
	daily	[ˈdeɪli]	e.g. a daily news update	täglich
	to **underline**	[ˌʌndəˈlaɪn]	to draw a line under sth	unterstreichen
10	to **take a message**	[ˌteɪk ə ˈmesɪdʒ]	e.g. I'm afraid Ms Meyer can't come to the phone. Can I take a message?	eine Nachricht entgegennehmen, etw ausrichten
	apprentice	[əˈprentɪs]	sb learning how to do a job	Auszubildende/r, Lehrling
	garage	[ˈgærɑːʒ]	a place where cars are repaired	Kfz-Werkstatt
	to **answer the phone**	[ˌɑːnsə ðə ˈfəʊn]	e.g. You answer the phone when it rings.	ans Telefon gehen
	while	[waɪl]	at the same time as sth else	während
	recording	[rɪˈkɔːdɪŋ]	*v* to record	Aufnahme
	to **complete a task**	[kəmˌpliːt ə ˈtɑːsk]	to finish doing sth	eine Aufgabe ausführen
	expression	[ɪkˈspreʃn]	*v* to express	Ausdruck
	to **put sb through to sb**	[ˌpʊt ˈθruː tə]	e.g. I'll just put you through to Mr Smith.	(Telefon:) jdn mit jdm verbinden
	to **spell**	[spel]	to say the letters of a word in the right order	buchstabieren
	surname	[ˈsɜːneɪm]	family name e.g. Schmidt, Yildiz, Sarova	Nachname

	wife	[waɪf]	a married woman	(Ehe-)Frau
	to **let sb know that ...**	[ˌlet ˈnəʊ ðət]	to give sb a message	jdm ausrichten, dass ...; jdm Bescheid sagen, dass ...
	to **leave sth**	[liːv]	e.g. I left my phone on the train.	etw liegen lassen, etw vergessen
	mobile (phone) ***BE***	[ˌməʊbaɪl ˈfəʊn]	*AE:* cell (phone)	Handy
	to **pass sth on**	[ˌpɑːs ˈɒn]	to give sth (e.g. information) to another person	etw weitergeben
	May I ...	[ˈmeɪ aɪ]	e.g. May I have the last biscuit, please?	Darf ich ...
	to **call sb back**	[ˌkɔːl ˈbæk]	to phone sb who has phoned you	jdn zurückrufen
	to **tell sb sth**	[tel]	to give information to sb	jdm etw sagen
	spelling	[ˈspelɪŋ]	*v* to spell	Schreibweise, Rechtschreibung
	to **match sth to sth**	[ˈmætʃ tə]	to put things together which are the same	etw einer Sache zuordnen
	phonetics	[fəˈnetɪks]	the study of speech sounds	Phonetik
11	to **be missing**	[bi ˈmɪsɪŋ]	not there	fehlen
	conversation	[ˌkɒnvəˈseɪʃn]	e.g. I had an interesting conversation with Jim.	Gespräch
	order	[ˈɔːdə]	*v* to order	Bestellung
	to **arrive**	[əˈraɪv]	e.g. The shoes I ordered arrived today.	eintreffen, ankommen
	diagram	[ˈdaɪəgræm]	a drawing which shows how sth works	Grafik, Diagramm
	to **practise sth**	[ˈpræktɪs]	to train to do sth better	etw trainieren, etw üben
	to **swap**	[swɒp]	to exchange sth for sth else	tauschen
	to **call sb**	[kɔːl]	e.g. Have you called Steve from HR?	jdn anrufen
12	**skills** ***pl***	[skɪlz]	things sb can do well	Kenntnisse, Fertigkeiten
	practice	[ˈpræktɪs]	training	Training, Übung
	change	[tʃeɪndʒ]	*v* to change	Änderung
	to **stay**	[steɪ]	e.g. I stay in a hotel when I'm on holiday.	bleiben, übernachten
	to **change sth**	[tʃeɪndʒ]	to make sth different	etw ändern
	bed and breakfast (B&B)	[ˌbed ən ˈbrekfəst]	e.g. A bed and breakfast is cheaper than a hotel.	(Frühstücks-)Pension
	response	[rɪˈspɒns]	reply	Antwort, Reaktion
	to **fit sth**	[fɪt]	to go together well with sth	in/zu etw passen
	gap	[gæp]	space, hole	Lücke
	... speaking.	[ˈspiːkɪŋ]	e.g. Good morning, this is Holly speaking.	(Telefon:) Sie sprechen mit ...
	Oh dear!	[əʊ ˈdɪə]	e.g. Oh dear! That's not good news.	Ach du liebe Güte!
	to **cancel sth**	[ˈkænsl]	e.g. I was ill, so I had to cancel my holiday.	etw stornieren, etw absagen
	booking	[ˈbʊkɪŋ]	reservation	Buchung, Reservierung
	That's fine.	[ðəts ˈfaɪn]	e.g. That's fine. Thanks for telling me.	Das ist (völlig) in Ordnung.
	easily	[ˈiːzəli]	*adj* easy	ohne weiteres
	You're welcome.	[jɔː ˈwelkəm]	what you say after sb says ‚Thank you'.	Gern geschehen.
	Have a lovely day.	[hæv ə ˌlʌvli ˈdeɪ]	sth nice you say at the end of a conversation	Einen schönen Tag noch!
	double room	[ˌdʌbl ˈruːm]	a hotel room with a double bed in it	Doppelzimmer
	with sb	[wɪð, wɪθ]	e.g. I'm travelling with my parents this summer.	bei jdm
13	**appointment**	[əˈpɔɪntmənt]	e.g. When is your appointment with the doctor?	Termin
	doctor	[ˈdɒktə]	sb who helps ill people	Arzt/Ärztin
	surgery	[ˈsɜːdʒəri]	a place where you can go and see a doctor	(Arzt-)Praxis
	ill	[ɪl]	<> well, healthy	krank
	to **see a doctor**	[ˌsiː ə ˈdɒktə]	to go to the doctor	zum Arzt gehen
	local	[ˈləʊkl]	near to where you are	örtlich, vor/am Ort, lokal
	clinic	[ˈklɪnɪk]	a place where a doctor works	Ambulanz, Klinik
	full name	[ˌfʊl ˈneɪm]	e.g. Angela Dorothea Merkel	vollständiger Name
	sick	[sɪk]	unwell, ill	krank, unwohl
	to **hurt**	[hɜːt]	to have pain	wehtun
14	to **create sth**	[kriˈeɪt]	to make sth	etw erstellen
	social media ***pl***	[ˌsəʊʃl ˈmiːdiə]	e.g. Facebook, Twitter, whatsapp	soziale Medien
	profile	[ˈprəʊfaɪl]	information about sb on an internet page	Profil
	basic	[ˈbeɪsɪk]	e.g. I can give give you some basic information.	grundlegend, wesentlich
	nickname	[ˈnɪkneɪm]	e.g. Some people don't like their nicknames.	Spitzname, Nickname
	favourite	[ˈfeɪvərɪt]	e.g. My favourite food is chocolate.	Lieblings-
	fridge	[frɪdʒ]	a machine that keeps food cold	Kühlschrank
	what else?	[wɒt ˈels]	e.g. What else do we have to take on holiday?	was (sonst) noch?
	to **include sth**	[ɪnˈkluːd]	<> to leave sth out	etw einbeziehen, etw verwenden
	drawing	[ˈdrɔːɪŋ]	a picture done with a pencil on paper	Zeichnung
	to **present sth to sb**	[prɪˈzent]	to show sth to other people	etw jdm vorstellen, etw jdm präsentieren
	snapshot	[ˈsnæpʃɒt]	summary	Schnappschuss
	important (to sb)	[ɪmˈpɔːtnt]	e.g. It is important to eat healthy food.	wichtig (für jdn)

	to **work on sth**	[ˈwɜːk ɒn]	to improve sth, to make sth better	an etw arbeiten

UNIT 2

15	**family tree**	[ˌfæməli ˈtriː]	a chart which shows people in a family	Stammbaum
	relationship	[rɪˈleɪʃnʃɪp]	a connection to sb else	Verwandtschaftsverhältnis
	nephew	[ˈnevjuː]	my brother or sister's son	Neffe
	niece	[niːs]	my brother or sister's daughter	Nichte
	brother-in-law	[ˈbrʌðər ɪn lɔː]	your brother or sister's husband	Schwager
	to **be close to sb**	[bi ˈkləʊs tə]	to have a good relationship with sb	jdm nahestehen
	to **number**	[ˈnʌmbə]	e.g. 1. Most important 2. Not very important 3. Not important	nummerieren
	priority	[praɪˈɒrəti]	the most important thing	Priorität, Vorrang
	to **give sb advice**	[gɪv ədˈvaɪs]	to tell sb what you think they should do	jdn beraten, jdm einen Rat geben
	to **criticize**	[ˈkrɪtɪsaɪz]	to tell sb they are doing sth wrong	Kritik üben
	to **cheer sb up**	[ˌtʃɪər ˈʌp]	to make sb feel happy	jdn aufmuntern, jdn aufheitern
	to **be down**	[bi ˈdaʊn]	to feel depressed	niedergeschlagen sein, nicht gut drauf sein
	practical	[ˈpræktɪkl]	<> theoretical	praktisch
	role model	[ˈrəʊl mɒdl]	sb you admire and want to be like	Vorbild
16	**title**	[ˈtaɪtl]	the name of a book, film, picture, etc	Titel
	to **be dyslexic**	[bi dɪsˈleksɪk]	e.g. I find it difficult to read. I'm dyslexic.	Legastheniker/in sein
	to **ride**	[raɪd]	e.g. My maths teacher rides a motorbike.	(Fahrrad, Motorrad) fahren
	to **climb**	[klaɪm]	*n* climbing	klettern
	rock climbing	[ˈrɒk klaɪmɪŋ]	a sport where you go up mountains with ropes	Klettern
	any more	[ˌeni ˈmɔː]	e.g. any more questions	weitere
	real	[rɪəl]	<> fake	wirklich, echt
	husband	[ˈhʌzbənd]	<> wife	(Ehe-)Mann
	to **start a business**	[ˌstɑːt ə ˈbɪznəs]	e.g. I would like to start a business.	ein Unternehmen gründen
	nurse	[nɜːs]	sb who helps ill people in hospital	Krankenschwester, Krankenpfleger
	mechanic	[mɪˈkænɪk]	sb who fixes cars	Mechaniker/in
	apprenticeship	[əˈprentɪʃɪp]	a course where you learn how to do a job	Lehre, Ausbildung
	boring	[ˈbɔːrɪŋ]	<> interesting	langweilig
	special	[ˈspeʃl]	<> normal, boring	besondere/r/s
	not ... until	[nɒt ənˈtɪl]	e.g. I cannot start university until I have finished school.	erst
	learning difficulty	[ˈlɜːnɪŋ dɪfɪkəlti]	a learning difficulty makes it hard for sb to learn things	Lernschwäche
	straight	[streɪt]	directly	direkt, geradewegs
	another	[əˈnʌðə]	one more, an alternative	ein/e andere/r/s
17	to **copy sth**	[ˈkɒpi]	e.g. I copied the cartoon and it looked exactly l ike the original.	etw abschreiben, etw übertragen, etw kopieren
	to **achieve sth**	[əˈtʃiːv]	to do sth successfully	etw erreichen
	once	[wʌns]	e.g. I go out with my friends once a week.	einmal
18	**work experience**	[ˈwɜːk ɪkspɪəriəns]	e.g. I did work experience in the holidays.	Praktikum
	working holiday	[ˌwɜːkɪŋ ˈhɒlədeɪ]	working while you are on holiday somewhere	Arbeitsurlaub
	intensive course	[ɪnˌtensɪv ˈkɔːs]	a lot of learning in a short space of time	Intensivkurs
	sandwich bar	[ˈsænwɪdʒ bɑː]	a shop selling snacks and sandwiches	Imbiss
	pastry chef	[ˈpeɪstri ʃef]	a cook who makes cakes, croissants, etc.	Konditor/in
	to **make friends**	[meɪk ˈfrendz]	to meet new people and get to know them	Feunde finden
	to **teach sb sth**	[tiːtʃ]	e.g. My mum is teaching me how to drive a car.	jdm etw beibringen
	baker	[ˈbeɪkə]	a cook who makes bread	Bäcker/in
	to **decide**	[dɪˈsaɪd]	e.g. After my accident, I decided to become an ambulance driver.	(sich) entscheiden, beschließen
	not quite	[nɒt ˈkwaɪt]	almost	nicht ganz, irgendwie nicht
	sb gets bored with sth	[sʌmbədi ˌgets ˈbɔːd wɪð]	e.g. I get bored with doing the same thing every day!	jdn langweilt etw, jdm geht etw auf die Nerven
	to **be worried**	[bi ˈwʌrid]	to feel troubled or concerned	besorgt sein, sich Sorgen machen
	alone	[əˈləʊn]	<> with others	alleine
	foreign	[ˈfɒrən]	from another country	ausländisch, fremd
	typical	[ˈtɪpɪkl]	normal, average	typisch
	eventually	[ɪˈventʃuəli]	in the end	schließlich, am Ende
	to **persuade sb**	[pəˈsweɪd]	e.g. Kim persuaded me to go to the party.	jdn überzeugen, jdn überreden

CV (= curriculum vitae)	[ˌsiː ˈviː, kəˌrɪkjələm ˈviːtaɪ]	information about sb's education and working life	Lebenslauf
to **apply for sth**	[əˈplaɪ fə]	e.g. She applied for a job as a waiter in a cafe.	sich für/um etw bewerben
professional	[prəˈfeʃənl]	<> amateur	professionell
way	[weɪ]	e.g. He said hello in a polite way.	Art (und Weise)
situation	[ˌsɪtʒuˈeɪʃn]	circumstance	Lage, Situation
chef	[ʃef]	sb who cooks food in a restuarant	Koch/Köchin
so	[səʊ]	e.g. The film was over, so I went home.	daher, deshalb
timeline	[ˈtaɪmlaɪn]	the order in which things happen or will happen	Zeitachse, Chronik
event	[ɪˈvent]	an important thing that happens	Ereignis
to **feel sth about sth**	[ˈfiːl əbaʊt]	*n* feeling	etw von etw halten
to **enjoy doing sth**	[ɪnˈdʒɔɪ]	e.g. Tom really enjoys playing football.	etw gern tun
to **match**	[mætʃ]	to put things together which are the same	zueinander passen
to **accept sth**	[əkˈsept]	<> to reject sth	etw akzeptieren
primary school	[ˈpraɪməri skuːl]	children go to this school when they are between 6 and 9 years old	Grundschule
age	[eɪdʒ]	e.g. In the USA, you can get your driver's licence at the age of 16.	Alter
to **call**	[kɔːl]	e.g. My friends call me Minnie, although my name is Miranda.	nennen
weather	[ˈweðə]	e.g. sunny, snowy, rainy, cloudy, etc.	Wetter
grandparents ***pl***	[ˈgrænpeərnts]	the parents of my parents	Großeltern
at first	[ət ˈfɜːst]	to begin with	zunächst, zuerst
to **miss sb**	[mɪs]	to feel sad because sb is not there	jdn vermissen
secondary school	[ˈsekəndri skuːl]	the school after primary school	weiterführende Schule
to **join sb**	[dʒɔɪn]	to do sth with sb else	sich jdm anschließen, bei jdm mitmachen
soccer	[ˈsɒkə]	e.g. soccer match, soccer ball	Fußball
to **get fit**	[ˌget ˈfɪt]	to exercise and become healthier	fit werden
brilliant	[ˈbrɪliənt]	fantastic, wonderful, excellent	super, toll, klasse
What next?	[ˌwɒt ˈnekst]	e.g. I have done that. What next?	Was kam danach? Und dann?
to **repeat sth**	[rɪˈpiːt]	to say sth again	etw wiederholen
to **remember**	[rɪˈmembə]	<> to forget	daran denken
You might as well be ...	[ju ˌmaɪt əz ˈwel]	e.g. You might as well be happy about the results!	Dann kannst du auch ... sein.
honest	[ˈɒnɪst]	e.g. To be honest, I think that's a bad idea.	ehrlich
Good point.	[ˌgʊd ˈpɔɪnt]	e.g. Good point. I agree.	Da hast du recht.
to **be/get bored**	[bi/get ˈbɔːt]	<> to be interested in sth	sich langweilen
academic	[ˌækəˈdemɪk]	educational, theoretical	akademisch, theoretisch, praxisfern
to **guess**	[ges]	e.g. It's midnight – I guess they're not coming.	vermuten
to **change sth**	[tʃeɪndʒ]	to swap, to switch	etw wechseln
subject	[ˈsʌbdʒɪkt]	e.g. My favourite subject at school is English!	(Schul-)Fach
motivated	[ˈməʊtɪveɪtɪd]	*n* motivation	motiviert
excellent	[ˈeksələnt]	<> awful	ausgezeichnet, hervorragend
to **coach sb**	[kəʊtʃ]	to train sb e.g. in a sport	jdn trainieren
responsibility	[rɪˌspɒnsəˈbɪləti]	being in charge of sth	Aufgabe, Verantwortung
you see	[ju ˈsiː]	e.g. You see? I told you it would work.	weißt du / wissen Sie
working hours ***pl***	[ˌwɜːkɪŋ ˈaʊəz]	the time you have to work	Arbeitszeiten
to **get up**	[ˌget ˈʌp]	<> go to bed	aufstehen
in the middle of	[ɪn ðə ˈmɪdl əv]	e.g. In the middle of the day, I have lunch.	mitten in
career	[kəˈrɪə]	a job or profession	Berufsweg, Laufbahn, Karriere
first of all	[ˌfɜːst əv ˈɔːl]	e.g. First of all I need to fill in the form.	zuallererst
voluntary work	[ˌvɒləntri ˈwɜːk]	work you don't earn any money for	Freiwilligendienst, ehrenamtliche Tätigkeit
charity	[ˈtʃærəti]	an organization that helps others	wohltätige Zwecke, Hilfsorganisation
experience	[ɪkˈspɪəriəns]	e.g. My first ride on a rollercoaster was a fantastic experience.	Erlebnis, Erfahrung(en)
sb enjoys sth	[ɪnˈdʒɔɪz]	e.g. My brother really enjoys ice cream.	jdm gefällt etw, jdm macht etw Spaß
to **improve sth**	[ɪmˈpruːv]	to make/do sth better	etw verbessern
19 **unhappy**	[ʌnˈhæpi]	<> happy	unzufrieden, unglücklich
role	[rəʊl]	e.g. What is your role in the company?	Funktion, Aufgabe, Rolle
coach	[kəʊtʃ]	sb who trains a team	Trainer/in
proud	[praʊd]	e.g. I am proud of my little brother.	stolz

20	**item**	[ˈaɪtəm]	thing, e.g. item of clothing	Punkt, Gegenstand
	nationality	[ˌnæʃəˈnæləti]	e.g. German, British, Irish, etc.	Staatsangehörigkeit
	professional	[prəˈfeʃənl]	e.g. Steve is a professional footballer.	beruflich, berufsbezogen
	summary	[ˈsʌməri]	the main points	Zusammenfassung, Kurzdarstellung, Resümee
	reliable	[rɪˈlaɪəbl]	e.g. My car is old but very reliable – it never breaks down!	zuverlässig
	hard-working	[ˌhɑːd ˈwɜːkɪŋ]	<> lazy	fleißig
	commercial	[kəˈmɜːʃl]	to do with business	gewerblich
	bakery	[ˈbeɪkəri]	a place where bread is made and sold	Bäckerei, Backhandwerk
	to **serve sb**	[sɜːv]	to sell things to sb, to help sb	jdn bedienen
	customer	[ˈkʌstəmə]	sb who buys goods and services	Kunde/Kundin
	work experience	[ˈwɜːk ɪkspɪəriəns]	the work sb has done	Berufserfahrung
	assistant	[əˈsɪstənt]	deputy	stellvertretende/r
	team leader	[ˈtiːm liːdə]	sb who is responsible for a group of people at work	Teamleiter/in
	voluntary	[ˈvɒləntri]	unpaid (e.g. work)	ehrenamtlich
	position	[pəˈzɪʃn]	place, job	Stelle, Position
	education	[ˌedʒuˈkeɪʃn]	learning at school and university	Schulbildung
	training	[ˈtreɪnɪŋ]	learning how to do a job	Ausbildung
	vocational college	[vəʊˌkeɪʃənl ˈkɒlɪdʒ]	a school where you learn skills for work	Berufsschule
	three-year course	[ˌθriː jɪə ˈkɔːs]	education that takes three years to complete	dreijährige Ausbildung
	academy	[əˈkædəmi]	a type of school	Akademie
	qualification	[ˌkwɒlɪfɪˈkeɪʃn]	e.g. A-levels, Bachelor's degree, MA, etc.	Qualifikation, Abschluss, Ausbildung
	certificate	[səˈtɪfɪkət]	a piece of paper that shows your qualification	Zeugnis, Nachweis, Diplom
	school leaving certificate	[ˌskuːl liːvɪŋ səˈtɪfɪkət]	a certificate that shows sb has finished their school education	Schulabschluss(zeugnis)
	grade	[greɪd]	e.g. A–E	Note
	average	[ˈævərɪdʒ]	e.g. On average you are late once a week.	Durchschnitt
	native language	[ˌneɪtɪv ˈlæŋgwɪdʒ]	the first language sb learns	Muttersprache
	foreign language	[ˌfɒrən ˈlæŋgwɪdʒ]	a language from a different country	Fremdsprache
	organizational	[ˌɔːgənaɪˈzeɪʃənl]	*v* to organize	organisatorisch, Organisations-
	creative	[kriˈeɪtɪv]	having many ideas	schöpferisch, kreativ
21	**food server**	[ˈfuːd sɜːvə]	sb who serves food in cafes or restaurants	Bedienung, Servierkraft
	document	[ˈdɒkjumənt]	pages that contain important information	Schriftstück, Datei, Dokument
	spreadsheet	[ˈspredʃiːt]	a table with numbers in it	Tabelle, Tabellenkalkulation
	to **organize sth**	[ˈɔːgənaɪz]	*n* organisation	etw organisieren
	fundraising	[ˈfʌndreɪzɪŋ]	collecting of money for a special reason	Mittelbeschaffung, Spendensammeln
	event	[ɪˈvent]	e.g. a concert	Veranstaltung, Aktion
	to **raise money for charity**	[reɪz ˌmʌni fə ˈtʃærəti]	to collect money for an organisation that helps others	Spenden(gelder) sammeln
	to **enjoy sth**	[ɪnˈdʒɔɪ]	e.g. Most people enjoy listening to music.	etw genießen
	different	[ˈdɪfrənt]	<> the same	verschieden, unterschiedlich
	kind	[kaɪnd]	sort, type	Art
	set of instructions	[ˌset əv ɪnˈstrʌkʃnz]	notes that tell sb how to do sth	Anleitung
	care assistant	[ˌkeər əˈsɪstənt]	sb whose job is to look after other people	Pfleger/in
	sales assistant	[ˈseɪlz əsɪstənt]	sb who sells things in a shop	Verkäufer/in
	to **be a good communicator**	[bi ə ˌgʊd kəˈmjuːnɪkeɪtə]	to be able to listen and talk to other people	kommunikativ sein
	listener	[ˈlɪsnə]	*v* to listen	Zuhörer/in
	problem solver	[ˈprɒbləm sɒlvə]	sb who is good at finding solutions	Problemlöser/in
	to **be able to do sth**	[bi ˈeɪbl tə duː]	e.g. He is able to drive a car.	in der Lage / fähig sein, etw zu tun; etw tun können
	criticism	[ˈkrɪtɪsɪzəm]	negative feedback	Kritik
	pressure	[ˈpreʃə]	e.g. We should not put children under pressure.	Druck
	to **be attentive to detail**	[bi əˌtentɪv tə ˈdiːteɪl]	to see or notice small, important things	auf Details achten, sorgfältig sein
	caring	[ˈkeərɪŋ]	*v* to care	fürsorglich, sozial
	empathetic	[empəˈθetɪk]	to feel what other people feel	einfühlsam, empathisch
	polite(ly)	[pəˈlaɪt]	e.g. saying please and thank you	höflich
	responsible	[rɪˈspɒnsəbl]	be trusted to do the right thing	verantwortungsbewusst
	self-confident	[ˌself ˈkɒnfɪdənt]	secure in yourself	selbstbewusst
	technically minded	[ˌteknɪkli ˈmaɪndɪd]	to like working with machines	technisch interessiert/begabt
	cartoon	[kɑːˈtuːn]	e.g. Mickey Mouse, Donald Duck	Illustration, Karikatur

	suitable	[ˈsuːtəbl]	e.g. Chocolate is not suitable food for dogs.	geeignet, passend
	to **give reasons for sth**	[ˌɡɪv ˈriːznz fə]	to say why you think sth	etw begründen
	to **employ sb**	[ɪmˈplɔɪ]	to hire sb	jdn einstellen, jdn beschäftigen
	accident	[ˈæksɪdənt]	e.g. a traffic accident	Unfall
	writing	[ˈraɪtɪŋ]	*v* to write	(Hand-)Schrift
22	**state**	[steɪt]	e.g. Hessen, Bavaria, Baden-Württemberg	Staat, (USA:) Bundesstaat
	called	[kɔːld]	e.g. We live in a town called Greenport.	namens
	to **grow up**	[ˌɡrəʊ ˈʌp]	to get older and become an adult	aufwachsen
	to **leave home**	[liːv ˈhəʊm]	to move away from your parents' house	von zu Hause weggehen
	empty	[ˈempti]	<> full	leer
	without	[wɪˈðaʊt]	<> with	ohne
	to **lose**	[luːz]	<> to find	verlieren
	to **move in with sb**	[ˌmuːv ˈɪn wɪð]	to go and live in a new place with sb	zu jdm ziehen, bei jdm einziehen
	to **move**	[muːv]	to go and live somewhere else	umziehen, (wohin) ziehen
	to **save money**	[ˌseɪv ˈmʌni]	<> spend money	Geld sparen
	while	[waɪl]	at the same time as sth else	Weile
	early	[ˈɜːli]	<> late	früh
	to **die**	[daɪ]	<> to live	sterben
	That won't do!	[ðæt ˌwəʊnt ˈduː]	e.g. That is not OK!	Das geht nicht!
	independent(ly)	[ˌɪndɪˈpendənt]	<> dependent(ly)	unabhängig
	lady	[ˈleɪdi]	woman	Dame
	roof	[ruːf]	stops buildings getting wet inside when it rains	Dach
	meal	[miːl]	e.g. breakfast, lunch, dinner	Essen, Mahlzeit
	dining table	[ˈdaɪnɪŋ teɪbl]	a special table, used for eating meals	Esstisch
	to **chat**	[tʃæt]	to have a conversation with sb	sich unterhalten, (miteinander) plaudern
	to **look after sb**	[lʊk ˈɑːftə]	to take care of sb	sich um jdn kümmern
	each other	[ˌiːtʃ ˈʌðə]	e.g. My sister and I trust each other.	einander
	sb/sth used to be sth	[ˈjuːs(t) tə]	previously, it was normal for sb/sth to be this way	jd/etw war früher etw
23	**flat** *BE*	[flæt]	e.g. *AE* apartment	Wohnung
	noisy	[ˈnɔɪzi]	<> quiet	laut, voller Lärm
	according to	[əˈkɔːdɪŋ tə]	e.g. According to my mother, breakfast is very important.	laut, gemäß, nach
	member	[ˈmembə]	sb who belongs to a club, organisation	Mitglied
	past	[pɑːst]	<> future	Vergangenheit
	mealtime	[ˈmiːltaɪm]	time when you eat a meal	Essenszeit
	to **spend**	[spend]	to use (time)	(Zeit) verbringen
24	**milestone**	[ˈmaɪlstəʊn]	an important place in a project / sb's life	Projektabschnitt, Meilenstein
	to **brainstorm**	[ˈbreɪnstɔːm]	to collect ideas	(Ideen) sammeln
	to **draw**	[drɔː]	*n* drawing	zeichnen, (Linie) ziehen
	sheet (of paper)	[ʃiːt]	one piece (of paper)	Blatt (Papier)

UNIT 3

25	**community**	[kəˈmjuːnəti]	the people who live around you	Gemeinde, Gemeinschaft
	angry	[ˈæŋɡri]	what you feel when sth is unfair or annoying	wütend, zornig
	bored	[bɔːd]	<> interested	gelangweilt
	in love	[ɪn ˈlʌv]	e.g. Valentine's Day is for people who are in love.	verliebt
	nervous	[ˈnɜːvəs]	<> calm	aufgeregt, nervös
	scared	[skeəd]	e.g. Many people are scared of spiders.	ängstlich, verängstigt
	surprised	[səˈpraɪzd]	*n* surprise	erstaunt, überrascht
	to **match sth**	[mætʃ]	e.g. My shoes match my hat – they're both red.	zu etw passen
	to **win**	[wɪn]	*n* winner	siegen, gewinnen
26	**strange**	[streɪndʒ]	<> normal	seltsam, komisch
	to **mean**	[miːn]	e.g. What does this message mean?	bedeuten, heißen
	to **be scared (of sb/sth)**	[bi ˈskeəd]	to be afraid	(vor jdm/etw) Angst haben
	heart	[hɑːt]	e.g. Your heart is an important part of your body.	Herz
	maybe	[ˈmeɪbi]	perhaps	vielleicht, womöglich
	usual	[ˈjuːʒuəl]	<> unusual	üblich, normal
	type	[taɪp]	sort, kind	Art, Typ
	quite	[kwaɪt]	e.g. She's quite pretty.	ziemlich, ganz

	serious	[ˈsɪəriəs]	e.g. Why are you laughing? Please be serious.	ernst
	not ... at all	[ˌnɒt ət ˈɔːl]	e.g. I don't like football at all.	überhaupt nicht
	chatty	[ˈtʃæti]	talkative	geschwätzig
	lazy	[ˈleɪzi]	<> hard-working	faul, träge
	quiet	[ˈkwaɪət]	<> loud	ruhig, still
	around sb	[əˈraʊnd]	near sb	in jds Nähe
	to have sth in common	[həv ɪn ˈkɒmən]	to like the same things as sb else	etw gemeinsam haben
	to chill out	[ˌtʃɪl ˈaʊt]	to relax	faulenzen, abhängen, chillen
	loud(ly)	[laʊd]	<> quiet(ly)	laut
27	**text (message)**	[ˈtekst (mesɪdʒ)]	short message sent on a phone	Textnachricht, SMS
	by mistake	[ˌbaɪ mɪˈsteɪk]	<> on purpose	aus Versehen
	to prefer sb/sth	[prɪˈfɜː]	to like sb/sth better than sb/sth else	jdn/etw bevorzugen
	description	[dɪˈskrɪpʃn]	*v* to describe	Beschreibung
	clever	[ˈklevə]	intelligent	intelligent, schlau
	confident	[ˈkɒnfɪdənt]	*n* confidence	selbstbewusst, zuversichtlich
	funny	[ˈfʌni]	e.g. That was a funny joke!	witzig, lustig
	sensitive	[ˈsensətɪv]	e.g. My mum is very sensitive about that.	sensibel
	strong	[strɒŋ]	<> weak	stark, kräftig
	to describe	[dɪˈskraɪb]	*n* description	beschreiben
	precise	[prɪˈsaɪs]	exact	genau, präzise
	to add sth	[æd]	e.g. We need bread. I'll add that to my list.	etw hinzufügen
	crowd	[kraʊd]	lots of people in one place	Menschenmenge
	exercise	[ˈeksəsaɪz]	*phr* to get some exercise	Bewegung, Sport
	ideal	[aɪˈdiːəl]	perfect	ideal
28	**training session**	[ˈtreɪnɪŋ seʃn]	sport's practice	Trainingseinheit
	martial arts *pl*	[ˌmɑːʃl ˈɑːts]	e.g. karate, judo, taekwondo, etc.	Kampfsport
	rule	[ruːl]	sth you should follow to do sth right	Regel, Vorschrift
	at least	[ət ˈliːst]	no less than	mindestens
	to treat	[triːt]	e.g. The students treat the teacher with respect.	behandeln
	to shoot	[ʃuːt]	to film	(Film) drehen
	to listen carefully	[ˌlɪsn ˈkeəfəli]	e.g. Always listen to the teacher carefully.	aufmerksam zuhören
	instructor	[ɪnˈstrʌktə]	teacher	Lehrer/in
	senior	[ˈsiːniə]	<> junior	älter, erfahren
	valuables *pl*	[ˈvæljuəblz]	expensive things e.g. jewellery	Wertsachen
	locker	[ˈlɒkə]	a small cupboard at school that you can lock your things in	Schließfach, Spind
	to leave sth	[liːv]	to go out of sth	etw verlassen
	urgent	[ˈɜːdʒənt]	sth that needs to be done immediately	dringend
	(phone) call	[(ˈfəʊn) kɔːl]	*phr* to make a call	Anruf, Telefongespräch
	to be unwell	[bi ˌʌnˈwel]	to be sick/ill	sich nicht wohl fühlen, krank sein
	injury	[ˈɪndʒəri]	*v* to injure	Verletzung
	to take sth off	[ˌteɪk ˈɒf]	<> to put sth on	etw (Kleidung usw.) ausziehen
	entrance	[ˈentrəns]	<> exit	Eingang
	to make sure	[ˌmeɪk ˈʃʊə]	e.g. Make sure you do all your homework before you go out.	dafür sorgen(, dass ...), sicherstellen(, dass ...)
	uniform	[ˈjuːnɪfɔːm]	special clothes that you have to wear at work or school	(Sport-)Anzug
	clean	[kliːn]	<> dirty	sauber
	tidy	[ˈtaɪdi]	<> messy	ordentlich, aufgeräumt
	to sweep	[swiːp]	*phr* to sweep the floor	kehren, (aus)fegen
	floor	[flɔː]	ground	Boden
	to bring sth out	[ˌbrɪŋ ˈaʊt]	<> to put sth away	etw (hervor)holen
	equipment	[ɪˈkwɪpmənt]	things you need to do sth	Geräte, Ausrüstung
	to tidy up	[ˌtaɪdi ˈʌp]	to put everything away	aufräumen
	possessions *pl*	[pəˈzeʃnz]	things you own	Habseligkeiten, Sachen
	heading	[ˈhedɪŋ]	title	Überschrift
	set of rules	[ˌset əv ˈruːlz]	list of things you have to do to do sth right	Regeln
	to clean	[kliːn]	*adj* clean	reinigen, säubern
	clothing	[ˈkləʊðɪŋ]	clothes	Kleidung
	communication	[kəˌmjuːnɪˈkeɪʃn]	*v* to communicate	Kommunikation
	health	[helθ]	*adj* healthy	Gesundheit
	hygiene	[ˈhaɪdʒiːn]	*adj* hygienic	Hygiene
	routine	[ruːˈtiːn]	e.g. daily routine	Routine
	to design sth	[dɪˈzaɪn]	to make sth	etw gestalten, etw entwerfen

	to explain sth	[ɪkˈspleɪn]	*n* explanation	etw erläutern, etw erklären
29	**to remind sb about sth**	[rɪˈmaɪnd əbaʊt]	*n* reminder	jdn an etw erinnern
	firstly	[ˈfɜːstli]	at first	erstens
	secondly	[ˈsekəndli]	after that	zweitens
	to turn sth off	[ˌtɜːn ˈɒf]	<> to turn sth on	etw ausschalten, etw ausmachen
	to keep sth	[kiːp]	<> to throw sth away	etw aufbewahren
	valuable items *pl*	[ˌvæljuəbl ˈaɪtəmz]	e.g. purse, mobile phone, jewellery	Wertgegenstände
	female changing rooms *pl*	[ˌfiːmeɪl ˈtʃeɪndʒɪŋ ruːmz]	where women and girls can change their clothes	Damenumkleide
	broken	[ˈbrəʊkən]	*v* to break	kaputt
	lock	[lɒk]	*v* to lock	Schloss
	female	[ˈfiːmeɪl]	<> male	weiblich
	by	[baɪ]	next to	neben
	out of the way	[ˌaʊt əv ðə ˈweɪ]	<> in the way	nicht im Weg
	final	[ˈfaɪnl]	last	letzte/r/s
	dirty	[ˈdɜːti]	<> clean	schmutzig, dreckig
	to surprise	[səˈpraɪz]	to shock, to amaze	überraschen, erstaunen
	to be responsible for sth	[bi rɪˈspɒnsəbl fə]	*n* responsibility	für etw zuständig/verantwortlich sein
	discipline	[ˈdɪsəplɪn]	*adj* disciplined	Disziplin
	to volunteer to do sth	[ˌvɒlənˈtɪə tə duː]	*adj* voluntary	sich bereiterklären, etw zu tun; sich freiwillig melden, etw zu tun
	to choose sb/sth	[tʃuːz]	to pick sb/sth	jdn/etw auswählen
	style	[staɪl]	design	Art, Stil
	to let sb know	[ˌlet ˈnəʊ]	to tell sb	jdm Bescheid geben/sagen
	to listen back	[ˌlɪsn ˈbæk]	to listen again	sich etw nochmals anhören
	to check	[tʃek]	e.g. Check your answers.	überprüfen, kontrollieren
	to attract attention	[əˌtrækt əˈtenʃn]	to get sb's attention	Aufmerksamkeit erregen
	excuse me	[ɪkˈskjuːz mi]	e.g. Excuse me. Can I ask you a question?	entschuldigen Sie
	to apologize	[əˈpɒlədʒaɪz]	*n* apology	sich entschuldigen
	to ask for sth	[ˈɑːsk fə]	to request	um etw bitten
	permission	[pəˈmɪʃn]	*v* to permit	Erlaubnis
	to shut sth	[ʃʌt]	to close sth	etw schließen, etw zumachen
	instruction	[ɪnˈstrʌkʃn]	*v* to instruct	Anweisung, Anleitung
	sign	[saɪn]	e.g. warning sign	Schild, Hinweis
	to ring	[rɪŋ]	e.g. to ring a bell	läuten, klingeln
	bell	[bel]	e.g. The church bell rings every hour.	Glocke, Klingel
	rubbish	[ˈrʌbɪʃ]	things you throw away	Abfall, Müll
	bin	[bɪn]	where you put rubbish	Mülleimer, Mülltonne
	to act sth	[ækt]	e.g. to act a play	etw spielen, etw aufführen
30	**trouble**	[ˈtrʌbl]	problems	Schwierigkeit(en), Problem(e), Ärger
	the other day	[ði ˌʌðə ˈdeɪ]	recently	neulich
	to try	[traɪ]	to attempt	versuchen
	to get along with sb	[ˌget əˈlɒŋ wɪð]	e.g. I get along with my family. We don't have any problems.	mit jdm (gut) auskommen
	colleague	[ˈkɒliːg]	sb you work with	Kollege/-in
	busy	[ˈbɪzi]	e.g. It's always busy in the morning.	arbeitsreich, betriebsam
	filling	[ˈfɪlɪŋ]	what you put in a sandwich	(Brot-)Belag, Aufstrich, Füllung
	and so on	[ənd ˈsəʊ ɒn]	etc.	und so weiter
	tired	[ˈtaɪəd]	sleepy	müde, erschöpft
	grumpy	[ˈgrʌmpi]	in a bad mood	mürrisch, schlecht gelaunt
	to make a comment	[ˌmeɪk ə ˈkɒmənt]	to say sth	eine Bemerkung machen
	as usual	[əz ˈjuːʒuəl]	as normal	wie üblich
	to try harder	[traɪ ˈhɑːdə]	e.g. You nearly did it. Try harder next time.	sich mehr bemühen/anstrengen
	on time	[ɒn ˈtaɪm]	<> late	pünktlich
	to criticize sb/sth	[ˈkrɪtɪsaɪz]	*n* criticism	jdn/etw kritisieren
	worker	[ˈwɜːkə]	employee	Arbeiter/in
	to hurt sb	[hɜːt]	to upset sb, to injure sb	jdn verletzen
	upset	[ˌʌpˈset]	unhappy or annoyed	aufgebracht, verärgert
	even though	[ˈiːvn ðəʊ]	although	obwohl
	to confuse sb	[kənˈfjuːz]	*n* confusion	jdn verwirren

	rude	[ruːd]	<> polite	derb, unfreundlich, unhöflich
	helpful	[ˈhelpfl]	useful	hilfreich, nützlich
31	**behaviour**	[bɪˈheɪvjə]	*v* to behave	Verhalten, Benehmen, Auftreten
	arrogant	[ˈærəgənt]	*n* arrogance	überheblich, arrogant
	informal	[ɪnˈfɔːml]	<> formal	zwanglos, informell
	attitude (to sth)	[ˈætɪtjuːd]	belief, view	Einstellung, Haltung (zu etw)
	to **interact with sb**	[ˌɪntərˈækt wɪð]	*n* interaction	mit jdm kommunizieren, sich mit jdm auseinandersetzen
	to **annoy sb**	[əˈnɔɪ]	to bother sb	jdn nerven, jdn ärgern
	action	[ˈækʃn]	*v* to act	Handlung
	opinion	[əˈpɪniən]	(point of) view	Meinung, Ansicht
	to **agree with sb's opinion**	[əˌgriː wɪð ˌsʌmbədiz əˈpɪniən]	to think the same as sb else	jds Meinung sein, jds Ansicht teilen
	to **be friendly with sb**	[bi ˈfrendli wɪð]	to be nice to sb	nett zu jdm sein, mit jdm befreundet sein
	to **remember sth**	[rɪˈmembə]	<> to forget sth	etw nicht vergessen, an etw denken
	to **share sth**	[ʃeə]	e.g. The children shared a packet of sweets.	(sich) etw teilen
	to **respect sb/sth**	[rɪˈspekt]	*n* respect	jdn/etw respektieren
32	**rack**	[ræk]	a place where clothes can hang	(Kleider-)Ständer, Regal
	size	[saɪz]	e.g. What size is this sweatshirt?	Größe
	to **try sth on**	[ˌtraɪ ˈɒn]	e.g. to try some new clothes on	etw anprobieren
	next door	[ˌnekst ˈdɔː]	in the next building	nebenan
	surprise	[səˈpraɪz]	*v* to surprise	Überraschung
	plain	[pleɪn]	<> patterned	einfach, einfarbig, uni
	to **be on sale**	[bi ɒn ˈseɪl]	to be reduced (in price)	im Angebot sein
	anyway	[ˈeniweɪ]	e.g. I don't like soup but I'll eat it anyway.	sowieso, ohnehin, trotzdem
	to **pay cash**	[ˌpeɪ ˈkæʃ]	<> to pay by card	bar zahlen
	to **tap the card**	[ˌtæp ðə ˈkɑːd]	e.g. Just tap your card here, please.	die Karte kurz auflegen (aufs Lesegerät)
	receipt	[rɪˈsiːt]	piece of paper you get when you buy sth	Quittung, Kassenbon
	trip	[trɪp]	journey	Reise
33	to **go for a walk**	[ˌgəʊ fər ə ˈwɔːk]	e.g. I went for a walk on the beach.	spazieren gehen
	to **be rubbish**	[bi ˈrʌbɪʃ]	to not be good	nichts taugen
	sky	[skaɪ]	e.g. The sun is high in the sky.	Himmel
	to **transmit**	[trænsˈmɪt]	to send	übertragen, senden
	messaging app	[ˈmesɪdʒɪŋ æp]	app used to send messages	Nachrichten-App
	to **keep in touch with sth**	[ˌkiːp ɪn ˈtʌtʃ wɪð]	to stay in contact with sb	auf dem Laufenden über etw bleiben
	to **burn**	[bɜːn]	e.g. I do lots of sport to burn calories.	verbrennen
	to **suppose**	[səˈpəʊz]	to think, to believe	vermuten, glauben, annehmen
	free	[friː]	at no cost	kostenlos, gratis
	news *pl*	[njuːz]	e.g. I watched the news on TV.	Nachrichten, aktuelle Meldungen
34	to **attend sth**	[əˈtend]	to go to	an etw teilnehmen
	intercultural	[ˌɪntəˈkʌltʃərəl]	*n* culture	interkulturell
	awareness	[əˈweənəs]	*v* to be aware	Bewusstsein, Sensibilität
	handout	[ˈhændaʊt]	e.g. He prepared a handout for the workshop.	Arbeitsblatt
	following	[ˈfɒləʊɪŋ]	*v* to follow	folgende/r/s
	ethnic	[ˈeθnɪk]	e.g. ethnic group	ethnisch
	minority	[maɪˈnɒrəti]	<> majority	Minderheit
	several	[ˈsevrəl]	a few, some	mehrere
	greeting	[ˈgriːtɪŋ]	*v* to greet	Begrüßung
	handshake	[ˈhændʃeɪk]	*v* to shake hands	Händeschütteln, Handschlag
	bow	[baʊ]	*v* to bow	Verbeugung
	first name	[ˈfɜːst neɪm]	<> surname	Vorname
	subject	[ˈsʌbdʒɪkt]	topic	Thema
	to **avoid**	[əˈvɔɪd]	to try not to do sth	vermeiden, meiden
	body language	[ˈbɒdi læŋgwɪdʒ]	what you communciate with your body	Körpersprache
	eye contact	[ˈaɪ kɒntækt]	looking sb in the eye	Blickkontakt
	physical	[ˈfɪzɪkl]	<> mental	körperlich
	distance	[ˈdɪstəns]	e.g. social distance	Abstand, Entfernung
	variation	[ˌveəriˈeɪʃn]	*v* to vary	Abweichung
	exception (to a rule)	[ɪkˈsepʃn]	sth that does not follow a rule	Ausnahme (von einer Regel)

	to **disagree with sth**	[ˌdɪsəˈgriː wɪð]	<> to agree with sth	mit etw nicht einverstanden sein
	to **get sth wrong**	[ˌget ˈrɒŋ]	to misunderstand	etw falsch verstehen
	to**pic**	[ˈtɒpɪk]	subject	Thema
	to **hand sth out**	[ˌhænd ˈaʊt]	to give sth out	etw austeilen
	to **shake hands**	[ʃeɪk ˈhændz]	*n* handshake	sich die Hand geben
	gently	[ˈdʒentli]	carefully	sanft, behutsam
	optional	[ˈɒpʃənl]	<> required, compulsory	fakultativ, optional
	to **nod one's head**	[ˌnɒd wʌnz ˈhed]	<> to shake one's head	mit dem Kopf nicken
	married	[ˈmærid]	<> single	verheiratet
	request	[rɪˈkwest]	*v* to request	Bitte, Anfrage
	to **give a strong opinion**	[gɪv ə ˌstrɒŋ əˈpɪniən]	to say what you think	(s)eine Meinung mit Nachdruck äußern
	to **smile**	[smaɪl]	*n* smile	lächeln
	modest	[ˈmɒdɪst]	<> arrogant	bescheiden
	formal	[ˈfɔːml]	<> informal	formell, förmlich
	to **touch**	[tʌtʃ]	*n* touch	berühren
	other than	[ˈʌðə ðən]	except, apart from	ausgenommen, außer
	to **wave around one's arms**	[weɪv əˌraʊnd wʌnz ˈɑːmz]	to move your arms a lot	mit den Armen fuchteln
	gesture	[ˈdʒestʃə]	sth you do with your hands	Geste
	in front of	[ɪn ˈfrʌnt əv]	<> behind	vor
	chest	[tʃest]	the front top part of your body	Brust
	to **bow the head**	[ˌbaʊ ðə ˈhed]	to lower your head	den Kopf neigen
	celebrity	[səˈlebrəti]	a famous person	Promi(nente/r)
	instead	[ɪnˈsted]	e.g. We didn't want to go so stayed home instead.	stattdessen
	to **stand close to sb**	[ˌstænd ˈkləʊs tə]	<> to stand apart from sb	dicht bei jdm stehen
	to **point one's finger at sb**	[ˌpɔɪnt wʌnz ˈfɪŋgər ət]	e.g. Don't point your finger at me.	mit dem Finger auf jdn zeigen
	for no reason	[fə nəʊ ˈriːzn]	without a reason	ohne Grund, einfach so
	appearance	[əˈpɪərəns]	*v* to appear	Aussehen
	expression	[ɪkˈspreʃn]	*v* to express	Gesichtsausdruck
	smile	[smaɪl]	*v* to smile	Lächeln
	to **earn sth**	[ɜːn]	to get money for doing work	etw verdienen
	to **keep far apart from sb**	[kiːp ˌfɑːr əˈpɑːt frəm]	<> to stay close together	große Distanz zu jdm halten
	fake	[feɪk]	<> real	gekünstelt, künstlich
	to **laugh**	[lɑːf]	<> to cry	lachen
	strong	[strɒŋ]	<> weak	(Händedruck:) fest; (Reaktion:) deutlich
	to **offer an opinion**	[ˌɒfər ən əˈpɪniən]	to say what you think	(s)eine Meinung äußern
	freely	[ˈfriːli]	e.g. to speak freely	offen, freimütig
	to **react (strongly) to sth**	[riˈækt tə]	*n* reaction	(heftig) auf etw reagieren
	lively	[ˈlaɪvli]	animated	lebhaft, lebendig

UNIT 4

35	**building**	[ˈbɪldɪŋ]	*v* to build	Gebäude
	around town	[əˌraʊnd ˈtaʊn]	in town	in der Stadt
	gym	[dʒɪm]	place where you exercise	Fitness-Studio
	library	[ˈlaɪbrəri]	you can borrow books from here	Bibliothek
	public	[ˈpʌblɪk]	<> private	öffentlich
	railway	[ˈreɪlweɪ]	e.g. railway station	Eisenbahn, Bahn
	taxi rank	[ˈtæksi ræŋk]	where taxis wait for customers	Taxistand
	area	[ˈeəriə]	region	Gegend
	survey	[ˈsɜːveɪ]	questionnaire	Umfrage
36	**climate**	[ˈklaɪmət]	e.g. a warm climate	Klima
	sight	[saɪt]	somewhere tourists visit	Sehenswürdigkeit
	map	[mæp]	picture showing where places are	(Land-)Karte, (Stadt-)Plan
	to **suggest**	[səˈdʒest]	*n* suggestion	vorschlagen
	southeast	[saʊθˈiːst]	<> northwest	Südosten
	not ... yet	[nɒt ˈjet]	<> already	noch nicht
	beach	[biːtʃ]	area of sand next to the sea	Strand
	coast	[kəʊst]	land next to the sea	Küste

	to sunbathe	[ˈsʌnbeɪð]	to lie in the sun	sonnenbaden
	famous	[ˈfeɪməs]	well known	berühmt, bekannt
	Outback ***AusE***	[ˈaʊtbæk]	countryside in Australia	Hinterland, Busch
	dry	[draɪ]	<> wet	trocken
	flat	[flæt]	level	flach
	to sound	[saʊnd]	e.g. That sounds great!	klingen
	horrible	[ˈhɒrəbl]	really bad	fürchterlich, schrecklich
	awesome	[ˈɔːsəm]	really good	fantastisch, großartig
	space	[speɪs]	*phr* lots of space	Platz, Raum, Fläche
	the whole of ...	[ðə ˈhəʊl əv]	all of	ganz ...
	to be called	[bi ˈkɔːld]	to be named	heißen
	Aussie ***AusE***	[ˈɒzi]	sb from Australia	Australier/in; australisch
	skiing	[ˈskiːɪŋ]	a winter sport	Skifahren
	to joke	[dʒəʊk]	*phr* You're joking!	scherzen, Witze machen
	ski resort	[ˈskiː rɪzɔːt]	place people stay on a skiing holiday	Wintersportort
	opportunity	[ˌɒpəˈtjuːnəti]	chance	Gelegenheit, Chance
37	**to invite sb**	[ɪnˈvaɪt]	*n* invitation	jdn einladen
	to guess sth	[ges]	to give an answer you don't know is correct	etw erraten
	maple syrup	[ˌmeɪpl ˈsɪrəp]	e.g. pancakes and maple syrup	Ahornsirup
	spicy	[ˈspaɪsi]	hot, with lots of chilli	pikant, würzig, scharf
	colourful	[ˈkʌləfl]	with lots of colour	farbenfroh, bunt
	festival	[ˈfestɪvl]	celebration	Fest, Festtag
38	**volunteer**	[ˌvɒlənˈtɪə]	*adj* voluntary	ehrenamtliche/r Helfer/in
	(job) advertisement	[ədˈvɜːtɪsmənt]	*v* to advertise	Stellenanzeige, Stellenangebot
	wanted	[ˈwɒntɪd]	needed	gesucht
	outgoing	[ˈaʊtgəʊɪŋ]	sociable	kontaktfreudig
	to spare sth	[speə]	e.g. to spare time for sth	etw erübrigen
	ambassador	[æmˈbæsədə]	e.g. tourist ambassador; sb who represents sth	Botschafter/in
	to give directions	[ˌgɪv dəˈrekʃnz]	to explain to sb where they need to go	den Weg erklären
	tourist attraction	[ˌtʊərɪst əˈtrækʃn]	a sight	Sehenswürdigkeit
	pack	[pæk]	e.g. information pack	Paket
	briefing session	[ˈbriːfɪŋ seʃn]	time when sb is told what they have to do	Einweisung
	public transport	[ˌpʌblɪk ˈtrænspɔːt]	e.g. buses, trains, trams, etc.	öffentliche Verkehrsmittel
	safety	[ˈseɪfti]	*adj* safe	Sicherheit
	busy	[ˈbɪzi]	popular, full of people	belebt, verkehrsreich
	during daylight hours	[ˌdjʊərɪŋ ˈdeɪlaɪt aʊəz]	during the day	tagsüber
	supervisor	[ˈsuːpəvaɪzə]	*v* to supervise	Betreuer/in, Vorgesetzte/r
	location	[ləʊˈkeɪʃn]	place	Standort
	voicemail	[ˈvɔɪsmeɪl]	message on an answerphone	Sprachnachricht
	to be fluent in a language	[bi ˌfluːənt ɪn ə ˈlæŋgwɪdʒ]	to speak a language very well	eine Sprache fließend sprechen
	visitor	[ˈvɪzɪtə]	guest	Besucher/in, Gast
	to mention sth	[ˈmenʃn]	to say or state sth	etw erwähnen
	application	[ˌæplɪˈkeɪʃn]	*v* to apply	Bewerbung
39	**to follow**	[ˈfɒləʊ]	e.g. to follow directions	folgen
	directions ***pl***	[dəˈrekʃnz]	e.g. to give directions	Wegbeschreibung
	destination	[ˌdestɪˈneɪʃn]	place you want to go	Ziel, Zielort
	over there	[ˌəʊvə ˈðeə]	e.g. The museum is over there.	da drüben
	opposite	[ˈɒpəzɪt]	on the other side	gegenüber (von)
	to cross sth	[krɒs]	to go from one side of sth to the other	etw überqueren
	to turn left/right	[ˌtɜːn ˈleft/ˈraɪt]	e.g. Turn right at the end of the road.	links/rechts abbiegen
	across	[əˈkrɒs]	e.g. across the road	über
	on the left/right (hand side)	[ɒn ðə ˈleft/ˈraɪt]	e.g. It's on the right hand side of the street.	links/rechts
	straight on	[ˌstreɪt ˈɒn]	straight ahead	geradeaus
	side	[saɪd]	e.g. on the left side	Seite
	a couple of	[ə ˈkʌpl əv]	one or two	ein paar
	to recommend sth	[ˌrekəˈmend]	*n* recommendation	etw empfehlen
	corner	[ˈkɔːnə]	e.g. on the corner of Main Street	Ecke
	around the corner	[əˌraʊnd ðə ˈkɔːnə]	to turn right/left at the corner	um die Ecke
	moving image	[ˌmuːvɪŋ ˈɪmɪdʒ]	film	bewegtes Bild, Film
	to ask for directions	[ˌɑːsk fə dəˈrekʃnz]	to ask how to get somewhere	nach dem Weg fragen
	store	[stɔː]	*BE*: shop	Laden, Geschäft
	cathedral	[kəˈθiːdrəl]	big church	Dom, Kathedrale
40	**neighbour**	[ˈneɪbə]	sb who lives next door to you	Nachbar/in

	cleaner	[ˈkliːnə]	*v* to clean	Reinigungskraft
	porter	[ˈpɔːtə]	sb who assists train passengers on the platform	Fahrgastbetreuer/in auf dem Bahnsteig
	signaller	[ˈsɪgnələ]	*v* to signal	Fahrdienstleiter/in, Bahnwärter/in
	station supervisor	[ˌsteɪʃn ˈsuːpəvaɪzə]	person in charge of a station	Bahnhofs-Chef/in
	ticket clerk	[ˈtɪkɪt klɑːk]	sb who sells tickets	Schalterbedienstete/r, Fahrkartenverkäufer/in
	train guard	[ˈtreɪn gɑːd]	sb who checks tickets	Zugbegleiter/in
	passenger	[ˈpæsɪndʒə]	sb who travels in a car, on a train, etc.	Fahrgast, Passagier
	luggage	[ˈlʌgɪdʒ]	bags, suitcases, etc.	Gepäck
	platform	[ˈplætfɔːm]	e.g. train platform	Bahnsteig
	concourse	[ˈkɒŋkɔːs]	hall	Bahnhofshalle
	movement	[ˈmuːvmənt]	*v* to move	Bewegung
	to **assist sb**	[əˈsɪst]	to help sb	jdm helfen, jdm assistieren
	goods *pl*	[gʊdz]	things to buy	Ware(n)
	sort	[sɔːt]	type	Art
	station manager	[ˌsteɪʃn ˈmænɪdʒə]	*v* to manage	Bahnhofsvorsteher/in
	to **be in charge of sth**	[bi ɪn ˈtʃɑːdʒ əv]	to be responsible for sth	für etw zuständig/ verantwortlich sein
	day-to-day operations *pl*	[ˌdeɪ tə deɪ ɒpəˈreɪʃnz]	things that happen every day	(operatives) Tagesgeschäft
	staff *pl*	[stɑːf]	people who work somewhere	Personal, Mitarbeiter
	to **supervise**	[ˈsuːpəvaɪz]	*n* supervisor	(Personal, Mitarbeiter) führen
	school leaver	[ˈskuːl liːvə]	*v* to leave school	Schulabgänger/in
	main	[meɪn]	central	Haupt-
	area	[ˈeəriə]	zone	Bereich, Gebiet
	ticket office	[ˈtɪkɪt ɒfɪs]	where people buy tickets	Fahrkartenschalter
	counter	[ˈkaʊntə]	e.g. ticket counter	Schalter, Tresen
	to **provide sth**	[prəˈvaɪd]	to give or offer sth	etw bieten, etw zur Verfügung stellen
	administrative	[ədˈmɪnɪstrətɪv]	e.g. administrative or office work	Verwaltungs-
	to **get on/off**	[ˌget ˈɒn/ˈɒf]	e.g. to get on or off a train or bus	ein-/aussteigen
	to **load sth**	[ləʊd]	e.g. to put things on/into sth	etw verladen
	to **unload sth**	[ˌʌnˈləʊd]	e.g. to take things off/out of sth	etw abladen, etw entladen
	announcement	[əˈnaʊnsmənt]	*v* to announce	Durchsage
	contractor	[kənˈtræktə]	a company sb hires to do sth	Auftragsunternehmen
	separate	[ˈseprət]	<> together	gesondert/e/s, eigene/r/s
	train network	[ˈtreɪn netwɜːk]	train company	Bahngesellschaft
	to **hire sb**	[ˈhaɪə]	e.g. to hire a cleaner	jdn beauftragen, jdn engagieren
	to **report to sb**	[rɪˈpɔːt tə]	to work under sb	jdm unterstellt sein, jdm unterstehen
	retail	[ˈriːteɪl]	e.g. to work in retail	Einzelhandel
	business	[ˈbɪznəs]	company or firm	Unternehmen, Geschäft
	train driver	[ˈtreɪn draɪvə]	person who drives a train	Lokführer/in, Zugführer/in
	responsible	[rɪˈspɒnsəbl]	*n* responsibility	verantwortungsvoll
	to **operate sth**	[ˈɒpəreɪt]	to work sth	etw bedienen
	engineering	[ˌendʒɪˈnɪərɪŋ]	*n* engineer	Technik, Ingenieurwesen
	maintenance	[ˈmeɪntənəns]	*v* to maintain	Instandhaltung, Wartung
	crew	[kruː]	team	Mannschaft, Team
	track	[træk]	e.g. train track	Gleis
41	**national park**	[ˌnæʃnəl ˈpɑːk]	protected parks	Nationalpark
	to **keep to sth**	[ˈkiːp tə]	e.g. to keep to the rules	sich an etw halten
	walking trail	[ˈwɔːkɪŋ treɪl]	hiking trail	Wanderweg
	bathroom facilities *pl*	[ˈbɑːθruːm fəsɪlətiz]	e.g. toilet and bath or shower	Sanitäranlagen
	driving licence	[ˈdraɪvɪŋ laɪsns]	card that says you are allowed to drive	Führerschein
	essential	[ɪˈsenʃl]	necessary	unerlässlich, unbedingt erforderlich
	to **use one's initiative**	[ˌjuːz wʌnz ɪˈnɪʃətɪv]	to do sth on your own without sb telling you to do it	Eigeninitiative zeigen
	snake	[sneɪk]	a long animal with no legs	Schlange
	island	[ˈaɪlənd]	land surrounded by water	Insel
	caretaker	[ˈkeəteɪkə]	sb who looks after a building	Hausmeister/in, Verwalter/in
	fresh water	[freʃ ˈwɔːtə]	clean water	Süßwasser, frisches Wasser

	electricity	[ɪˌlekˈtrɪsəti]	*adj* electrical	Strom
	to **paint sth**	[peɪnt]	e.g. to paint a picture or a building	etw (an)streichen
	to **relax**	[rɪˈlæks]	to chill, n relaxation	sich erholen, sich entspannen
	to **go for a swim**	[gəʊ fər ə ˈswɪm]	*n* swimming	schwimmen gehen
	station hand ***AusE***	[ˈsteɪʃn hænd]	sb who works on a farm in the outback	landwirtschaftliche/r Hilfsarbeiter/in
	a range of ...	[ə ˈreɪndʒ əv]	a variety or selection of	eine Reihe (von) ...
	to **ride a horse**	[ˌraɪd ə ˈhɔːs]	*n* horse riding	reiten
	dirt bike	[ˈdɜːt baɪk]	e.g. to ride a dirt bike	Geländemotorrad
	to **be confident around ...**	[bi ˈkɒnfɪdənt əraʊnd]	*n* confidence	sicher mit Umgang mit ... sein, sich sicher in der Nähe von ... fühlen
	lonely	[ˈləʊnli]	alone	einsam
	close community	[ˌkləʊs kəˈmjuːnəti]	e.g. We live in a close community.	eingeschworene Gemeinschaft
	meaning	[ˈmiːnɪŋ]	*v* to mean	Bedeutung
	to **mark**	[mɑːk]	to highlight	markieren, kennzeichnen
42	**importance**	[ɪmˈpɔːtns]	*adj* important	Bedeutung, Wichtigkeit
	entertainment	[ˌentəˈteɪnmənt]	*adj* entertaining	Unterhaltung, Vergnügen
43	**travel**	[ˈtrævl]	holiday or journey	Reisen
	to **travel**	[ˈtrævl]	to go on a trip or journey	reisen
44	**placemat**	[ˈpleɪsmæt]	a mat on the table you put your plate on	Tischset
	to **agree on sth**	[əˈgriː ɒn]	<> to disagree about sth	sich auf etw einigen
	to **miss sth**	[mɪs]	to not see sth	etw verpassen
	bullet point	[ˈbʊlɪt pɔɪnt]	used to list items	(Aufzählungs-)Punkt

UNIT 5

45	**free time**	[ˌfriː ˈtaɪm]	leisure time, time when you are not working	Freizeit
	to **fit sth**	[fɪt]	to be right for sth	zu etw passen, sich für etw eignen
	to **work out**	[ˌwɜːk ˈaʊt]	e.g. to work out at the gym	trainieren
	to **volunteer**	[ˌvɒlənˈtɪə]	*adj* voluntary	ehrenamtlich tätig sein
	to **surf the internet for information**	[ˌsɜːf ði ˌɪntənet fər ɪnfəˈmeɪʃn]	to look for sth online	im Internet nach Informationen suchen
	social	[ˈsəʊʃl]	*n* society	sozial, gesellig, gesellschaftlich
	entertaining	[ˌentəˈteɪnɪŋ]	<> boring	unterhaltsam
	educational	[ˌedʒuˈkeɪʃənl]	informative	informativ, (weiter)bildend
	spare time	[ˌspeə ˈtaɪm]	free time	Freizeit
	to **spend time on sth**	[ˌspend ˈtaɪm ɒn]	to take time to do sth	Zeit in etw investieren, Zeit für etw aufwenden
	pie chart	[ˈpaɪ tʃɑːt]	type of graph in the shape of a circle	Tortendiagramm
46	**thief, thieves**	[θiːf, θiːvz]	sb who steals things	Dieb, Diebe; Räuber
	outside	[ˈaʊtsaɪd]	<> inside	(draußen) vor
	impatient	[ɪmˈpeɪʃnt]	<> patient	ungeduldig
	scooter	[ˈskuːtə]	a small motorcycle	(Motor-)Roller
	We won't be long!	[wiː ˌwəʊnt bi ˈlɒŋ]	e.g. Wait for us! We won't be long!	Wir kommen gleich nach!
	relaxed	[rɪˈlækst]	<> stressed	entspannt, locker
	to **mean**	[miːn]	*n* meaning	meinen
	How do you mean?	[ˌhaʊ duː ju ˈmiːn]	e.g. How do you mean? I don't understand.	Wie meinst du das?
	part-time	[ˌpɑːt ˈtaɪm]	<> full-time	Teilzeit(-)
	to **fail an exam**	[ˌfeɪl ən ɪgˈzæm]	<> to pass an exam	bei einer Prüfung durchfallen, eine Prüfung nicht bestehen
	to **stay up**	[ˌsteɪ ˈʌp]	*phr* to stay up late	aufbleiben, wach bleiben
	to **make a choice**	[ˌmeɪk ə ˈtʃɔɪs]	to decide	eine Entscheidung treffen, sich entscheiden
	to **steal**	[stiːl]	to take sth you shouldn't	stehlen, rauben
	to **be about to do sth**	[bi əˈbaʊt tə]	e.g. We need to hurry. The film's about to start.	etw gleich tun; gerade dabei sein, etw zu tun; im Begriff sein, etw zu tun
	advert	[ˈædvɜːt]	short for 'advertisement'	Werbespot
	although	[ɔːlˈðəʊ]	even though	obwohl
47	to **give sth up**	[ˌgɪv ˈʌp]	to stop doing sth	etw aufgeben
	to **sell sth**	[sel]	<> to buy sth	etw verkaufen
	waste of time	[ˌweɪst əf ˈtaɪm]	e.g. Watching that film was a waste of time.	Zeitverschwendung
	to **pass an exam**	[ˌpɑːs ən ɪgˈzæm]	<> to fail an exam	eine Prüfung bestehen
	necessary	[ˈnesəsəri]	needed, required	nötig
	tiring	[ˈtaɪərɪŋ]	*v* to tire	anstrengend, ermüdend

	stressed	[strest]	<> relaxed	erschöpft, gestresst
48	**DIY**	[ˌdiː aɪ ˈwaɪ]	short for ‚do it yourself'	Heimwerken, Heimwerker-
	lovely	[ˈlʌvli]	very nice	schön, nett, hübsch
	shared flat	[ˌʃeəd ˈflæt]	<> flat of your own	Wohngemeinschaft
	furniture	[ˈfɜːnɪtʃə]	e.g. table, chairs, bed, etc.	Möbel
	though	[ðəʊ]	however	allerdings, jedoch, aber
	flat-pack furniture	[ˌflæt pæk ˈfɜːnɪtʃə]	furniture you have to build yourself	Selbstbau-Möbel
	to **turn out sth**	[ˌtɜːn ˈaʊt]	e.g. It didn't turn out like I thought.	sich als etw herausstellen, am Ende etw sein
	to **be supposed to be**	[bi səˈpəʊzd tə]	e.g. That test was supposed to be easy.	etw sein sollen
	to **break sth**	[breɪk]	<> to fix sth	etw kaputt machen, etw zerbrechen
	electric drill	[ɪˌlektrɪk ˈdrɪl]	tool you use to make holes in things	Bohrmaschine, Akkuschrauber
	instructions *pl*	[ɪnˈstrʌkʃnz]	*v* to instruct	Anleitung
	complicated	[ˈkɒmplɪkeɪtɪd]	<> easy	kompliziert
	explanation	[ˌekspləˈneɪʃn]	*v* to explain	Erklärung, Erläuterung
	to **roll up one's sleeves**	[rəʊl ˌʌp wʌnz ˈsliːvz]	to pull your sleeves up	die Ärmel hochkrempeln
	to **grab sth**	[græb]	to take hold of sth	sich etw schnappen
	screwdriver	[ˈskruːdraɪvə]	tool you use to turn screws	Schraubenzieher
	nail	[neɪl]	sth you use to fix two things together	Nagel
	to **smash sth up**	[ˌsmæʃ ˈʌp]	to break sth up	etw zertrümmern
	solution	[səˈluːʃn]	answer; *v* to solve	Lösung
	step	[step]	*phr* step by step	Schritt
	order	[ˈɔːdə]	sequence	Reihenfolge
	drill bit	[ˈdrɪl bɪt]	part of a drill	Bohrer
	ear protection	[ˌɪə prəˈtekʃn]	sth that stops you hurting your ears	Gehörschutz
	eye protection	[ˈaɪ prətekʃn]	sth that stops you hurting your eyes	Schutzbrille
	to **turn**	[tɜːn]	to rotate, to move in a circle	sich drehen
	to **adjust sth**	[əˈdʒʌst]	to adapt/change sth	etw einstellen, etw regeln
	force	[fɔːs]	*adj* forceful	Stärke
	to **drill**	[drɪl]	to make a hole in sth	bohren
	to **fit sth into sth**	[ˈfɪt ɪntə]	to put sth into sth	etw in etw einpassen
	firm(ly)	[fɜːm]	tight(ly)	fest
	chuck	[tʃʌk]	mouth in the drill for the drill bit	Bohrfutter
	hole	[həʊl]	gap	Loch
	to **overheat sth**	[ˌəʊvəˈhiːt]	to let sth get too hot	etw überhitzen
	to **hold sth steady**	[həʊld ˈstedi]	to hold sth still	etw festhalten
49	**caption**	[ˈkæpʃn]	explanation under a picture	Überschrift, Bildunterschrift
	video frame	[ˈvɪdiəʊ freɪm]	picture taken from a video	Videobild
	component	[kəmˈpəʊnənt]	piece, part	Bauteil
	to **follow sth closely**	[ˌfɒləʊ ˈkləʊsli]	e.g. to follow the instructions closely	sich genau an etw halten
	to **look at sth carefully**	[ˌlʊk ət ˈkeəfəli]	to study sth	sich etw genau ansehen
	tool	[tuːl]	e.g. This is not the right tool for the job.	Werkzeug
	to **fit**	[fɪt]	e.g. Something's wrong. This piece doesn't fit.	passen
	to **open sth carefully**	[ˌəʊpən ˈkeəfəli]	e.g. Open it carefully so you don't break it.	etw vorsichtig öffnen
	to **tighten a screw**	[ˌtaɪtn ə ˈskruː]	e.g. The legs of the chair are loose – I'll have to tighten the screws.	eine Schraube anziehen/festziehen
	to **build sth**	[bɪld]	to make sth	etw bauen, etw aufbauen
	piece of furniture	[ˌpiːs əf ˈfɜːnɪtʃə]	e.g. desk, table, chair	Möbelstück
	to **demonstrate sth**	[ˈdemənstreɪt]	*n* demonstration	etw vorführen, etw demonstrieren
	to **cover sth**	[ˈkʌvə]	to put sth over sth else to protect it	etw bedecken, etw abdecken
	coat (of paint)	[ˌkəʊt (əf ˈpeɪnt)]	layer (of paint)	(Farb-)Schicht, Anstrich
	to **plant sth**	[plɑːnt]	e.g. to plant some flowers	etw pflanzen
	herbs *pl*	[hɜːbz]	e.g. basil, oregano, etc.	Kräuter
	pot	[pɒt]	e.g. flower pot	Topf
	compost	[ˈkɒmpɒst]	earth you use to grow plants	Pflanzerde
	seeds *pl*	[siːdz]	what plants and flowers grow from	Samen
	to **dye sth**	[daɪ]	to make sth a different colour	etw färben
	gloves *pl*	[glʌvz]	clothes you wear on your hands	Handschuhe
	to **apply sth**	[əˈplaɪ]	to put on sth	etw (Creme usw.) auftragen
	dye	[daɪ]	*v* to dye	Farbe
	timer	[ˈtaɪmə]	e.g. I set the timer so I know when to take it out.	(Küchen-)Wecker

	to **cook**	[kʊk]	e.g. Shall we cook the meat in the oven?	(Fleisch) braten
	to **slice sth**	[slaɪs]	to cut sth	etw in Scheiben schneiden
	burger bap	[ˈbɜːgə bæp]	bread you use to make a burger	Burgerbrötchen
	ingredients ***pl***	[ɪnˈgriːdiənts]	foods you need to make sth	Zutaten
	to **assemble sth**	[əˈsembl]	to put sth together	etw zusammensetzen
	to **hang sth on a wall**	[ˌhæŋ ɒn ə ˈwɔːl]	e.g. to hang a picture on the wall	etw an die Wand hängen
	tyre	[ˈtaɪə]	e.g. a bike tyre	Reifen
	to **mend a flat tyre**	[ˌmend ə ˌflæt ˈtaɪə]	to fix a broken tyre	einen Platten flicken
	to **load the dishwasher**	[ˌləʊd ðə ˈdɪʃwɒʃə]	to put things in the dishwasher	die Spülmaschine befüllen
50	**on the job**	[ɒn ðə ˈdʒɒb]	at work	bei der Arbeit
	landscape	[ˈlændskeɪp]	scenery	Landschaft
	gardener	[ˈgɑːdnə]	sb who looks after gardens	Gärtner/in
	outdoor	[ˈaʊtdɔː]	<> indoor	im Freien
	venue	[ˈvenjuː]	place where an event takes place	Veranstaltungsort
	builder	[ˈbɪldə]	*v* to build	Bauarbeiter/in
	delivery driver	[dɪˈlɪvəri draɪvə]	sb who delivers parcels	Lieferwagenfahrer/in, (Kraft-) Fahrer/in
	electrician	[ɪˌlekˈtrɪʃn]	sb who works with electricity	Elektriker/in
	security officer	[sɪˈkjʊərəti ɒfɪsə]	sb in charge of security in a place	Sicherheitskraft
	forklift operator	[ˌfɔːklɪft ˈɒpəreɪtə]	sb who drives a forklift	Gabelstaplerfahrer/in
	paramedic	[ˌpærəˈmedɪk]	emergency healthcare worker	Sanitäter
	sound engineer	[ˌsaʊnd endʒɪˈnɪə]	person in charge of sound at an event	Tontechniker/in
	to **arrange sth**	[əˈreɪndʒ]	to organize or prepare sth	etw aufstellen, etw vorbereiten, etw sortieren
	to **install sth**	[ɪnˈstɔːl]	*n* installation	etw aufbauen, etw einrichten, etw installieren
	sale	[seɪl]	*phr* for sale	Verkauf
	lighting	[ˈlaɪtɪŋ]	lights	Beleuchtung
	patient	[ˈpeɪʃnt]	sb being treated for a medical problem	Patient/in
	security pass	[sɪˈkjʊərəti pɑːs]	e.g. You need a security pass to go backstage.	Ausweis, (Backstage-)Pass
	sound equipment	[ˈsaʊnd ɪkwɪpmənt]	e.g. loudspeakers etc.	Beschallungsanlage
51	**job description**	[ˈdʒɒb dɪskrɪpʃn]	list of things you have to do in a job	Stellenbeschreibung, Tätigkeitsbeschreibung
	duty	[ˈdjuːti]	task	Aufgabe, Pflicht
	assistant	[əˈsɪstnt]	*v* to assist	Hilfs-
	plant	[plɑːnt]	e.g. There are lots of plants in her garden.	Pflanze
	gardening	[ˈgɑːdnɪŋ]	*v* to garden	Gartenarbeit, Gärtnern
	lawnmower	[ˈlɔːnməʊə]	sth you use to cut grass	Rasenmäher
	to **mow**	[məʊ]	to cut grass	mähen
	grass	[grɑːs]	e.g. We have to cut the grass at the weekend.	Rasen, Gras
	fit	[fɪt]	healthy, in shape	gut in Form, fit
	to **involve sth**	[ɪnˈvɒlv]	*n* involvement	etw umfassen, etw einschließen, etw einbeziehen
	to **carry sth**	[ˈkæri]	e.g. A gardener has to carry heavy plants.	etw tragen
	heavy	[ˈhevi]	<> light	schwer
	load	[ləʊd]	*phr* a heavy load	Last
	outdoors	[ˌaʊtˈdɔːz]	<> indoors	draußen
	job ad	[ˈdʒɒb æd]	short for 'job advertisement'	Stellenanzeige
	learner's permit ***AE***	[ˌlɜːnəz ˈpɜːmɪt]	document that allows you to drive before you have passed your test	Lernführerschein
	to **wonder**	[ˈwʌndə]	to question	sich fragen, sich Gedanken machen
	to **be busy**	[bi ˈbɪzi]	to have a lot to do	viel zu tun haben
	flower bed	[ˈflaʊə bed]	e.g. We have a big flowerbed in our garden.	Blumenbeet
	hard worker	[ˌhɑːd ˈwɜːkə]	sb who works hard	fleißige/r Arbeiter/in
	required	[rɪˈkwaɪəd]	necessary	erforderlich, nötig
	to **take an order**	[ˌteɪk ən ˈɔːdə]	to note down what sb wants in a restaurant	eine Bestellung aufnehmen
	to **add sth up**	[ˌæd ˈʌp]	to work sth out	etw ausrechnen, etw zusamenzählen
	bill	[bɪl]	sth which tells you how much you have to pay	Rechnung
	flexible	[ˈfleksəbl]	happy to change	flexibel
	to **communicate**	[kəˈmjuːnɪkeɪt]	*n* communication	kommunizieren
	to **evaluate sth**	[ɪˈvæljueɪt]	*n* evaluation	etw beurteilen, etw einschätzen

	medical	[ˈmedɪkl]	*n* medicine	medizinisch
	injection	[ɪnˈdʒekʃn]	*v* to inject	Injektion, Spritze
	medicine	[ˈmedsn]	e.g. The doctor gave me some medicine.	Medikament(e)
	to **stay calm**	[ˌsteɪ ˈkɑːm]	<> to get stressed	die Ruhe bewahren, ruhig bleiben
	emergency	[ɪˈmɜːdʒənsi]	e.g. In an emergency, call 999.	Notfall
	medical equipment	[ˌmedɪkl ɪˈkwɪpmənt]	things doctors and nurses use	Medizingeräte
	ID	[ˌaɪ ˈdiː]	short for ‚identification'	Ausweis
	wristband	[ˈrɪstbænd]	sth you wear on your lower arm	Armband
	effective(ly)	[ɪˈfektɪv]	efficient(ly)	effektiv, kompetent
	to **identify sth**	[aɪˈdentɪfaɪ]	*n* identification	etw erkennen, etw identifizieren
	security risk	[sɪˈkjʊərəti rɪsk]	sth that could be dangerous	Sicherheitsrisiko
	police officer	[pəˈliːs ɒfɪsə]	policeman or policewoman	Polizeibeamte/r
	to **set sth up**	[ˌset ˈʌp]	to get sth ready	etw aufbauen
	audio equipment	[ˈɔːdiəʊ ɪkwɪpmənt]	sound equipment	Tonanlage, Beschallungsanlage
	to **repair sth**	[rɪˈpeə]	to fix sth	etw reparieren
	to **maintain sth**	[meɪnˈteɪn]	*n* maintenance	etw warten, etw instandhalten
	to **mix sth**	[mɪks]	*n* mixture	etw mischen
	sound	[saʊnd]	sth you can hear	Klang, Ton
	musician	[mjuːˈzɪʃn]	sb who plays music	Musiker/in
	event manager	[ɪˈvent mænɪdʒə]	person in charge of an event	Veranstaltungsleiter/in
	to **pack sth up**	[ˌpæk ˈʌp]	to put sth away	etw zusammenpacken
	to **be one's turn**	[bi wʌnz ˈtɜːn]	e.g. It's my turn to choose a song to listen to.	an der Reihe sein
	law	[lɔː]	*adj* legal	Gesetz, Recht
	aged	[eɪdʒd]	at the age of	im Alter von
52	to **check in on**	[ˌtʃek ˌɪn ɒn]	e.g. to check in on social media	einchecken
	to **share sth**	[ʃeə]	e.g. She shared her photos on social media.	etw teilen
	annoying	[əˈnɔɪɪŋ]	irritating	nervig, ärgerlich
	to **look out across sth**	[ˌlʊk ˈaʊt əkrɒs]	e.g. The window looked out across the sea.	über etw blicken
	audience	[ˈɔːdiəns]	the people watching sth	Publikum, Zuschauer
	bright	[braɪt]	<> dark	hell
	screen	[skriːn]	display on an electronic device, e.g. phone or tablet	Bildschirm
	high above sth	[ˌhaɪ əˈbʌv]	e.g. I waved my hand high above my head.	hoch über etw
	shot	[ʃɒt]	*phr* to get a good shot	Aufnahme, Einstellung
	performer	[pəˈfɔːmə]	*v* to perform	Künstler/in
	to **be allowed to do sth**	[bi əˈlaʊd tə duː]	to be permitted to do sth	etw tun dürfen
	zone	[zəʊn]	area	Bereich
	magnetic bag	[mægˌnetɪk ˈbæg]	a bag which you close using a magnet	magnetisch abgeschirmte Tasche
	member of staff	[ˌmembər əf ˈstɑːf]	sb who works at a place	Mitarbeiter/in
	to **lock sth**	[lɒk]	to close sth with a key	etw abschließen, etw verschließen
53	to **seem**	[siːm]	to appear	scheinen
	to **upload sth**	[ˌʌpˈləʊd]	<> to download sth	etw hochladen
	advertising	[ˈædvətaɪzɪŋ]	e.g. flyer, TV advert, etc.	Werbung
	sponsorship	[ˈspɒnsəʃɪp]	*v* to sponsor	finanzielle Unterstützung, Sponsoring
	sadly	[ˈsædli]	unfortunately	leider, bedauerlicherweise
	It's not quite that simple.	[ɪts nɒt kwaɪt ˌðæt ˈsɪmpl]	e.g. It looks easy but it's not quite that simple.	Es ist nicht ganz so einfach.
	reality	[riˈæləti]	the real world	Wirklichkeit
	talented	[ˈtæləntɪd]	*n* talent	begabt, talentiert
	professional	[prəˈfeʃənl]	<> amateur	Profi
	result	[rɪˈzʌlt]	product, outcome	Ergebnis, Resultat
	research	[rɪˈsɜːtʃ]	*v* to research	Recherche, Forschung
	attempt	[əˈtempt]	try	Versuch
	to **set sth**	[set]	to decide sth	etw festlegen
	schedule	[ˈʃedjuːl]	timetable	Zeitplan
	brand	[brænd]	e.g. a brand name	Marke
	to **work on sth**	[ˈwɜːk ɒn]	e.g. to work on a project	sich mit etw beschäftigen
	truly	[ˈtruːli]	really, actually	wirklich
	on the other hand	[ɒn ði ˈʌðə hænd]	however	andererseits

	balance	[ˈbæləns]	*phr* to get the balance right	Gleichgewicht
	to **be enthusiastic about sth**	[bi ɪnˌθjuːziˈæstɪk əbaʊt]	to be excited about sth	von etw begeistert sein, sich für etw begeistern
	after all	[ˌɑːftər ˈɔːl]	in the end	schließlich
	influence	[ˈɪnfluəns]	sth that changes sb/sth	Einfluss
	authentic	[ɔːˈθentɪk]	real	authentisch
	trust	[trʌst]	*v* to trust	Vertrauen
	to **gain sth**	[geɪn]	to get sth	etw erwerben, etw erlangen
	furthermore	[ˌfɜːðəˈmɔː]	moreover	außerdem, darüber hinaus
	job security	[ˌdʒɒb sɪˈkjʊərəti]	e.g. I never know if I will keep my job so I have no job security.	sicherer Arbeitsplatz
54	**practical**	[ˈpræktɪkl]	suitable	geeignet, umsetzbar
	visual	[ˈvɪʒuəl]	*n* vision	anschaulich, visuell
	viewer	[ˈvjuːə]	sb who watches sth	Zuschauer/in
	to **try sth**	[traɪ]	to attempt sth	etw ausprobieren
	to **decide sth**	[dɪˈsaɪd]	*n* decision	etw festlegen
	producer	[prəˈdjuːsə]	*v* to produce	Produzent/in
	script	[skrɪpt]	text of a video	Drehbuch
	to **select sth**	[sɪˈlekt]	to choose sth	etw auswählen
	(film) location	[ləʊˈkeɪʃn]	where sth is filmed	Drehort
	director	[dəˈrektə]	*v* to direct	Regisseur/in
	to **run sth**	[rʌn]	to manage sth	etw leiten, etw durchführen
	shoot	[ʃuːt]	filming	Dreh, Filmaufnahmen
	camera operator	[ˌkæmərə ˈɒpəreɪtə]	sb who does the filming	Kameramann/-frau
	props manager	[ˈprɒps mænɪdʒə]	sb who finds all the objects needed in a film	Requisiteur/in
	to **take care of sb/sth**	[ˌteɪk ˈkeər əv]	to look after sb/sth	sich um jdn/etw kümmern
	lighting engineer	[ˈlaɪtɪŋ endʒɪnɪə]	sb who operates the lights	Beleuchter/in
	actor	[ˈæktə]	*v* to act	Schauspieler/in, Darsteller/in
	to **appear in a video**	[əˌpɪər ɪn ə ˈvɪdiəʊ]	to be in a video	in einem Video auftreten/mitspielen
	to **be good at sth**	[bi ˈgʊd ət]	<> to be bad at sth	etw gut können
	to **offer sth**	[ˈɒfə]	to provide sth	etw anbieten, etw bieten
	to **reach an agreement**	[ˌriːtʃ ən əˈgriːmənt]	to agree on sth	eine Einigung erzielen
	to **agree**	[əˈgriː]	sich einig sein	
	to **separate sth**	[ˈsepəreɪt]	to share sth out	etw unterteilen
	section	[ˈsekʃn]	part	Abschnitt
	introduction	[ˌɪntrəˈdʌkʃn]	*v* to introduce	Einleitung

UNIT 6

55	to **label sth**	[ˈleɪbl]	to identify sth	etw bezeichnen, etw beschriften
	respect	[rɪˈspekt]	e.g. It is important to treat people with respect.	Achtung, Respekt
	status	[ˈsteɪtəs]	prestige	Ansehen, Prestige, (soziale) Stellung
	mind map	[ˈmaɪnd mæp]	a type of diagram	Mindmap
	to **pick sth**	[pɪk]	to choose sth	sich etw aussuchen, etw wählen
	to **agree (strongly) with sth**	[əˈgriː wɪð]	to firmly agree with sth	einer Sache (voll und ganz) zustimmen
	self-starter	[ˌself ˈstɑːtə]	sb who is very active and willing to do things	jd mit Eigenitiative
	to **work sth out**	[ˌwɜːk ˈaʊt]	to solve sth	etw herausfinden, etw erledigen
	breadwinner	[ˈbredwɪnə]	sb who earns money	Geldverdiener/in
	individual	[ˌɪndɪˈvɪdʒuəl]	a person	Einzelperson, Einzelne/r
	to **do one's share**	[ˌduː wʌnz ˈʃeə]	e.g. Everybody has to do their share.	seinen Beitrag leisten
	to **be involved in sth**	[bi ɪnˈvɒlvd ɪn]	*n* involvement	an etw beteiligt sein/werden
	to **take a decision**	[ˌteɪk ə dɪˈsɪʒn]	to decide	eine Entscheidung fällen
	to **do well**	[ˌduː ˈwel]	to be successful	erfolgreich sein, gut abschneiden
	to **motivate**	[ˈməʊtɪveɪt]	*n* motivation	motivieren
	to **stand out from the crowd**	[ˌstænd ˈaʊt frəm ðə ˈkraʊd]	to be noticeable	sich von der Masse abheben, auffallen
	to **impress sb**	[ɪmˈpres]	*n* impression	jdn beeindrucken

	to **take control**	[ˌteɪk kənˈtrəʊl]	to lead	die Führung übernehmen, führen
56	**care home**	[ˈkeə həʊm]	where elderly people live and are looked after	Pflegeheim
	to **skim a text**	[ˌskɪm ə ˈtekst]	to read a text quickly	einen Text überfliegen
	resident	[ˈrezɪdənt]	*v* to reside	Bewohner/in
	mostly	[ˈməʊstli]	most of the time	größtenteils, meistens
	working conditions ***pl***	[ˌwɜːkɪŋ kənˈdɪʃnz]	e.g. The working conditions are bad – we have no breaks and don't get much money.	Arbeitsbedingungen
	to **provide a service to sb**	[prəˌvaɪd ə ˈsɜːvɪs tə]	e.g. We provide a good service for our customers.	jdm eine Dienstleistung erbringen
	proper(ly)	[ˈprɒpə]	right, correct(ly)	ordentlich, richtig, sachgerecht
	in my opinion	[ɪn ˌmaɪ əˈpɪnɪən]	e.g. I think …	meiner Meinung/Ansicht nach
	carer	[ˈkeərə]	*v* to care	Pfleger/in, Betreuer/in
	all day	[ɔːl ˈdeɪ]	the whole day	den ganzen Tag lang
	manager	[ˈmænɪdʒə]	*v* to manage	Leiter/in, Chef/in
	to **afford sb/sth**	[əˈfɔːd]	to be able to buy sth	sich jdn/etw leisten
	I disagree.	[aɪ ˌdɪsəˈgriː]	e.g. I think I'm very good at playing the guitar. – I disagree.	Da bin ich anderer Meinung. Das finde ich nicht.
	to **mean to do sth**	[ˌmiːn tə ˈduː]	to want to do sth	beabsichtigen, etw zu tun; etw tun wollen
	to **supervise sb**	[ˈsuːpəvaɪz]	*n* supervisor	jdn beaufsichtigen, jdn (als Vorgesetze/r) betreuen
	to **do sth about sth**	[ˈduː əbaʊt]	e.g. I don't know what I can do about it to make it better.	etw in einer Angelegenheit unternehmen, etw machen
	to **complain to sb**	[kəmˈpleɪn tə]	*n* complaint	sich bei jdm beschweren
	trainee	[treɪˈniː]	apprentice	Auszubildende/r
	to **give up**	[ˌgɪv ˈʌp]	to stop trying	aufgeben
	to **solve a problem**	[ˌsɒlv ə ˈprɒbləm]	*n* solution to a problem	ein Problem lösen
	for a while	[fər ə ˈwaɪl]	for a short time	eine Zeitlang, eine Weile
57	to **spend**	[spend]	*phr* to spend money	(Geld) ausgeben
	to **run sth**	[rʌn]	to manage sth	(Firma usw.:) etw betreiben, etw führen
	staff meeting	[ˈstɑːf miːtɪŋ]	meeting for everybody who works somewhere	Personalversammlung
	to **hold a meeting**	[ˌhəʊld ə ˈmiːtɪŋ]	to run a meeting	eine Versammlung abhalten
58	**ethical**	[ˈeθɪkl]	*n* ethics	ethisch (handelnd)
	employer	[ɪmˈplɔɪə]	a person who gives sb a job	Arbeitgeber/in
	painting and decorating business	[ˌpeɪntɪŋ ən ˈdekəreɪtɪŋ bɪznəs]	e.g. We paid for a painting and decorating business to make the bedroom look nice.	Malerei- und Dekorateurbetrieb
	pay	[peɪ]	money from a job	Bezahlung, Lohn
	paint	[peɪnt]	e.g. wall paint, oil paint	Farbe
	to **contain sth**	[kənˈteɪn]	e.g. Wine contains alcohol.	etw enthlaten
	chemicals ***pl***	[ˈkemɪklz]	e.g. water, oxygen, etc.	Chemikalien
	headaches ***pl***	[ˈhedeɪks]	pain in the head	Kopfschmerzen
	skin	[skɪn]	e.g. The face cream we used damaged our skin.	Haut
	environmentally friendly	[ɪnˌvaɪrənˌmentəli ˈfrendli]	not harmful to the environment	umweltfreundlich
	protective equipment	[prəˌtektɪv ɪˈkwɪpmənt]	e.g. safety glasses, hard hat	Schutzausrüstung
	faulty	[ˈfɔːlti]	broken or damaged	mangelhaft, defekt
	workplace	[ˈwɜːkpleɪs]	where sb works	Arbeitsplatz, Arbeitsstätte
	unsafe	[ˌʌnˈseɪf]	<> safe	unsicher, gefährlich
	to **do better**	[du ˈbetə]	to improve	es besser machen
	vision	[ˈvɪʒn]	idea	Vision
	non-toxic	[ˌnɒn ˈtɒksɪk]	<> toxic, poisonous	ungiftig
	natural	[ˈnætʃrəl]	<> artificial	natürlich
	raw materials ***pl***	[ˌrɔː məˈtɪəriəlz]	materials used to make sth	Rohstoffe
	to **last**	[lɑːst]	e.g. My phone battery doesn't last long.	halten
	toxic	[ˈtɒksɪk]	poisonous	giftig
	healthy	[ˈhelθi]	<> ill, sick	gesund
	paint brush	[ˈpeɪnt brʌʃ]	sth you use to paint	Pinsel
	paint roller	[ˈpeɪnt rəʊlə]	sth you use to paint	Farbwalze, Streichrolle
	supplier	[səˈplaɪə]	*v* to supply	Lieferant/in, Zulieferer
	wage	[weɪdʒ]	pay, money from a job	Lohn
	employee	[ɪmˈplɔɪiː]	a person who has a job	Arbeitnehmer/in
	eco-friendly	[ˈiːkəʊ frendli]	environmentally friendly	umweltfreundlich

	electric	[ɪˈlektrɪk]	e.g. an electric bike	elektrisch, Elektro-
	van	[væn]	e.g. delivery van	Lieferwagen
	to **support sb/sth**	[səˈpɔːt]	*n* support	jdn/etw unterstützen
	financial(ly)	[faɪˈnænʃl]	to do with money	finanziell
	homeless	[ˈhəʊmləs]	without a home	obdachlos
	youth	[juːθ]	*adj* young	Jugend, Jugendliche
	per year	[pə ˈjɪə]	each year	pro Jahr
	either ... or	[ˌaɪðə ˈɔː]	this one or that one	entweder ... oder
	insecure housing	[ɪnsɪˌkjʊə ˈhaʊzɪŋ]	being in constant danger of losing your home	prekäre Wohnverhältnisse
	equal opportunities ***pl***	[ˌiːkwəl ɒpəˈtjuːnətiz]	e.g. We are an equal opportunities employer, who employs the best person for the job.	Chancengleichheit, Gleichstellung
	to **discriminate (against sb)**	[dɪˈskrɪmɪneɪt]	*n* discrimination	(jdn) diskriminieren, (jdn) benachteiligen
	gender	[ˈdʒendə]	sex, male or female	Geschlecht
	sexual orientation	[ˌsekʃuəl ɔːriənˈteɪʃn]	e.g. straight, gay or bisexual	sexuelle Orientierung
	ethnic background	[ˌeθnɪk ˈbækgraʊnd]	where your family comes from	ethnische Herkunft
	physical ability	[ˌfɪzɪkl əˈbɪləti]	how well you can move physically	körperliche Fähigkeiten
	target funding	[ˌtɑːgɪt ˈfʌndɪŋ]	*v* to fund	Finanzierungsziel
59	**qualified**	[ˈkwɒlɪfaɪd]	*v* to qualify	qualifiziert, ausgebildet, mit Abschluss
	to **hurt oneself**	[ˈhɜːt wʌnself]	to injure oneself	sich verletzen
	particular	[pəˈtɪkjələ]	certain	bestimmte/r/s, speziell
	treatment	[ˈtriːtmənt]	*v* to treat	Behandlung
	of one's own	[əv wʌnz ˈəʊn]	belonging to you	eigene/r/s
	to **work sth out**	[ˌwɜːk ˈaʊt]	to figure sth out	etw herausarbeiten
	benefits ***pl***	[ˈbenɪfɪts]	extras, perks	Zusatzleistungen
60	**(It's) All in a day's work.**	[ˌɔːl ɪn ə ˌdeɪz ˈwɜːk]	e.g. It was nothing special. Just all in a day's work.	Das gehört zum (Arbeits-) Alltag.
	freelance	[ˈfriːlɑːns]	self-employed	selbständig
	event technician	[ɪˈvent teknɪʃn]	sb who looks after technology at an event	Veranstaltungstechniker/in
	basically	[ˈbeɪsɪkli]	essentially, practically	eigentlich, im Grunde genommen
	similar	[ˈsɪmələ]	<> different	ähnlich
	space	[speɪs]	area	Ort, Platz, Fläche, Raum
	organizer	[ˈɔːgənaɪzə]	*v* to organize	Organisator/in, Veranstalter/in
	need	[niːd]	requirement	Bedürfnis
	buzz	[bʌz]	e.g. I love the buzz of an exciting festival.	Nervenkitzel, Kick
	excitement	[ɪkˈsaɪtmənt]	*adj* exciting	Anspannung, Aufregung
	downside	[ˈdaʊnsaɪd]	disadvantage	Kehrseite, Nachteile
	accurate(ly)	[ˈækjərət]	precise(ly)	genau, präzise
	to **be methodical**	[bi məˈθɒdɪkl]	to work carefully	systematisch vorgehen
	lifestyle	[ˈlaɪfstaɪl]	way of life	Lebensweise
	as a result	[əz ə rɪˈzʌlt]	therefore	demzufolge
	antisocial	[ˌæntɪˈsəʊʃl]	<> social	nicht sozialverträglich
	to **get to do sth**	[ˌget tə ˈduː]	to be able to do sth	die Möglichkeit haben, etw zu tun
	to **serve sth**	[sɜːv]	to bring sb sth	etw servieren
	hectic	[ˈhektɪk]	busy, chaotic	hektisch
	regular	[ˈregjələ]	sb who goes somewhere regularly	Stammkunde/-in
	a real character	[ə ˌrɪəl ˈkærəktə]	sb unique	ein Charakterkopf, ein Unikum
	machine	[məˈʃiːn]	appliance	Maschine, Gerät
	to **bang sth out**	[ˌbæŋ ˈaʊt]	e.g. I have to bang out the cup to make sure it is empty.	etw herausschlagen
	coffee grounds ***pl***	[ˈkɒfi graʊndz]	leftover coffee	Kaffeesatz, Kaffeemehl
	aside from that	[əˌsaɪd frəm ˈðæt]	apart from that	abgesehen davon
	management	[ˈmænɪdʒmənt]	*v* to manage	Geschäftsführung
	media designer	[ˈmiːdiə dɪzaɪnə]	*v* to design media	Mediengestalter/in
	to **turn sth into sth**	[ˈtɜːn ɪntə]	to make sth into sth else	etw zu etw machen
	restoring	[rɪˈstɔːrɪŋ]	*v* to restore	Restaurierung
	to **upcycle**	[ʌpˈsaɪkl]	to make sth old new and better	aufwerten, veredeln, upcyceln
	junk	[dʒʌŋk]	sth nobody wants	Müll
	rubbish	[ˈrʌbɪʃ]	waste	Abfall, Müll
	object	[ˈɒbdʒɪkt]	item	Gegenstand, Objekt
	environment	[ɪnˈvaɪrənmənt]	the atmosphere and things around us	Umwelt
	workshop	[ˈwɜːkʃɒp]	place where things are made	Werkstatt
	through	[θruː]	over, using	durch, über

	to **drop in**	[ˌdrɒp ˈɪn]	e.g. I just dropped in to see how you are.	(bei jdm) vorbeikommen
	occasionally	[əˈkeɪʒənəli]	not very often	gelegentlich
	lack (of sth)	[læk]	not enough of sth	Mangel (an etw)
	by oneself	[baɪ wʌnˈself]	on your own	allein
	except	[ɪkˈsept]	apart from	außer
	delivery guy	[dɪˈlɪvəri gaɪ]	man who delivers things	Zusteller
	to **pick sth up**	[ˌpɪk ˈʌp]	to collect sth	etw abholen
	finished product	[ˌfɪnɪʃt ˈprɒdʌkt]	end product	fertiges Produkt
	worry	[ˈwʌri]	*adj* worried	Sorge
	furniture maker	[ˈfɜːnɪtʃə meɪkə]	sb who makes furniture	Möbelbauer/in
	grid	[grɪd]	table	Raster, Tabelle
	variety	[vəˈraɪəti]	range of different things	Abwechslung
61	**vocational training**	[vəʊˌkeɪʃənl ˈtreɪnɪŋ]	job training	Berufsausbildung
	Things are busy here.	[ˌθɪŋz ɑː ˈbɪzi hɪə]	e.g. There's a lot going on here.	Hier ist eine Menge los.
	plumbing	[ˈplʌmɪŋ]	to do with (water) pipes	Klempnerei, Gas-/Wasserinstallation
	course	[kɔːs]	training	Ausbildung(sgang)
	strict	[strɪkt]	e.g. It's a strict system. You have to do things the right way.	streng
	skilled	[skɪld]	qualified	qualifiziert
	compulsory	[kəmˈpʌlsəri]	<> optional	zwingend (vorgeschrieben), obligatorisch
	joiner	[ˈdʒɔɪnə]	carpenter	Schreiner/in
	to **manage sth**	[ˈmænɪdʒ]	to run sth	etw leiten, etw führen
	unskilled	[ˌʌnˈskɪld]	unqualified	ungelernt, nicht ausgebildet
	to **train sb**	[treɪn]	to teach sb how to do sth	jdn schulen, jdn ausbilden
	quality	[ˈkwɒləti]	*phr* good quality	Qualität
	bank clerk	[ˈbæŋk klɑːk]	sb who works in a bank	Bankangestellte/r
	all the same	[ˌɔːl ðə ˈseɪm]	however, nevertheless	immerhin, dennoch
	to **reinvent oneself**	[ˌriːɪnˈvent wʌnself]	e.g. I'm going to reinvent myself and start a completely new job.	sich neu erfinden
	advantage	[ədˈvɑːntɪdʒ]	benefit	Vorteil
	disadvantage	[ˌdɪsədˈvɑːntɪdʒ]	downside	Nachteil
62	**surprising**	[səˈpraɪzɪŋ]	*v* to surprise	überraschend, erstaunlich
	benefit	[ˈbenɪfɪt]	advantage	Nutzen, Vorteil
	mental	[ˈmentl]	<> physical	mental, geistig
	particularly	[pəˈtɪkjələli]	especially	insbesondere, besonders
	to **find sth**	[faɪnd]	to discover sth	etw herausfinden
	generally	[ˈdʒenrəli]	normally, in general	im Allgemeinen
	researcher	[rɪˈsɜːtʃə]	*v* to research	Forscher/in, Wissenschaftler/in
	inner city	[ˌɪnə ˈsɪti]	close to the middle of a city	Innenstadt
	suburban area	[səˌbɜːbən ˈeəriə]	an area around or on the edge of a city	Vorstadt, Stadtrand
	rural area	[ˈrʊərl eəriə]	not near any towns or cities	ländliches Gebiet
	after-school activities *pl*	[ɑːftə ˌskuːl ækˈtɪvətiz]	sth you do once school is finished	außerschulische Aktivitäten
	dance class	[ˈdɑːns klɑːs]	where you learn how to dance	Tanzkurs
	drama class	[ˈdrɑːmə klɑːs]	where you learn how to act	Schauspielkurs
	to **take part in sth**	[ˌteɪk ˈpɑːt ɪn]	to participate in sth	an etw teilnehmen
	to **prepare sb for sth**	[prɪˈpeə fə]	to get sb ready for sth	jdn auf etw vorbereiten
	world of work	[ˌwɜːld əv ˈwɜːk]	e.g. An apprenticeship prepares you for the world of work.	Arbeitswelt
	to **fit in with sth**	[ˌfɪt ˈɪn wɪð]	to match sth	mit etw übereinstimmen
	recent	[ˈriːsnt]	current, up to date	aktuell
	average	[ˈævərɪdʒ]	normal	durchschnittlich
	amount of time	[əˌmaʊnt əf ˈtaɪm]	length of time	Zeit, Dauer, Zeitaufwand
	to **sink**	[sɪŋk]	to go down	sinken
	to **do exercise**	[duː ˈeksəsaɪz]	to do sport	Sport treiben, sich bewegen
	outside	[ˈaʊtsaɪd]	<> inside	außerhalb von
	effect	[ɪˈfekt]	e.g. What is the effect on the environment?	Auswirkung, Effekt
	educational	[ˌedʒuˈkeɪʃənl]	*n* education	Bildungs-
	concentration	[ˌkɒnsnˈtreɪʃn]	*v* to concentrate	Konzentration
	ability	[əˈbɪləti]	*adj* able	Fähigkeit
	self-confidence	[ˌself ˈkɒnfɪdəns]	*adj* confident	Selbstvertrauen, Selbstbewusstsein
	social skills *pl*	[ˌsəʊʃl ˈskɪlz]	e.g. ability to communicate well etc.	Sozialkompetenz

63	**study**	['stʌdi]	research	Studie
	equally	['iːkwəli]	just as	gleichermaßen, ebenso
	performance	[pə'fɔːməns]	*v* to perform	Leistung, Abschneiden
	to **distract sb from sth**	[dɪ'strækt frəm]	*n* distraction	jdn von etw ablenken
	nearly	['nɪəli]	almost	fast
	to **look at sth**	['lʊk ət]	to study sth	etw untersuchen
	to **lead to sth**	['liːd tə]	to result in	zu etw führen
	planning	['plænɪŋ]	*v* to plan	Planung, Vorbereitung
64	**care assistant**	[ˌkeər ə'sɪstənt]	carer	Pflegeassistent/in
	chimney sweep	['tʃɪmni swiːp]	sb who cleans chimneys	Schornsteinfeger/in
	courier	['kʊriə]	sb who delivers things	Bote/Botin, Zusteller/in
	fire officer	['faɪər ɒfɪsə]	fireman or firewoman	Feuerwehrmann
	tailor	['teɪlə]	sb who makes clothes	Schneider/in
	make-up artist	[ˌmeɪk ʌp 'ɑːtɪst]	sb who does people's make-up	Maskenbildner/in
	market researcher	[ˌmɑːkɪt rɪ'sɜːtʃə]	*n* market research	Marktforscher/in
	veterinary assistant	[ˌvetnri ə'sɪstənt]	sb who helps look after sick animals	tiermedizinische/r Fachangestellte/r
	manual skill	[ˌmænjuəl 'skɪl]	physical skill	handwerkliches Geschick
	numerical skill	[njuːˌmerɪkl 'skɪl]	skill to do with numbers	Zahlenverständnis, Rechenkompetenz
	pile	[paɪl]	e.g. The books were in a pile on her desk.	Stapel
	to **deal**	[diːl]	to hand out cards	(Karten) austeilen, geben
	skill level	['skɪl levl]	e.g. What skill level do you need to be a carpenter?	Kompetenzniveau, -stufe
	to **collect sth**	[kə'lekt]	to gather sth together	etw einsammeln

UNIT 7

65	**goal**	[gəʊl]	sth you aim for	Ziel
	future	['fjuːtʃə]	*n* future	zukünftig
	to **explore sth**	[ɪk'splɔː]	*n* explorer	etw erkunden, etw erforschen
	to **save up**	[ˌseɪv 'ʌp]	to keep money to spend later	sparen
	to **start a family**	[ˌstɑːt ə 'fæmli]	e.g. We started a family after we got married.	eine Familie gründen
	to **predict sth**	[prɪ'dɪkt]	*n* prediction	etw vorhersagen
	to **happen**	['hæpən]	e.g. What happened in the film?	geschehen, passieren
	path	[pɑːθ]	you walk on this next to the road	Weg, Pfad
	to **look forward to sth**	[ˌlʊk 'fɔːwəd tə]	e.g. I look forward to meeting you.	sich auf etw freuen
66	**career plans** ***pl***	[kə'rɪə plænz]	e.g. I talked to my parents about my career plans.	Berufspläne, berufliche Vorstellungen
	convinced (of sth)	[kən'vɪnst]	e.g. He wasn't convinced it was a good idea.	(von etw) überzeugt
	to **laugh at sb/sth**	['lɑːf ət]	*n* laugh	sich über jdn/etw lustig machen, jdn auslachen
	energetic	[ˌenə'dʒetɪk]	*n* energy	tatkräftig, energiegeladen, dynamisch
	interpersonal skills ***pl***	[ˌɪntə'pɜːsənl skɪlz]	e.g. If you can communicate well, you have good interpersonal skills.	soziale Kompetenz
	careers adviser	[kə'rɪəz ədvaɪzə]	e.g. The careers adviser gave him some good advice.	Berufsberater/in
	definitely	['defɪnətli]	e.g. We are definitely getting a new dog tomorrow.	auf jeden Fall, absolut, ganz bestimmt
	ugly	['ʌgli]	<> pretty	hässlich
	with a bad temper	[wɪð ə ˌbæd 'tempə]	e.g. Be careful! Her dog has a bad temper!	jähzornig, aufbrausend
	cute	[kjuːt]	<> ugly	niedlich, süß
	walk	[wɔːk]	*v* to walk	Spaziergang
	fat	[fæt]	<> thin	dick
	to **bark**	[bɑːk]	*n* bark	bellen
	to **get angry**	[ˌget 'æŋgri]	e.g. My dad gets angry when I'm late.	sich aufregen, sich ärgern, böse werden
	dog walker	['dɒg wɔːkə]	sb who takes dogs for walks	jd, der Hunde ausführt
	to **work sth out**	[ˌwɜːk 'aʊt]	e.g. You can work out a fitness plan for me.	etw erstellen
	owner	['əʊnə]	*v* to own	Besitzer/in
	to **trust sb**	[trʌst]	e.g. I trust him to tell me the truth.	jdm vertrauen
	to **respect sb/sth**	[rɪ'spekt]	*n* respect	jdn/etw respektieren

	ad	[ˌeɪˈdiː]	e.g. There was an ad in the newspaper for the new vet.	Werbung, Anzeige, (Werbe-) Aushang
	vet	[vet]	a doctor for animals	Tierarzt/-ärztin
	at the vet's	[ət ðə ˈvets]	e.g. My phone rang when we were at the vet's.	in der Tierarztpraxis, beim Tierarzt
67	to **turn out to be sth**	[ˌtɜːn ˈaʊt tə]	e.g. It turned out to be a wrong number.	sich als etw erweisen, sich als etw herausstellen
	to **succeed**	[səkˈsiːd]	*adj* successful	erfolgreich sein, Erfolg haben
	vocational qualification	[vəʊˌkeɪʃənl kwɒlɪfɪˈkeɪʃn]	e.g. There are vocational qualifications for some jobs.	Berufsabschluss, berufliche Qualifikation
	to **live on sth**	[ˌlɪv ˈɒn]	e.g. We live on the money my mum earns.	von etw leben
	crazy	[ˈkreɪzi]	e.g. It was a crazy idea that we had.	verrückt
	animal shelter	[ˌænɪml ˈʃeltə]	e.g. We got our dog from the animal shelter.	Tierheim
	to **advise sb to do sth**	[ədˈvaɪz tə duː]	*n* advice	jdm (dazu) raten, etw zu tun
68	**unexpected**	[ˌʌnɪkˈspektɪd]	<> expected	unerwartet, überraschend
	career path	[kəˈrɪə pɑːθ]	e.g. I'm not sure which career path to follow.	Berufsweg, beruflicher Werdegang
	smooth(ly)	[smuːð]	<> rough(ly)	reibungslos, glatt
	change	[tʃeɪndʒ]	*v* to change	Veränderung
	to **turn into sth**	[ˈtɜːn ɪntə]	e.g. The idea turned into a new job.	(zu) etw werden, sich in etw verwandeln
	sb realizes sth	[ˈrɪəlaɪzɪz]	e.g. He realized he was going to miss the bus.	jdm wird etw klar, jd stellt etw fest
	pregnant	[ˈpregnənt]	going to have a baby	schwanger
	to **keep sth**	[kiːp]	e.g. I kept the information to myself.	etw behalten
	couple	[ˈkʌpl]	two people who are in a relationship	Paar
	relationship	[rɪˈleɪʃnʃɪp]	e.g. a good relationship, a bad relationship	Beziehung
	to **argue**	[ˈɑːgjuː]	*n* argument	sich streiten
	to **split up**	[ˌsplɪt ˈʌp]	e.g. They split up after three years.	sich trennen
	neither ... nor	[ˌnaɪðə ˈnɔː]	e.g. They were neither happy nor in love.	weder ... noch
	to **drop out of school**	[ˌdrɒp aʊt əf ˈskuːl]	e.g. He dropped out of school when he was 15.	die Schule abbrechen
	depressed	[dɪˈprest]	*n* depression	deprimiert
	reaction	[riˈækʃn]	*v* to react	Reaktion
	strategy	[ˈstrætədʒi]	e.g. We have to come up with a new strategy.	Strategie
	to **make sth up**	[ˌmeɪk ˈʌp]	e.g. Don't believe him. He made the story up.	sich etw ausdenken
	commentary	[ˈkɒməntri]	e.g. sports commentary	(laufender) Kommentar
	to **beat sb**	[biːt]	e.g. The other team beat us.	jdn schlagen
	deal	[diːl]	e.g. He got a good deal when he bought his car.	Angebot, Vertrag
	past sth	[pɑːst]	e.g. Don't just walk past me! Say hello!	an etw vorbei
	waste	[weɪst]	rubbish	Abfall
	to **throw sth away**	[ˌθrəʊ əˈweɪ]	e.g. Throw your rubbish away carefully.	etw wegwerfen
	to **grow sth**	[grəʊ]	e.g. I grew tomatoes in my garden.	(Pflanze:) etw anbauen, etw ziehen
	mushroom	[ˈmʌʃrʊm]	e.g. My favourite pizza has mushrooms on it.	Pilz
	to **do research**	[du rɪˈsɜːtʃ]	e.g. Do some research on the internet!	recherchieren
	cheap	[tʃiːp]	<> expensive	billig
	gourmet	[ˈgʊəmeɪ]	e.g. We had a gourmet meal on my birthday.	Feinschmecker(-), Edel-, Gourmet(-)
	expensive	[ɪkˈspensɪv]	<> cheap	teuer
	community college *AE*	[kəˈmjuːnəti kɒlɪdʒ]	e.g. You can do vocational qualifications at a community college.	zweijährige Berufsschule zur Studienvorbereitung in den USA
	financial	[faɪˈnænʃl]	e.g. financial help, financial advisor	Finanz-, finanziell
	financial adviser	[faɪˌnænʃl ədˈvaɪzə]	e.g. My parents spoke to a financial adviser before they bought a house.	Finanzberater/in
	adult	[ˈædʌlt]	<> child	Erwachsene/r
	to **be friends with sb**	[bi ˈfrendz wɪð]	e.g. Sarah and Anne are friends with each other.	mit jdm befreundet sein
	to **make friends with sb**	[meɪk ˈfrendz wɪð]	e.g. Jack made friends with Mo.	sich mit jdm anfreunden
	to **get one's life back together**	[ˌget wʌnz laɪf ˌbæk təˈgeðə]	e.g. After the accident he had to get his life back together.	sein Leben wieder auf die Reihe kriegen
	hairdresser	[ˈheədresə]	sb who cuts and styles hair	Friseur/in
	assistant manager	[əˌsɪstənt ˈmænɪdʒə]	e.g. He asked the assistant manager for a job.	stellvertretende/r Leiter/in
	to **go wrong**	[ˌgəʊ ˈrɒŋ]	e.g. Everything went wrong at the weekend.	schieflaufen

	to **become ill**	[bɪˌkʌm ˈɪl]	e.g. She became ill and went into hospital.	krank werden
	not any more	[nɒt ˌeni ˈmɔː]	e.g. He doesn't want to go to school any more.	nicht mehr
	plumber	[ˈplʌmə]	sb who repairs pipes and bathrooms	Installateur/in, Klempner/in
	atmosphere	[ˈætməsfɪə]	e.g. There was a funny atmosphere in the room.	Atmosphäre
	to **feel like sth**	[ˈfiːl laɪk]	e.g. I didn't know that I could feel like this.	sich wie etw anfühlen
	to **try hard**	[ˌtraɪ ˈhɑːd]	e.g. If you try hard, you will do well.	sich (sehr) anstrengen
	plumbing company	[ˈplʌmɪŋ kʌmpəni]	where a plumber works	Installateurbetrieb, Sanitärfirma
	success	[səkˈses]	*adj* successful	Erfolg
69	to **learn a lesson from sth**	[ˌlɜːn ə ˈlesn frəm]	e.g. She learnt a lesson from that mistake.	eine Lehre aus etw ziehen
	possibility	[ˌpɒsəˈbɪləti]	*adj* possible	Möglichkeit
	listener	[ˈlɪsnə]	*v* to listen	Hörer/in
	kind	[kaɪnd]	e.g. The woman in the shop was very kind.	freundlich, nett, liebenswürdig
	to **forgive sb**	[fəˈgɪv]	e.g. The teacher forgave her for being late.	jdm verzeihen, jdm vergeben
	to **work out**	[ˌwɜːk ˈaʊt]	e.g. Everything worked out for Dave in the end.	klappen, gut laufen
	to **be afraid of sth**	[bi əˈfreɪd əv]	*adj* afraid	vor etw Angst haben
	to **get worse**	[get ˈwɜːs]	e.g. His cough got worse and he went to see the doctor.	sich verschlimmern, sich verschlechtern
	to **turn one's life around**	[ˌtɜːn wʌnz ˈlaɪf əraʊnd]	e.g. Her mentor helped her turn her life around.	sein Leben umkrempeln
	to **share sth with sb**	[ˈʃeə wɪð]	e.g. She shared her story with her mentor.	jdm von etw erzählen, jdm etw anvertrauen
	to **come up with sth**	[ˌkʌm ˈʌp wɪð]	e.g. Together they came up with a good plan.	auf etw kommen, sich etw einfallen lassen
	perspective	[pəˈspektɪv]	e.g. We have different perspectives on this topic.	Blickwinkel, Sicht, Perspektive
	underdog	[ˈʌndədɒg]	e.g. He was a bit of an underdog, but he won.	Außenseiter/in, Underdog
	to **arrange sth**	[əˈreɪndʒ]	e.g. He arranged a surprise for his parents.	etw organisieren
	to **fall apart**	[ˌfɔːl əˈpɑːt]	e.g. The skirt was so old it fell apart.	auseinanderfallen, sich auflösen
	fight	[faɪt]	*v* to fight	Streit, Schlägerei
	to **get into trouble with sb**	[ˌget ɪntə ˈtrʌbl wɪð]	e.g. The girl got into trouble with her parents.	Schwierigkeiten mit jdm bekommen
70	**fashion**	[ˈfæʃn]	e.g. Fashion really interests me.	Mode, Kollektion
	to **seek sb/sth**	[siːk]	to look for sb/sth	jdn/etw suchen
	reviewer	[rɪˈvjuːə]	*v* to review	Kritiker/in, Rezensent/in
	sample	[ˈsɑːmpl]	e.g. They sent me a sample of the paint.	Muster, Probe
	product line	[ˈprɒdʌkt laɪn]	e.g. This is a very new product line.	Produktlinie
	review	[rɪˈvjuː]	*v* to review	Kritik, Rezension, Besprechung
	payment	[ˈpeɪmənt]	*v* to pay	Bezahlung
	to **be free to do sth**	[bi ˈfriː tə duː]	e.g. You are free to do whatever you want here.	etw tun dürfen/können
	unbiased	[ˌʌnˈbaɪəst]	<> biased	unvoreingenommen, neutral
	tester	[ˈtestə]	*v* to test	Prüfer/in
	cruelty-free	[ˈkruːəlti friː]	e.g. All our products are cruelty-free.	ohne Tierquälerei hergestellt
	carbon neutral	[ˌkɑːbən ˈnjuːtrəl]	e.g. These are carbon neutral products.	CO2-neutral
	sweatshop	[ˈswetʃɒp]	e.g. There are lots of sweatshops in India.	Ausbeuterbetrieb, Sweatshop
	natural fibre	[ˌnætʃrəl ˈfaɪbə]	e.g. Our clothes are made using natural fibres.	Naturfaser
	exciting	[ɪkˈsaɪtɪŋ]	e.g. We had an exciting holiday.	spannend, aufregend
	public relations *pl* **(PR)**	[ˌpʌblɪk rɪˈleɪʃnz]	e.g. I think a job in public relations is exciting.	Pressearbeit
	PR manager	[ˌpiː ˈɑː mænɪdʒə]	e.g. PR managers work long hours.	Pressechef/in
	subject line	[ˈsʌbdʒɪkt laɪn]	e.g. Don't forget the subject line in your email.	Betreff(zeile)
	personality	[ˌpɜːsəˈnæləti]	*adj* personal	Persönlichkeit
	to **fit with sth**	[ˈfɪt wɪð]	e.g. That shirt fits well with those trousers.	zu etw passen
	to **include sth**	[ɪnˈkluːd]	e.g. Include your CV with your application.	etw beifügen, etw einfügen
	to **review sth**	[rɪˈvjuː]	*n* review	etw besprechen, etw rezensieren
	leisure	[ˈleʒə]	e.g. leisure time	Freizeit
	reason	[ˈriːzn]	e.g. Give me a reason why I should do go.	Grund, Motiv
71	to **reply to sth**	[rɪˈplaɪ tə]	*n* reply	auf etw antworten
	reply	[rɪˈplaɪ]	*v* to reply	Antwort
	service	[ˈsɜːvɪs]	e.g. Our service is better than anyone else's.	Dienst
	channel	[ˈtʃænl]	e.g. a TV channel	Kanal
	to **suit sth**	[suːt]	e.g. I think I would suit the job very well.	zu etw passen, sich für etw eignen
	to **feature sth**	[ˈfiːtʃə]	e.g. Our posts feature the latest fashions.	etw vorstellen, etw zeigen

	Yours sincerely,	[ˌjɔːz sɪnˈsɪəli]	sth you write at the end of a letter or email	(Brief, E-Mail) Mit freundlichen Grüßen
	greeting	[ˈgriːtɪŋ]	*v* to greet	(Brief, E-Mail) Anrede
	close	[kləʊz]	*v* to close	(Brief, E-Mail) Schluss, Schlussformel
	Yours faithfully,	[jɔːz ˈfeɪθfəli]	sth you write at the end of a letter or email	(Brief, E-Mail) Mit freundlichen Grüßen
	over to you	[ˌəʊvə tə ˈjuː]	e.g. I have said all I want to, now over to you.	jetzt bist du dran
	content	[ˈkɒntent]	e.g. There is a lot of content in this book.	Inhalt(e)
72	to **manage sth**	[ˈmænɪdʒ]	e.g. We managed to organize our finances.	mit etw zurechtkommen, etw bewältigen
	to **be hopeless with sth**	[bi ˈhəʊpləs wɪð]	<> to be good with sth	mit etw überhaupt nicht zurechtkommen
73	to **keep hold of sth**	[ˌkiːp ˈhəʊld əv]	<> to let go of sth	etw festhalten
74	**cloud**	[klaʊd]	e.g. There are lots of black clouds in the sky.	Wolke
	board	[bɔːd]	e.g. Write the answers on the board.	Tafel, Brett
	adventure	[ədˈventʃə]	e.g. The holiday was a great adventure.	Abenteuer

UNIT 8

75	**summer job**	[ˈsʌmə dʒɒb]	e.g. Sarah got a summer job in a theme park.	Ferienjob
	comic strip	[ˈkɒmɪk strɪp]	e.g. There's a good comic strip in the paper.	Blldgeschichte, Comic
	summer camp	[ˈsʌmə kæmp]	e.g. Paul helped at the summer camp.	Ferienlager
	spoilt	[spɔɪlt]	e.g. My nephew is very spoilt.	(Kind:) verwöhnt, ungezogen
	backstage	[ˌbækˈsteɪdʒ]	e.g. We went backstage after the concert.	hinter der Bühne, backstage
	pros and cons *pl*	[ˌprəʊz ənd ˈkɒnz]	advantages and disadvantages	Für und Wider, Vor- und Nachteile
76	to **get ready (for sth)**	[get ˈredi]	to prepare	sich (für etw) bereit machen, sich (auf etw) vorbereiten
	relative	[ˈrelətɪv]	family member	Verwandte/r
	vacancy	[ˈveɪkənsi]	e.g. a job vacancy	freie/offene Stelle
	to **search for sth**	[ˈsɜːtʃ fə]	to look for sth	(nach) etw suchen
	to **fill sth out**	[ˌfɪl ˈaʊt]	e.g. to fill out a form	etw ausfüllen
	interview	[ˈɪntəvjuː]	*v* to interview	Vorstellungsgespräch
	fundraiser	[ˈfʌndreɪzə]	e.g. There was a fundraiser to raise money.	Spendenbeschaffer/in
	form	[fɔːm]	e.g. I completed a form with my name and address.	Formular
	smart	[smɑːt]	e.g. You should wear smart clothes for an interview.	(Kleidung:) schick, elegant, gepflegt
	to **research sth**	[rɪˈsɜːtʃ]	*n* research	etw recherchieren, Nachforschungen über etw anstellen
	to **review sth**	[rɪˈvjuː]	*n* review	etw überprüfen, etw überarbeiten
	to **prepare sth**	[prɪˈpeə]	*n* preparation	etw vorbereiten
	to **be ready to do sth**	[bi ˈredi tə duː]	to be prepared	bereit sein, etw zu tun
	to **give details**	[ˌgɪv ˈdiːteɪlz]	e.g. Please give us details about the accident.	Einzelheiten mitteilen
77	to **prepare (for sth)**	[prɪˈpeə]	*n* preparation	sich (auf etw) vorbereiten
	since	[sɪns]	e.g. I have been waiting since 3 o'clock.	seit
78	**theme park**	[ˈθiːm pɑːk]	e.g. A new theme park has opened nearby.	Freizeitpark, Themenpark
	to **recruit sb**	[rɪˈkruːt]	e.g. The theme park is recruiting new people.	jdn einstellen
	ride	[raɪd]	e.g. I don't like fast rides.	Fahrgeschäft
	attendant	[əˈtendənt]	*v* to attend	Betreuer/in, Wärter/in
	to **meet sth**	[miːt]	e.g. Did we meet the requirements for the job?	etw (Vorschrift usw.) erfüllen
	height	[haɪt]	e.g. Your height is how tall you are.	Höhe, Größe
	restriction	[rɪˈstrɪkʃn]	*v* to restrict	Beschränkung
	diplomatic	[ˌdɪpləˈmætɪk]	e.g. She was very diplomatic when she asked what had happened.	diplomatisch
	roving	[ˈrəʊvɪŋ]	e.g. a roving photographer	mobil
	photographer	[fəˈtɒgrəfə]	*n* photograph	Fotograf/in
	temporary post	[ˌtemprəri ˈpəʊst]	<> permanent post	befristete Stelle
	for free	[fə ˈfriː]	when sth doesn't cost anything	umsonst
	to **have the time of one's life**	[həv ðə ˌtaɪm əv wʌnz ˈlaɪf]	to have the best time ever	sich großartig amüsieren
	to **appeal to sb**	[əˈpiːl tə]	e.g. This jobs really appeals to me.	jdn ansprechen, für jdn attraktiv sein
	adventurous	[ədˈventʃərəs]	*n* adventure	abenteuerlustig

	beverage	[ˈbevərɪdʒ]	e.g. tea, coffee	Getränk(e)
	food and beverage worker	[ˌfuːd ənd ˈbevərɪdʒ wɜːkə]	sb who makes and sells food and drinks	Gastronomie-Mitarbeiter/in
	varied	[ˈveərid]	e.g. The work is very varied.	abwechslungsreich
	behind the scenes	[bɪˌhaɪnd ðə ˈsiːnz]	e.g. We were allowed to look behind the scenes.	hinter den Kulissen
	rather than	[ˈrɑːðə ðən]	instead of	eher/lieber ... als
	permanent staff	[ˌpɜːmənənt ˈstɑːf]	<> temporary staff	festangestellte Mitarbeiter/innen
	engineer	[ˌendʒɪˈnɪə]	e.g. You have to study to become an engineer.	Techniker/in, Ingenieur/in
	entertainer	[ˌentəˈteɪnə]	*v* to entertain	Unterhaltungskünstler/in
	to **juggle**	[ˈdʒʌgl]	e.g. She can't juggle, she drops the balls.	jonglieren
	to **do magic tricks**	[duː ˌmædʒɪk ˈtrɪks]	e.g. A magician does magic tricks.	zaubern
	to **dress up as sth**	[ˌdres ˈʌp əz]	e.g. The people all dressed up as film stars.	sich als etw verkleiden
	mascot	[ˈmæskət]	e.g. Our soccer team has a bear as its mascot.	Maskottchen
	fun-loving	[ˈfʌn lʌvɪŋ]	e.g. She is fun-loving and has lots of friends.	lebenslustig
	cheerful	[ˈtʃɪəfl]	<> sad	vergnügt, gut gelaunt, fröhlich
	covering letter	[ˈkʌvərɪŋ letə]	e.g. Send a covering letter with your CV.	Anschreiben, Begleitschreiben
	HR department	[ˌeɪtʃ ˈɑː dɪpɑːtmənt]	e.g. Send your application to the HR department.	Personalabteilung
	PO box	[ˌpiː ˈəʊ bɒks]	e.g. A PO box is a box at the post office for letters.	Postfach
	to **wash the dishes**	[ˌwɒʃ ðə ˈdɪʃɪz]	e.g. After a meal you have to wash the dishes.	Geschirr spülen
	to **be tough to please**	[bi ˌtʌf tə ˈpliːz]	e.g. I don't know what to buy him. He is very tough to please.	schwer zufriedenzustellen sein
	to **be on one's feet**	[be ɒn ˌwʌnz ˈfiːt]	e.g. A waiter is on his feet all day.	auf den Beinen sein
	hardly	[ˈhɑːdli]	e.g. A waitress hardly has time to sit down.	kaum
79	**rollercoaster**	[ˈrəʊləkəʊstə]	e.g. Look, there's a new rollercoaster.	Achterbahn
	opposite	[ˈɒpəzɪt]	'hot' is the opposite of 'cold'	Gegenteil, Gegensatz
	nightmare	[ˈnaɪtmeə]	<> dream	Albtraum
	steward ***BE***	[stjuːəd]	sb who works in a bar or a restaurant	Oberkellner/in
	car park attendant	[ˌkɑː pɑːk əˈtendənt]	sb who works in a car park	Parkwächter/in
	nursery assistant	[ˈnɜːsəri əsɪstənt]	sb who works in a play school	Kinderbetreuer/in
	housekeeping assistant	[ˈhaʊskiːpɪŋ əsɪstənt]	sb who works in a hotel	Reinigungskraft, Zimmermädchen
	security guard	[sɪˈkjʊərəti gɑːd]	sb who works in a bank or at a nightclub	Sicherheitskraft
	ticket attendant	[ˈtɪkɪt ətendənt]	sb who checks tickets at the cinema	Kartenabreißer/in, Kartenverkäufer/in
	waiter	[ˈweɪtə]	sb who works in a café or restaurant	Kellner
	waitress	[ˈweɪtrɪs]	sb who works in a café or restaurant	Kellnerin
	to **vote on sth**	[ˈvəʊt ɒn]	e.g. The class voted on the class speaker.	über etw abstimmen
80	to **take a seat**	[ˌteɪk ə ˈsiːt]	to sit down	Platz nehmen
	ordinary	[ˈɔːdnri]	e.g. It was just an ordinary day.	gewöhnlich, normal
	mark	[mɑːk]	e.g. My marks are better than last year.	Note
	challenge	[ˈtʃælɪndʒ]	*adj* challenging	Herausforderung, (schwierige) Aufgabe
	to **be in touch**	[bi ɪn ˈtʌtʃ]	to contact sb	sich melden
	Good luck!	[ˌgʊd ˈlʌk]	e.g. Good luck! Everything will be OK.	Viel Glück! Viel Erfolg!
	sociable	[ˈsəʊʃəbl]	<> antisocial	gesellig, kontaktfreudig
	safety conscious	[ˈseɪfti kɒnʃəs]	*adj* safe	sicherheitsbewusst
	silly	[ˈsɪli]	<> sensible	albern, dumm
	to **put oneself in danger**	[ˌpʊt wʌnself ɪn ˈdeɪndʒə]	to do sth dangerous	sich in Gefahr bringen
	to **be honest**	[tə bi ˈɒnɪst]	to tell the truth	ehrlich gesagt
	to **prefer to do sth**	[prɪˌfɜː tə ˈduː]	e.g. She prefers to play tennis than read.	etw lieber tun
	at least	[ət ˈliːst]	e.g. At least you can help me tidy up.	wenigstens, zumindest
	Not at all.	[ˌnɒt ət ˈɔːl]	e.g. Thank you so much! – Not at all.	Nichts zu danken!
	as soon as	[əz ˈsuːn əz]	e.g. I'll be with you as soon as I finish work.	sobald
	to **get on with sb**	[ˌget ˈɒn wɪð]	e.g. She really gets on with her new colleagues.	mit jdm zurechtkommen, mit jdm auskommen
	drama group	[ˈdrɑːmə gruːp]	e.g. We're doing „Romeo and Juliet" with our drama group at school.	Theater-AG
	charity run	[ˈtʃærəti rʌn]	e.g. There was a charity run to raise money.	Benefizlauf
	right away	[ˌraɪt əˈweɪ]	immediately	sofort
	candidate	[ˈkændɪdət]	sb who applies for a job	Bewerber/in
	to **interview sb**	[ˈɪntəvjuː]	*n* interview	mit jdm ein Vorstellungsgespräch führen

	unclear	[ˌʌnˈklɪə]	<> clear	undeutlich, vage
	strength	[streŋθ]	<> weakness	Stärke
	weakness	[ˈwiːknəs]	<> strength	Schwäche
	weak	[wiːk]	<> strong	schwach
	panel	[ˈpænl]	e.g. There was a panel of three interviewers.	Gremium, (Experten-)Gruppe
	job requirements ***pl***	[ˈdʒɒb rɪkwaɪəmənts]	e.g. what you need to be able to do a job	Stellenanforderungen
	to **vote for sb**	[ˈvəʊt fə]	e.g. Who did you vote for in the elections?	für jd stimmen
81	**personal qualities** ***pl***	[ˌpɜːsənl ˈkwɒlətiz]	e.g. Write your personal qualities on your CV.	persönliche Eigenschaften
	to **look sth up in a dictionary**	[lʊk ˌʌp ɪn ə ˈdɪkʃənri]	e.g. What does it mean? – I don't know. Look it up in a dictionary.	etw im Wörterbuch nachschlagen
	interviewee	[ˌɪntəvjuːˈiː]	*v* to interview	jd, mit dem ein Vorstellungsgespräch geführt wird
	interviewer	[ˈɪntəvjuːə]	*n* interview	jd, der Vorstellungsgespräch führt
	on one's own	[ɒn wʌnz ˈəʊn]	e.g. I stayed at home on my own and my parents went to the concert.	alleine
	suggestion	[səˈdʒestʃən]	*v* to suggest	Vorschlag
82	**composition**	[ˌkɒmpəˈzɪʃn]	e.g. You have to write a composition in the exam.	(kurzer) Aufsatz, Text
	spring	[sprɪŋ]	one of the four seasons	Frühling
	bike ride	[ˈbaɪk raɪd]	e.g. We went for a bike ride with our friends.	Fahrradtour
	emotion	[ɪˈməʊʃn]	e.g. Some people can't show their emotions.	Gefühl, Emotion

Video Wortliste

Video 1

to **go a long way with sth**	[ɡəʊ ə ˌlɒŋ ˈweɪ wɪð]	mit etw weit kommen
area	[ˈeəriə]	Bereich, Gebiet
native language	[ˌneɪtɪv ˈlæŋɡwɪdʒ]	Muttersprache
light blue	[ˌlaɪt ˈbluː]	hellblau
The clue is in the name.	[ðə ˌkluː ɪz ɪn ðə ˈneɪm]	Wie der Name schon sagt.
to **be called**	[bi ˈkɔːld]	heißen
original	[əˈrɪdʒənl]	ursprünglich
complicated	[ˈkɒmplɪkeɪtɪd]	kompliziert
aboriginal language	[æbəˌrɪdʒənl ˈlæŋɡwɪdʒ]	Eingeborenensprache
meaning	[ˈmiːnɪŋ]	Bedeutung
main	[meɪn]	Haupt-

Video 2

whole	[həʊl]	ganze/r/s
sheet (of paper)	[ʃiːt]	Blatt (Papier)
to **panic**	[ˈpænɪk]	in Panik geraten
Don't panic!	[ˌdəʊnt ˈpænɪk]	Keine Panik!
standard	[ˈstændəd]	genormt, Standard-
heading	[ˈhedɪŋ]	Überschrift
employer	[ɪmˈplɔɪə]	Arbeitgeber/in
to **be allowed to do sth**	[bi əˈlaʊd tə duː]	etw tun dürfen
to **look closely at sth**	[ˌlʊk ˈkləʊsli ət]	sich etw genau ansehen
firstly	[ˈfɜːstli]	erstens
application	[ˌæplɪˈkeɪʃn]	Bewerbung
to **try**	[traɪ]	versuchen
instead	[ɪnˈsted]	stattdessen
work-relevant	[ˈwɜːk reləvənt]	arbeitsbezogen, wichtig für die Arbeit
to **raise money for charity**	[reɪz ˌmʌni fə ˈtʃærəti]	Spenden(gelder) sammeln
responsible	[rɪˈspɒnsəbl]	verantwortungsvoll, verantwortlich
personal qualities ***pl***	[ˌpɜːsənl ˈkwɒlətiz]	persönliche Eigenschaften
focused	[ˈfəʊkəst]	konzentriert, zielorientiert
impressive	[ɪmˈpresɪv]	beeindruckend, eindrucksvoll
to **mention sth**	[ˈmenʃn]	etw erwähnen
to **communicate**	[kəˈmjuːnɪkeɪt]	kommunizieren
hands-on	[ˌhændz ˈɒn]	praktisch, praxisbezogen
to **depend on sth**	[dɪˈpend ɒn]	von etw abhängen, auf etw ankommen

Video 3

except	[ɪkˈsept]	außer
pitch	[pɪtʃ]	Fußballplatz, Spielfeld
queue	[kjuː]	Warteschlange
to **form sth**	[fɔːm]	etw bilden
respect	[rɪˈspekt]	Achtung, Respekt
in case	[ɪn ˈkeɪs]	falls; für den Fall, dass
not ever	[nɒt ˈevə]	nie, niemals
obviously	[ˈɒbviəsli]	natürlich, selbstverständlich
to **reply**	[rɪˈplaɪ]	antworten
to **join a company**	[ˌdʒɔɪn ə ˈkʌmpəni]	bei einer Firma anfangen
Good luck!	[ˌɡʊd ˈlʌk]	Viel Glück! Viel Erfolg!
slice of lemon	[ˌslaɪs əv ˈlemən]	Zitronenscheibe
to **mind**	[maɪnd]	etw dagegen haben
to **give sb attention**	[ˌɡɪv əˈtenʃn]	auf jdn achten
specific	[spəˈsɪfɪk]	bestimmt, speziell
occasion	[əˈkeɪʒn]	Anlass, Gelegenheit

Video 4

deadly	[ˈdedli]	tödlich
surf	[sɜːf]	Brandung

shark	[ʃɑːk]	Hai
to **snack on sb**	[ˈsnæk ɒn]	jdn verspeisen
to **watch out for sth**	[ˌwɒtʃ ˈaʊt fə]	nach etw Ausschau halten, auf etw achten
billabong ***AusE***	[ˈbɪləbɒŋ]	Wasserloch, toter Flussarm
tasty	[ˈteɪsti]	lecker
drop	[drɒp]	Fall (aus großer Höhe)
bear	[beə]	Bär
to **exist**	[ɪgˈzɪst]	existieren
to **make sth up**	[ˌmeɪk ˈʌp]	sich etw ausdenken
to **scare sb**	[skeə]	jdn erschrecken
cute	[kjuːt]	niedlich, süß
dangerous	[ˈdeɪndʒərəs]	gefährlich
spider	[ˈspaɪdə]	Spinne

Video 5

to **end up with sth**	[ˌend ˈʌp wɪð]	am Ende etw haben
brief	[briːf]	Anweisung, Vorgabe
resources ***pl***	[rɪˈsɔːsɪz]	Mittel, Ressourcen
theory	[ˈθɪəri]	Theorie
in practice	[ɪn ˈpræktɪs]	in der Praxis
to **grow sth**	[grəʊ]	(Pflanze:) etw anbauen, etw ziehen
to **label sth**	[ˈleɪbl]	etw bezeichnen, etw beschriften

Video 6

It's up to you.	[ɪts ˌʌp tə ˈjuː]	Es liegt ganz an dir.
It doesn't matter.	[ɪt ˌdʌznt ˈmætə]	Es ist egal.
artist	[ˈɑːtɪst]	Künstler/in, Grafiker/in
marker	[ˈmɑːkə]	Filzstift
pen	[pen]	Stift
pencil	[ˈpensl]	Bleistift
bold	[bəʊld]	plakativ, auffallend
to **connect**	[kəˈnekt]	verbinden
whole	[həʊl]	ganze/r/s
original	[əˈrɪdʒənl]	eigene/r/s
thought	[θɔːt]	Gedanke, Idee
to **join sth**	[dʒɔɪn]	etw verbinden
stage	[steɪdʒ]	Phase
to **highlight sth**	[ˈhaɪlaɪt]	etw hervorheben

Video 7

to **generate sth**	[ˈdʒenəreɪt]	etw erzeugen, etw entwickeln
to **pop out**	[ˌpɒp ˈaʊt]	rauskommen
to **free up your mind**	[friː ˌʌp jɔː ˈmaɪnd]	den Kopf freimachen
literally	[ˈlɪtərəli]	im wörtlichen Sinn, wortwörtlich
to **relieve stress**	[rɪˌliːv ˈstres]	Stress abbauen
to **pop into your head**	[ˌpɒp ɪntə jɔː ˈhed]	in den Sinn kommen
irrelevant	[ɪˈreləvənt]	unwichtig, belanglos
to **highlight sth**	[ˈhaɪlaɪt]	etw hervorheben
to **connect**	[kəˈnekt]	verbinden
hopefully	[ˈhəʊpfli]	hoffentlich

Video 8

interviewer	[ˈɪntəvjuːə]	jd, der Vorstellungsgespräch führt
to **talk sb/sth up**	[ˌtɔːk ˈʌp]	jdn/etw anpreisen
seriously	[ˈsɪəriəsli]	im Ernst
comfortable	[ˈkʌmftəbl]	bequem
upright	[ˈʌpraɪt]	aufrecht
enemy	[ˈenəmi]	Feind
candidate	[ˈkændɪdət]	Bewerber/in
hopefully	[ˈhəʊpfli]	hoffentlich

The English alphabet

a	[eɪ]	**h**	[eɪtʃ]	**o**	[əʊ]	**u**	[juː]
b	[biː]	**i**	[aɪ]	**p**	[piː]	**v**	[viː]
c	[siː]	**j**	[dʒeɪ]	**q**	[kjuː]	**w**	[ˈdʌbljuː]
d	[diː]	**k**	[keɪ]	**r**	[ɑː]	**x**	[eks]
e	[iː]	**l**	[el]	**s**	[es]	**y**	[waɪ]
f	[ef]	**m**	[em]	**t**	[tiː]	**z**	[zed]
g	[dʒiː]	**n**	[en]				

Alphabetische Wortliste

Dieses Wörterverzeichnis enthält alle Wörter aus Do it! 2nd Edition in alphabetischer Reihenfolge. Wörter, die in den Audio- und Videotexten vorkommen, sind mit einem T bzw. einem V, Wörter, die in den *Differentiation files* vorkommen, mit einem D und Wörter, die in den *Pairwork files* vorkommen, mit einem P hinter der Seitenzahl gekennzeichnet.

A

ability *62* Fähigkeit; **physical ~** *58* körperliche Fähigkeiten
able, to be ~ to do sth *21P* in der Lage / fähig sein, etw zu tun; etw tun können
aboriginal language *9V* Eingeborenensprache
about, to **be ~ to do sth** *46* etw gleich tun; gerade dabei sein, etw zu tun; im Begriff sein, etw zu tun; to **do sth ~ sth** *56* etw in einer Angelegenheit unternehmen, etw machen
above, high ~ sth *52* hoch über etw
academic *19T* akademisch, theoretisch, praxisfern
academy *20* Akademie
to **accept sth** *18D* etw akzeptieren
accident *21* Unfall
according to *23* laut, gemäß, nach
accurate(ly) *60T* genau, präzise
to **achieve sth** *17* etw erreichen
across *39T* über; to **look out ~ sth** *52* über etw blicken
to **act sth** *29* etw spielen, etw aufführen
action *31* Handlung
activities ***pl*****, after-school ~** *62* außerschulische Aktivitäten
actor *54* Schauspieler/in, Darsteller/in
actually *6* übrigens, wirklich, eigentlich, tatsächlich
ad *66* Werbung, Anzeige, (Werbe-) Aushang; **job ~** *51T* Stellenanzeige, Stellenangebot
to **add: ~ sth** *27* etw hinzufügen; **~ sth up** *51* etw ausrechnen, etw zusamenzählen
to **adjust sth** *48* etw einstellen, etw regeln
administrative *40T* Verwaltungs-
adult *68P* Erwachsene/r
advantage *61* Vorteil
adventure *74* Abenteuer
adventurous *78* abenteuerlustig
advert *46* Werbespot
advertising *53* Werbung
advertisement, job ~ *38* Stellenanzeige, Stellenangebot
advice, to give sb ~ *15* jdn beraten, jdm einen Rat geben
to **advise sb to do sth** *67* jdm (dazu) raten, etw zu tun
adviser, careers ~ *66* Berufsberater/in; **financial ~** *68P* Finanzberater/in
to **afford sb/sth** *56* sich jdn/etw leisten
afraid, to be ~ of sth *69T* vor etw Angst haben
after all *53* schließlich
after-school activities ***pl*** *62* außerschulische Aktivitäten
age *19T* Alter
aged *51* im Alter von
to **agree** *54* sich einig sein; **~ on sth** *44* sich auf etw einigen; **~ (strongly) with sth** *55* einer Sache (voll und ganz) zustimmen; **~ with sb** *5* jdm zustimmen, der gleichen Meinung wie jd sein; **~ with sb's opinion** *31* jds Meinung sein, jds Ansicht teilen
agreement, to reach an ~ *54* eine Einigung erzielen
all, after ~ *53* schließlich; **first of ~** *19T* zuallererst; **not ... at ~** *26* überhaupt nicht; **Not at ~.** *80T* Nichts zu danken!; **~ the same** *61* immerhin, dennoch; **~ day** *56* den ganzen Tag lang;
allowed, to be ~ to do sth *20V, 52* etw tun dürfen
alone *18* alleine
although *46* obwohl
ambassador *38* Botschafter/in
amount of time *62* Zeit, Dauer, Zeitaufwand
and so on *30* und so weiter
angry *25* wütend, zornig; to **get ~** *66* sich aufregen, sich ärgern, böse werden
animal shelter *67* Tierheim
announcement *40T* Durchsage
to **annoy sb** *31* jdn nerven, jdn ärgern
annoying *52* nervig, ärgerlich
another *16* ein/e andere/r/s
to **answer the phone** *10* ans Telefon gehen
antisocial *60T* nicht sozialverträglich
any more *16* weitere; **not ~** *68P* nicht mehr
anyway *32T* sowieso, ohnehin, trotzdem
apart, to keep far ~ from sb *34P* große Distanz zu jdm halten
to **apologize** *29* sich entschuldigen
to **appeal to sb** *78* jdn ansprechen, für jdn attraktiv sein
to **appear in a video** *54* in einem Video auftreten/mitspielen
appearance *34P* Aussehen
application 20V, *38* Bewerbung
to **apply: ~ for sth** *18* sich für/um etw bewerben; **~ sth** *49* etw (Creme usw.) auftragen
appointment *13* Termin
apprentice *10* Auszubildende/r, Lehrling
apprenticeship *16* Lehre, Ausbildung
area *9V, 40T* Bereich, Gebiet; *35* Gegend; **suburban ~** *62* Vorstadt, Stadtrand
to **argue** *68* sich streiten
argument *6* Diskussion, Streit
around *8* ungefähr; **~ sb** *26* in jds Nähe; **~ the corner** *39T* um die Ecke; **~ the world** *8* auf der ganzen Welt; **~ town** *35* in der Stadt
to **arrange sth** *50* etw aufstellen, etw vorbereiten, etw sortieren; *69* etw organisieren
to **arrive** *11* eintreffen, ankommen
arrogant *31* überheblich, arrogant
artist *57V* Künstler/in, Grafiker/in; **make-up ~** *64* Maskenbildner/in
as: ~ soon as *80T* sobald; **~ usual** *30* wie üblich; **~ a result** *60T* demzufolge
aside from that *60T* abgesehen davon
to **ask: ~ for sth** *29* um etw bitten; **~ for directions** *39* nach dem Weg fragen
to **assemble sth** *49* etw zusammensetzen
to **assist sb** *40* jdm helfen, jdm assistieren
assistant *20* stellvertretende/r; *51T* Hilfs-; **housekeeping ~** *79* Reinigungskraft, Zimmermädchen; **nursery ~** *79* Kinderbetreuer/in; **sales ~** *21P* Verkäufer/in; **veterinary ~** *64* tiermedizinische/r Fachangestellte/r; **~ manager** *68P* stellvertretende/r Leiter/in
atmosphere *68P* Atmosphäre
attempt *53* Versuch
to **attend sth** *34* an etw teilnehmen
attendant *78* Betreuer/in, Wärter/in; **car park ~** *79* Parkwächter/in; **ticket ~** *79* Kartenabreißer/in, Kartenverkäufer/in
attention, to attract ~ *29* Aufmerksamkeit erregen; to **give sb ~** *34V* auf jdn achten
attentive, to be ~ to detail *21P* auf Details achten, sorgfältig sein

attitude (to sth) *31* Einstellung, Haltung (zu etw)
to **attract attention** *29* Aufmerksamkeit erregen
attraction, tourist ~ *38* Sehenswürdigkeit
audience *52* Publikum, Zuschauer
audio equipment *51* Tonanlage, Beschallungsanlage
Aussie AusE *36* Australier/in; australisch
authentic *53* authentisch
average *20* Durchschnitt; *62* durchschnittlich
to **avoid** *34* vermeiden, meiden
awareness *34* Bewusstsein, Sensibilität
away, right ~ *80T* sofort
awesome *36* fantastisch, großartig

B

background, ethnic ~ *58* ethnische Herkunft
backstage *75* hinter der Bühne, backstage
bad, to be ~ at sth *7* etw nicht gut können, in etw nicht gut sein; **with a ~ temper** *66* jähzornig, aufbrausend; **That's too ~!** *8* Das ist schade! Zu dumm!
baker *18* Bäcker/in
bakery *20* Bäckerei, Backhandwerk
balance *53* Gleichgewicht
to **bang sth out** *60T* etw herausschlagen
bank clerk *61* Bankangestellte/r
bap, burger ~ *49* Burgerbrötchen
to **bark** *66* bellen
basic *14* grundlegend, wesentlich
basically *60T* eigentlich, im Grunde genommen
bathroom facilities *pl* *41* Sanitäranlagen
beach *36* Strand
bear *36V* Bär
to **beat sb** *68* jdn schlagen
to **become ill** *68P* krank werden
bed and breakfast (B&B) *12* (Frühstücks-)Pension
behaviour *31* Verhalten, Benehmen, Auftreten
behind the scenes *78* hinter den Kulissen
beige *5* beige
bell *29D* Glocke, Klingel
below *6* unten, untenstehend
benefit *62* Nutzen, Vorteil
benefits *pl* *59* Zusatzleistungen
better, to do ~ *58* es besser machen
beverage *78* Getränk(e); **food and ~ worker** *78* Gastronomie-Mitarbeiter/in
bike, dirt ~ *41* Geländemotorrad; **~ ride** *82* Fahrradtour
bill *51* Rechnung
billabong AusE *36V* Wasserloch, toter Flussarm
bin *29D* Mülleimer, Mülltonne
bit, drill ~ *48* Bohrer
board *74* Tafel, Brett
body language *34* Körpersprache
bold *57V* plakativ, auffallend
booking *12* Buchung, Reservierung
boomerang *22* Bumerang
bored *25* gelangweilt; to **be/get ~** *19T* sich langweilen; **sb gets ~ with sth** *18* jdn langweilt etw, jdm geht etw auf die Nerven
boring *16* langweilig
bow *34* Verbeugung
to **bow the head** *34P* den Kopf neigen
to **brainstorm** *24* (Ideen) sammeln
brand *53* Marke
breadwinner *55* Geldverdiener/in
to **break sth** *48* etw kaputt machen, etw zerbrechen
brief *54V* Anweisung, Vorgabe
briefing session *38* Einweisung
bright *52* hell
brilliant *19T* super, toll, klasse
to **bring sth out** *28* etw (hervor) holen
broken *29T* kaputt
brother-in-law *15* Schwager
brush, paint ~ *58* Pinsel
to **build sth** *49* etw bauen, etw aufbauen
builder *50* Bauarbeiter/in
building *35* Gebäude
bullet point *44* (Aufzählungs-)Punkt
burger bap *49* Burgerbrötchen
to **burn** *33T* verbrennen
business *8* Wirtschaft; *40T* Unternehmen, Geschäft; to **start a ~** *16* ein Unternehmen gründen
busy *30* arbeitsreich, betriebsam, hektisch; *38* belebt, verkehrsreich; to **be ~** *51T* viel zu tun haben; **Things are ~ here.** *61* Hier ist eine Menge los.
buzz *60T* Nervenkitzel, Kick
by *29T* neben; **~ oneself** *60T* allein; **~ mistake** *27* aus Versehen; **~ the way** *6* übrigens

C

call *28* Anruf, Telefongespräch
to **call** *19T* nennen; to call sb *11* jdn anrufen; **~ sb back** *10* jdn zurückrufen
called *22* namens; **to be ~** *9V, 36* heißen
calm, to stay ~ *51* die Ruhe bewahren, ruhig bleiben
camera operator *54* Kameramann/-frau
camp, summer ~ *75* Ferienlager
to **cancel sth** *12* etw stornieren, etw absagen
candidate *80T* Bewerber/in
caption *49* Überschrift, Bildunterschrift
car park attendant *79* Parkwächter/in
carbon neutral *70* CO2-neutral
care, to take ~ of sb/sth *54* sich um jdn/etw kümmern; **~ assistant** *21P* Pfleger/in; *64* Pflegeassistent/in; **~ home** *56* Pflegeheim
career *19T* Berufsweg, Laufbahn, Karriere; **~ path** *68* Berufsweg, beruflicher Werdegang; **~ plans *pl*** *66* Berufspläne, berufliche Vorstellungen
careers adviser *66* Berufsberater/in
carefully, to listen ~ *28* aufmerksam zuhören; to **look at sth ~** *49* sich etw genau ansehen; to **open sth ~** *49* etw vorsichtig öffnen
carer *56* Pfleger/in, Betreuer/in
caretaker *41* Hausmeister/in, Verwalter/in
caring *21P* fürsorglich, sozial
to **carry sth** *51T* etw tragen
cartoon *21* Illustration, Karikatur
case, in ~ *34V* falls; für den Fall, dass
cash, to pay ~ *32T* bar zahlen
cathedral *39* Dom, Kathedrale
celebrity *34P* Promi(nente/r)
certificate *20* Zeugnis, Nachweis, Diplom; **school leaving ~** *20* Schulabschluss(zeugnis)
challenge *80T* Herausforderung, (schwierige) Aufgabe
change *12* Änderung; *68* Veränderung
to **change: ~ sth** *12* etw ändern; *19T* etw wechseln; **~ one's mind** *6* es sich anders überlegen, seine Meinung ändern
changing rooms *pl*, female ~ *29T* Damenumkleide
channel *71* Kanal
character, a real ~ *60T* ein Charakterkopf, ein Unikum
charge, to be in ~ of sth *40T* für etw zuständig/verantwortlich sein
charity *19T* wohltätige Zwecke, Hilfsorganisation; to **raise money for ~** *20V, 21* Spenden(gelder) sammeln; **~ run** *80T* Benefizlauf
chart, pie ~ *45* Tortendiagramm
to **chat** *22* sich unterhalten, (miteinander) plaudern
chat *5* Unterhaltung, Gespräch
chatty *26* geschwätzig
cheap *68* billig

to **check** *29* überprüfen, kontrollieren; ~ **sth out** *7* sich etw (genau) ansehen; ~ **in on** *52* einchecken
to **cheer sb up** *15* jdn aufmuntern, jdn aufheitern
cheerful *78* vergnügt, gut gelaunt, fröhlich
chef *18* Koch/Köchin
chemicals ***pl*** *58* Chemikalien
chest *34P* Brust
to **chill out** *26* faulenzen, abhängen, chillen
chimney sweep *64* Schornsteinfeger/in
choice, to make a ~ *46* eine Entscheidung treffen, sich entscheiden
to **choose sb/sth** *29T* jdn/etw auswählen
chuck *48* Bohrfutter
class, dance ~ *62* Tanzkurs; **drama ~** *62* Schauspielkurs
to **clean** *28* reinigen, säubern
clean *28* sauber
cleaner *40* Reinigungskraft
clerk, bank ~ *61* Bankangestellte/r; **ticket ~** *40* Schalterbedienstete/r, Fahrkartenverkäufer/in
clever *27* intelligent, schlau
climate *36* Klima
to **climb** *16* klettern
climbing, rock ~ *16* Klettern
clinic *13* Ambulanz, Klinik
close *71* (Brief, E-Mail:) Schluss, Schlussformel; to **be ~ to sb** *15* jdm nahestehen; to stand **~ to sb** *34P* dicht bei jdm stehen; **~ community** *41* eingeschworene Gemeinschaft
closely, to follow sth ~ *49* sich genau an etw halten; to **look ~ at sth** *20V* sich etw genau ansehen
clothing *28* Kleidung
cloud *74* Wolke
clue: The ~ is in the name. *9V* Wie der Name schon sagt.
coach *19* Trainer/in
to **coach sb** *19T* jdn trainieren
coast *36* Küste
coat (of paint) *49* (Farb-)Schicht, Anstrich
coffee grounds ***pl*** *60T* Kaffeesatz, Kaffeemehl
colleague *30* Kollege/-in
to **collect sth** *64* etw einsammeln
college, community ~ AE *68P* zweijährige Berufsschule zur Studienvorbereitung in den USA; **vocational ~** *20* Berufsschule
colourful *37D* farbenfroh, bunt
to **come up with sth** *69T* auf etw kommen, sich etw einfallen lassen
comfortable *80V* bequem
comic strip *75* BIldgeschichte, Comic

comment *8* Bemerkung, Kommentar; to **make a ~** *30* eine Bemerkung machen
commentary *68* (laufender) Kommentar
commercial *20* gewerblich
common *6* üblich, verbreitet; to **have sth in ~** *26* etw gemeinsam haben
to **communicate 20V,** *51* kommunizieren
communication *28* Kommunikation
communicator, to **be a good ~** *21P* kommunikativ sein
community *25* Gemeinde, Gemeinschaft; **close ~** *41* eingeschworene Gemeinschaft; **~ college** ***AE*** *68P* zweijährige Berufsschule zur Studienvorbereitung in den USA
company *8* Unternehmen, Firma; to **join a ~** *34V* bei einer Firma anfangen
to **compare sth** *7* etw vergleichen
to **complain to sb** *56* sich bei jdm beschweren
to **complete a task** *10* eine Aufgabe ausführen
complicated 9V, *48* kompliziert
component *49* Bauteil
composition *82* (kurzer) Aufsatz, Text
compost *49* Pflanzerde
compulsory *61* zwingend (vorgeschrieben), obligatorisch
concentration *62* Konzentration
concourse *40* Bahnhofshalle
conditions ***pl*****, working ~** *56* Arbeitsbedingungen
confident *27* selbstbewusst, zuversichtlich; to **be ~ around ...** *41* sicher mit Umgang mit ... sein, sich sicher in der Nähe von ... fühlen
to **confuse sb** *30* jdn verwirren
to **connect** *57V* verbinden
conscious, safety ~ *80T* sicherheitsbewusst
contact, eye ~ *34* Blickkontakt
to **contain sth** *58* etw enthlaten
content *71* Inhalt(e)
contractor *40T* Auftragsunternehmen
control, to take ~ *55P* die Führung übernehmen, führen
conversation *11* Gespräch
convinced (of sth) *66* (von etw) überzeugt
to **cook** *49* (Fleisch) braten
to **copy sth** *17* etw abschreiben, etw übertragen, etw kopieren
corner *39T* Ecke; **around the ~** *39T* um die Ecke
counter *40T* Schalter, Tresen
couple *68* Paar; **a ~ of** *39T* ein paar
courier *64* Bote/Botin, Zusteller/in

course *61* Ausbildung(sgang); **intensive ~** *18* Intensivkurs; **three-year ~** *20* dreijährige Ausbildung
to **cover sth** *49* etw bedecken, etw abdecken
covering letter *78* Anschreiben, Begleitschreiben
crazy *67* verrückt
to **create sth** *14* etw erstellen
creative *20* schöpferisch, kreativ
crew *40T* Mannschaft, Team
criticism *21P* Kritik
to **criticize** *15* Kritik üben; **~ sb/sth** *30* jdn/etw kritisieren
to **cross sth** *39T* etw überqueren
crowd *27* Menschenmenge; to **stand out from the ~** *55P* sich von der Masse abheben, auffallen
cruelty-free *70* ohne Tierquälerei hergestellt
customer *20* Kunde/Kundin
cute 36V, *66* niedlich, süß
CV (= curriculum vitae) *18* Lebenslauf

D

daily *9* täglich
dance class *62* Tanzkurs
danger, to put oneself in ~ *80T* sich in Gefahr bringen
dangerous *36V* gefährlich
day, all ~ *56* den ganzen Tag lang; **the other ~** *30* neulich; **Have a lovely ~.** *12* Einen schönen Tag noch!; **All in a ~ work.** *60* Das gehört zum (Arbeits-)Alltag.; **~-to-day operations** ***pl*** *40T* (operatives) Tagesgeschäft
daylight, during ~ hours *38* tagsüber
deadly *36V* tödlich
to **deal** *64* (Karten) austeilen, geben
deal *68* Angebot, Vertrag
dear: Oh ~! *12* Ach du liebe Güte!
to **decide** *18* (sich) entscheiden, beschließen; **~ sth** *54* etw festlegen
decision, to take a ~ *55* eine Entscheidung fällen
definitely *66* auf jeden Fall, absolut, ganz bestimmt
delivery: ~ driver *50* Lieferwagenfahrer/in, (Kraft-)Fahrer/in; **~ guy** *60T* Zusteller
to **demonstrate sth** *49* etw vorführen, etw demonstrieren
department, HR ~ *78* Personalabteilung
to **depend on sth** *20V* von etw abhängen, auf etw ankommen
depressed *68* deprimiert
to **describe** *27* beschreiben

description *27* Beschreibung; **job ~** *51* Stellenbeschreibung, Tätigkeitsbeschreibung
to **design sth** *28* etw gestalten, etw entwerfen
destination *39* Ziel, Zielort
detail, to be attentive to ~ *21P* auf Details achten, sorgfältig sein; to **give ~s** *76* Einzelheiten mitteilen
diagram *11* Grafik, Diagramm
dictionary, to look sth up in a ~ *81* etw im Wörterbuch nachschlagen
to **die** *22* sterben
different *21* verschieden, unterschiedlich
difficult *9* schwierig, schwer
difficulty, learning ~ *16* Lernschwäche
dining table *22* Esstisch
diplomatic *78* diplomatisch
directions ***pl*** *39* Wegbeschreibung; to **ask for ~** *39* nach dem Weg fragen; to **give ~** *38* den Weg erklären
director *54* Regisseur/in
dirt bike *41* Geländemotorrad
dirty *29T* schmutzig, dreckig
disadvantage *61* Nachteil
to **disagree: ~ (with sb)** *5* anderer Meinung (als jd) sein; **~ with sth** *34* mit etw nicht einverstanden sein: **I ~.** *56* Da bin ich anderer Meinung. Das finde ich nicht.
discipline *29T* Disziplin
to **discriminate (against sb)** *58* (jdn) diskriminieren, (jdn) benachteiligen
to **discuss sth** *9* etw besprechen, etw diskutieren
dishes ***pl*****, to wash the ~** *78* Geschirr spülen
dishwasher, to load the ~ *49* die Spülmaschine befüllen
dislikes ***pl*****, likes and ~** *5* Vorlieben und Abneigungen
distance *34* Abstand, Entfernung
to **distract sb from sth** *63* jdn von etw ablenken
DIY *48* Heimwerken, Heimwerker-
to **do: ~ well** *55P* erfolgreich sein, gut abschneiden; **~ better** *58* es besser machen; **~ one's share** *55* seinen Beitrag leisten; **~ sth about sth** *56* etw in einer Angelegenheit unternehmen, etw machen; to **get to ~ sth** *60T* die Möglichkeit haben, etw zu tun; **That won't ~!** *22* Das geht nicht!
doctor *13* Arzt/Ärztin; to **see a ~** *13* zum Arzt gehen
document *21* Schriftstück, Datei, Dokument
dog walker *66* jd, der Hunde ausführt
door, next ~ *32T* nebenan
double room *12* Doppelzimmer
down, to be ~ *15* niedergeschlagen sein, nicht gut drauf sein
downside *60T* Kehrseite, Nachteile
drama: ~ class *62* Schauspielkurs; **~ group** *80T* Theater-AG
to **draw** *24* zeichnen, (Linie) ziehen
drawing *14* Zeichnung
to **dress up as sth** *78* sich als etw verkleiden
to **drill** *48* bohren
drill, electric ~ *48* Bohrmaschine, Akkuschrauber; **~ bit** *48* Bohrer
driver, delivery ~ *50* Lieferwagenfahrer/in, (Kraft-)Fahrer/in; **train ~** *40T* Lokführer/in, Zugführer/in
driving licence *41* Führerschein
drop *36V* Fall (aus großer Höhe)
to **drop: ~ in** *60T* (bei jdm) vorbeikommen; **~ out of school** *68* die Schule abbrechen
dry *36* trocken
duty *51T* Aufgabe, Pflicht
dye *49* Farbe
to **dye sth** *49* etw färben
dyslexic, to be ~ *16* Legastheniker/in sein

E

each other *22* einander
ear protection *48* Gehörschutz
early *22* früh
to **earn sth** *34P* etw verdienen
easily *12* ohne weiteres
eco-friendly *58* umweltfreundlich
education *20* Schulbildung
educational *45* informativ, (weiter) bildend; *62* Bildungs-
effect *62* Auswirkung, Effekt
effective(ly) *51* effektiv, kompetent
either ... or *58* entweder ... oder
electric *58* elektrisch, Elektro-; **~ drill** *48* Bohrmaschine, Akkuschrauber
electrician *50* Elektriker/in
electricity *41* Strom
else, what ~? *14* was (sonst) noch?
emergency *51* Notfall
emotion *84* Gefühl, Emotion
empathetic *21P* einfühlsam, empathisch
to **employ sb** *21* jdn einstellen, jdn beschäftigen
employee *58* Arbeitnehmer/in
employer *20V, 58* Arbeitgeber/in
empty *22* leer
to **end up with sth** *54V* am Ende etw haben
enemy *80V* Feind
energetic *66* tatkräftig, energiegeladen, dynamisch
engineer *78* Techniker/in, Ingenieur/in; **lighting ~** *54* Beleuchter/in
engineering *40T* Technik, Ingenieurwesen
English speaker *9* Englischsprachige/r
to **enjoy: ~ doing sth** *18* etw gern tun; **~ sth** *21* etw genießen; **sb ~s sth** *19T* jdm gefällt etw, jdm macht etw Spaß
entertainer *78* Unterhaltungskünstler/in
entertaining *45* unterhaltsam
entertainment *42* Unterhaltung, Vergnügen
enthusiastic, to be ~ about sth *53* von etw begeistert sein, sich für etw begeistern
entrance *28* Eingang
environment *60T* Umwelt
environmentally friendly *58* umweltfreundlich
equal opportunities ***pl*** *58* Chancengleichheit, Gleichstellung
equally *63* gleichermaßen, ebenso
equipment *28* Geräte, Ausrüstung; **audio ~** *51* Tonanlage, Beschallungsanlage; **medical ~** *51* Medizingeräte; **protective ~** *58* Schutzausrüstung; **sound ~** *50* Beschallungsanlage
essential *41* unerlässlich, unbedingt erforderlich
ethical *58* ethisch (handelnd)
ethnic *34* ethnisch; **~ background** *58* ethnische Herkunft
to **evaluate sth** *51* etw beurteilen, etw einschätzen
even *8* sogar; **~ though** *30* obwohl
event *18* Ereignis; *21* Veranstaltung, Aktion; **~ manager** *51* Veranstaltungsleiter/in; **~ technician** *60T* Veranstaltungstechniker/in
eventually *18* schließlich, am Ende
ever, not ~ *34V* nie, niemals
exam, to fail an ~ *46* bei einer Prüfung durchfallen, eine Prüfung nicht bestehen; to **pass an ~** *47* eine Prüfung bestehen
example, for ~ *8* zum Beispiel
excellent *19T* ausgezeichnet, hervorragend
except 34V, *60T* außer
exception (to a rule) *34* Ausnahme (von einer Regel)
exercise, to do ~ *62* Sport treiben, sich bewegen
excitement *60T* Anspannung, Aufregung
exciting *70* spannend, aufregend
excuse me *29* entschuldigen Sie
exercise *27* Bewegung, Sport
to **exist** *36V* existieren

to **expect sb to do sth** *8* von jdm erwarten, etw zu tun; erwarten, dass jd etw tut
expensive *68* teuer
experience *19T* Erlebnis, Erfahrung(en); **work** ~ *18* Praktikum; *20* Berufserfahrung
to **explain sth** *28* etw erläutern, etw erklären
explanation *48* Erklärung, Erläuterung
to **explore sth** *65* etw erkunden, etw erforschen
expression *10* Ausdruck; *34P* Gesichtsausdruck
eye: ~ **contact** *34* Blickkontakt; ~ **protection** *48* Schutzbrille

F

facilities ***pl*****, bathroom** ~ *41* Sanitäranlagen
to **fail an exam** *46* bei einer Prüfung durchfallen, eine Prüfung nicht bestehen
faithfully: Yours ~**,** *71* (Brief, E-Mail:) Mit freundlichen Grüßen
fake *34P* gekünstelt, künstlich; ~ **news** *7* Falschmeldungen, verdrehte Fakten
to **fall apart** *69* auseinanderfallen, sich auflösen
false *7* falsch, unzutreffend
family, to start a ~ *65* eine Familie gründen; ~ **tree** *15* Stammbaum
famous *36* berühmt, bekannt
far apart, to keep ~ **from sb** *34P* große Distanz zu jdm halten
fashion *70* Mode, Kollektion
fat *66* dick
faulty *58* mangelhaft, defekt
favourite *14* Lieblings-
to **feature sth** *71* etw vorstellen, etw zeigen
to **feel:** ~ **sth about sth** *18* etw von etw halten; ~ **like sth** *68P* sich wie etw anfühlen
female *29T* weiblich; ~ **changing rooms** ***pl*** *29T* Damenumkleide
festival *37D* Fest, Festtag
fibre, natural ~ *70* Naturfaser
fight *69* Streit, Schlägerei
to **fill sth out** *76* etw ausfüllen
filling *30* (Brot-)Belag, Aufstrich, Füllung
film location *54* Drehort
final *29T* letzte/r/s
financial *58* Finanz-, finanziell; ~ **adviser** *68P* Finanzberater/in
to **find sth** *62* etw herausfinden
finished, to have ~ *9* fertig sein; ~ **product** *60T* fertiges Produkt
fire officer *64* Feuerwehrmann
firm(ly) *48* fest
first, at ~ *19T* zunächst, zuerst; ~ **of all** *19T* zuallererst; ~ **name** *34* Vorname
firstly 20V, *29T* erstens
to **fit** *49* passen; ~ **sth** *12* in/zu etw passen; *45* sich für etw eignen; ~ **with sth** *70* zu etw passen; ~ **in with sth** *62* mit etw übereinstimmen; ~ **sth into sth** *48* etw in etw einpassen
fit *51T* gut in Form, fit; to **get** ~ *19T* fit werden
flat *23* Wohnung BE; **shared** ~ *48* Wohngemeinschaft; *36* flach; to **mend a** ~ **tyre** *49* eine Platten flicken; ~**-pack furniture** *48* Selbstbau-Möbel
flexible *51* flexibel
floor *28* Boden
flower bed *51T* Blumenbeet
fluent, to be ~ **in a language** *38* eine Sprache fließend sprechen
focused *20V* konzentriert, zielorientiert
to **follow** *39* folgen; ~ **sth closely** *49* sich genau an etw halten
following *34* folgende/r/s
food: ~ **server** *21* Bedienung, Servierkraft; ~ **and beverage worker** *78* Gastronomie-Mitarbeiter/in
foot: to be on one's feet *78* auf den Beinen sein
force *48* Stärke
foreign *18* ausländisch, fremd
foreign language *20* Fremdsprache
to **forgive sb** *69T* jdm verzeihen, jdm vergeben
forklift operator *50* Gabelstaplerfahrer/in
form *76* Formular
to **form sth** *34V* etw bilden
formal *34P* formell, förmlich
frame, video ~ *49* Videobild
free *33T* kostenlos, gratis; **for** ~ *78* umsonst; to **be** ~ **to do sth** *70* etw tun dürfen/können; ~ **time** *45* Freizeit
to **free up your mind** *69V* den Kopf freimachen
freelance *60T* selbständig
freely *34P* offen, freimütig
fresh water *41* Süßwasser, frisches Wasser
friend, to make ~**s** *18* Feunde finden; to **make** ~**s with sb** *68P* sich mit jdm anfreunden; to **be** ~**s with sb** *68P* mit jdm befreundet sein
friendly, to be ~ **with sb** *31* nett zu jdm sein, mit jdm befreundet sein
fridge *14* Kühlschrank
front, in ~ **of** *34P* vor
full name *13* vollständiger Name
fundraiser *76* Spendenbeschaffer/in
fundraising *21* Mittelbeschaffung, Spendensammeln, Fundraising
fun-loving *78* lebenslustig
funny *27* witzig, lustig
furniture *48* Möbel; **flat-pack** ~ *48* Selbstbau-Möbel; **piece of** ~ *49* Möbelstück; ~ **maker** *60* Möbelbauer/in
furthermore *53* außerdem, darüber hinaus
future *65* zukünftig

G

to **gain sth** *53* etw erwerben, etw erlangen
gap *12* Lücke
garage *10* Kfz-Werkstatt; *60T* Garage
gardener *50* Gärtner/in
gardening *51T* Gartenarbeit, Gärtnern
gender *58* Geschlecht
general *6* allgemein
generally *62* im Allgemeinen
to **generate sth** *69V* etw erzeugen, etw entwickeln
gently *34P* sanft, behutsam
gesture *34P* Geste
to **get:** ~ **up** *19T* aufstehen; ~ **on/off** *40T* ein-/aussteigen; ~ **on with sb** *80T* mit jdm zurechtkommen, mit jdm auskommen; ~ **along with sb** *30* mit jdm (gut) auskommen; ~ to **do sth** *60T* die Möglichkeit haben, etw zu tun; ~ to **know sb** *5* jdn kennenlernen; ~ **sth right** *6* etw richtig machen, etw hinbekommen; ~ **sth wrong** *34* etw falsch verstehen; ~ **worse** *69T* sich verschlimmern, sich verschlechtern; ~ **angry** *66* sich aufregen, sich ärgern, böse werden; ~ **ready (for sth)** *76* sich (für etw) bereit machen, sich (auf etw) vorbereiten
to **give:** ~ **up** *56* aufgeben; ~ **sth up** *47* etw aufgeben; ~ **reasons for sth** *21* etw begründen
gloves ***pl*** *49* Handschuhe
to **go:** ~ **wrong** *68P* schieflaufen; ~ **a long way with sth** *9V* mit etw weit kommen
goal *65* Ziel
good, to be ~ **at sth** *54* etw gut können; **G**~ **luck!** *34V, 80T* Viel Glück! Viel Erfolg!; **G**~ **point.** *19T* Da hast du recht.
goods ***pl*** *40* Ware(n)
gourmet *68* Feinschmecker(-), Edel-, Gourmet(-)
to **grab sth** *48* sich etw schnappen
grade *20* Note
grandparents ***pl*** *19T* Großeltern
grass *51T* Rasen, Gras

to **greet sb** *6* jdn begrüßen
greeting *34* Begrüßung; *71* (Brief, E-Mail:) Anrede
grid *60* Raster, Tabelle
to **grow:** ~ **sth 54V,** *68* (Pflanze:) etw anbauen, etw ziehen; ~ **up** *22* aufwachsen
grumpy *30* mürrisch, schlecht gelaunt
guard, security ~ *79* Sicherheitskraft; **train** ~ *40* Zugbegleiter/in
to **guess** *19T* vermuten; ~ **sth** *37* etw erraten
guy, delivery ~ *60T* Zusteller; ~**s** ***pl*** *6* Leute
gym *35* Fitness-Studio

H

hairdresser *68P* Friseur/in
hand, on the other ~ *53* andererseits; **on the left/right** ~ **side** *39T* links/rechts; **station** ~ ***AusE*** *41* landwirtschaftliche/r Hilfsarbeiter/in; to **shake** ~**s** *34P* sich die Hand geben
to **hand sth out** *34* etw austeilen
handout *34* Arbeitsblatt
handshake *34* Händeschütteln, Handschlag
hands-on *20V* praktisch, praxisbezogen
to **hang sth on a wall** *49* etw an die Wand hängen
to **happen** *65* geschehen, passieren
hard worker *51* fleißige/r Arbeiter/in
hard-working *20* fleißig
hardly *78* kaum
head, to bow the ~ *34P* den Kopf neigen; to **nod one's** ~ *34P* mit dem Kopf nicken; to **pop into your** ~ *69V* in den Sinn kommen
headaches ***pl*** *58* Kopfschmerzen
heading 20V, *28* Überschrift
health *28* Gesundheit
healthy *58* gesund
heart *26* Herz
heavy *51T* schwer
hectic *60T* hektisch
height *78* Höhe, Größe
helpful *30* hilfreich, nützlich
herbs ***pl*** *49* Kräuter
high above sth *52* hoch über etw
to **highlight sth** *57V* etw hervorheben
hint *6* Hinweis, Tipp
to **hire sb** *40T* jdn beauftragen, jdn engagieren
to **hold:** ~ **sth steady** *48* etw festhalten; ~ **a meeting** *57* eine Versammlung abhalten
hold, to keep ~ **of sth** *73* etw festhalten
hole *48* Loch
holiday, working ~ *18* Arbeitsurlaub
home, to leave ~ *22* von zu Hause weggehen
homeless *58* obdachlos
honest *19T* ehrlich; to **be** ~ *80T* ehrlich gesagt
to **hope** *8* hoffen
hopefully *69V* hoffentlich
hopeless, to be ~ **with sth** *72* mit etw überhaupt nicht zurechtkommen
horrible *36* fürchterlich, schrecklich
horse, to ride a ~ *41* reiten
hours ***pl*, working** ~ *19T* Arbeitszeiten
housekeeping assistant *79* Reinigungskraft, Zimmermädchen
housing, insecure ~ *58* prekäre Wohnverhältnisse
HR department *78* Personalabteilung
to **hurt** *13* wehtun; ~ **oneself** *59* sich verletzen; ~ **sb** *30* jdn verletzen
husband *16* (Ehe-)Mann
hygiene *28* Hygiene

I

ID *51* Ausweis
ideal *27* ideal
to **identify sth** *51* etw erkennen, etw identifizieren
ill *13* krank
image, moving ~ *39T* bewegtes Bild, Film
impatient *46* ungeduldig
importance *42* Bedeutung, Wichtigkeit
important (to sb) *14* wichtig (für jdn)
to **impress sb** *55P* jdn beeindrucken
impressive *20V* beeindruckend, eindrucksvoll
to **improve sth** *19T* etw verbessern
to **include sth** *14* etw einbeziehen, etw verwenden; *70* etw beifügen, etw einfügen
independent(ly) *22* unabhängig
individual *55* Einzelperson, Einzelne/r
influence *53* Einfluss
informal *31* zwanglos, informell
ingredients ***pl*** *49* Zutaten
initiative, to use one's ~ *41* Eigeninitiative zeigen
injection *51* Injektion, Spritze
injury *28* Verletzung
inner city *62* Innenstadt
insecure housing *58* prekäre Wohnverhältnisse
to **install sth** *50* etw aufbauen, etw einrichten, etw installieren
instead 20V, *34P* stattdessen
instruction *29* Anweisung, Anleitung; **(set of)** ~**s** ***pl*** *21* Anleitung
instructor *28* Lehrer/in
intensive course *18* Intensivkurs
to **interact with sb** *31* mit jdm kommunizieren, sich mit jdm auseinandersetzen
intercultural *34* interkulturell
interpersonal skills ***pl*** *66* soziale Kompetenz
interview *76* Vorstellungsgespräch
to **interview sb** *80T* mit jdm ein Vorstellungsgespräch führen
interviewee *81* jd, mit dem ein Vorstellungsgespräch geführt wird
interviewer *80V, 81* jd, der Vorstellungsgespräch führt
to **introduce sb/oneself to sb** *6* jdn/sich jdm vorstellen
introduction *54* Einleitung
to **invite sb** *37* jdn einladen
to **involve sth** *51T* etw umfassen, etw einschließen, etw einbeziehen
involved, to be ~ **in sth** *55* an etw beteiligt sein/werden
irrelevant *69V* unwichtig, belanglos
island *41* Insel
item *20* Punkt, Gegenstand; **valuable** ~**s** ***pl*** *29T* Wertgegenstände

J

job, summer ~ *75* Ferienjob; **on the** ~ *50* bei der Arbeit; ~ **ad(vertisement)** *38* Stellenanzeige, Stellenangebot; ~ **description** *51* Stellenbeschreibung, Tätigkeitsbeschreibung; ~ **requirements** ***pl*** *80* Stellenanforderungen; ~ **security** *53* sicherer Arbeitsplatz
to **join:** ~ **sb** *19T* sich jdm anschließen, bei jdm mitmachen; ~ **sth** *57V* etw verbinden; ~ **a company** *34V* bei einer Firma anfangen
joiner *61* Schreiner/in
to **joke** *36* scherzen, Witze machen
to **juggle** *78* jonglieren
junk *60T* Müll

K

to **keep:** ~ **sth** *29T* etw aufbewahren; *68* etw behalten; ~ **to sth** *41* sich an etw halten; ~ **far apart from sb** *34P* große Distanz zu jdm halten; ~ **hold of sth** *73* etw festhalten; ~ **in touch with sth** *33T* auf dem Laufenden über etw bleiben
kind *21* Art; *69T* freundlich, nett, liebenswürdig

to **know: to get to ~ sb** *5* jdn kennenlernen; to **let sb ~ (that ...)** *10T* jdm Bescheid sagen(, dass ...); jdm ausrichten, dass ...

L

to **label sth 54V,** *55* etw bezeichnen, etw beschriften
lack (of sth) *60T* Mangel (an etw)
lady *22* Dame
landscape *50* Landschaft
language, aboriginal ~ *9V* Eingeborenensprache; **body ~** *34* Körpersprache; **foreign ~** *20* Fremdsprache; **native ~** *9V, 20* Muttersprache; **official ~** *8* Amtssprache; to **be fluent in a ~** *38* eine Sprache fließend sprechen
to **last** *58* halten
to **laugh** *34P* lachen; **~ at sb/sth** *66* sich über jdn/etw lustig machen, jdn auslachen
law *51* Gesetz, Recht; **brother-in-~** *15* Schwager
lawnmower *51T* Rasenmäher
lazy *26* faul, träge
to **lead to sth** *63* zu etw führen
to **learn a lesson from sth** *69* eine Lehre aus etw ziehen
learner's permit AE *51T* Lernführerschein
learning difficulty *16* Lernschwäche
least, at ~ *28* mindestens; *80T* wenigstens, zumindest
to **leave sth** *8* etw hinterlassen; *10T* etw liegen lassen, etw vergessen; *28* etw verlassen; **~ home** *22* von zu Hause weggehen; **~ school** *9* von der Schule abgehen, mit der Schule fertig sein, den Schulabschluss machen
leaver, school ~ *40T* Schulabgänger/in
leisure *70* Freizeit
lemon, slice of ~ *34V* Zitronenscheibe
lesson, to learn a ~ from sth *69* eine Lehre aus etw ziehen
to **let sb know (that ...)** *10T* jdm Bescheid sagen(, dass ...); jdm ausrichten, dass ...
letter, covering ~ *78* Anschreiben, Begleitschreiben
level, skill ~ *64* Kompetenzniveau, -stufe
library *35* Bibliothek
licence, driving ~ *41* Führerschein
life, to get one's ~ back together *68P* sein Leben wieder auf die Reihe kriegen; to **turn one's ~ around** *69T* sein Leben umkrempeln; to **have the time of one's ~** *78* sich großartig amüsieren
lifestyle *60T* Lebensweise
light blue *9V* hellblau
lighting *50* Beleuchtung; **~ engineer** *54* Beleuchter/in
likes and dislikes *pl* *5* Vorlieben und Abneigungen
line, product ~ *70* Produktlinie; **subject ~** *70* Betreff(zeile)
to **listen: ~ back** *29* sich etw nochmals anhören; **~ carefully** *28* aufmerksam zuhören
listener *21P* Zuhörer/in; *69T* Hörer/in
literally *69V* im wörtlichen Sinn, wortwörtlich
to **live on sth** *67* von etw leben
lively *34P* lebhaft, lebendig
load *51T* Last
to **load: ~ sth** *40T* etw verladen; **~ the dishwasher** *49* die Spülmaschine befüllen
local *13* örtlich, vor/am Ort, lokal
location *38* Standort; **film ~** *54* Drehort
lock *29T* Schloss
to **lock sth** *52* etw abschließen, etw verschließen
locker *28* Schließfach, Spind
lonely *41* einsam
long: We won't be ~! *46* Wir kommen gleich nach!
to **look: ~ after sb** *22* sich um jdn kümmern; **~ at sth** *63* etw untersuchen; **~ at sth carefully** *49* sich etw genau ansehen; **~ closely at sth** *20V* sich etw genau ansehen; **~ forward to sth** *65* sich auf etw freuen; **~ out across sth** *52* über etw blicken; **~ sth up in a dictionary** *81* etw im Wörterbuch nachschlagen
to **lose** *22* verlieren
loud(ly) *26* laut
love, in ~ *25* verliebt
lovely *48* schön, nett, hübsch; **Have a ~ day.** *12* Einen schönen Tag noch!
luck: Good ~! 34V, *80T* Viel Glück! Viel Erfolg!
luckily *8* glücklicherweise, zum Glück
luggage *40* Gepäck

M

machine *60T* Maschine, Gerät
magic tricks *pl*, to do ~ *78* zaubern
magnetic bag *52* magnetisch abgeschirmte Tasche
main *9V, 40T* Haupt-
to **maintain sth** *51* etw warten, etw instandhalten
maintenance *40T* Instandhaltung, Wartung
to **make: ~ sth up** *36V, 68* sich etw ausdenken; **~ sure** *28* dafür sorgen(, dass ...), sicherstellen(, dass ...)
make-up artist *64* Maskenbildner/in
to **manage sth** *61* etw leiten, etw führen; *72* mit etw zurechtkommen, etw bewältigen
management *60T* Geschäftsführung
manager *56* Leiter/in, Chef/in; **assistant ~** *68P* stellvertretende/r Leiter/in; **event ~** *51* Veranstaltungsleiter/in; **PR ~** *70* Pressechef/in; **props ~** *54* Requisiteur/in; **station ~** *40T* Bahnhofsvorsteher/in
manual skill *64* handwerkliches Geschick
map *36* (Land-)Karte, (Stadt-)Plan
maple syrup *37D* Ahornsirup
to **mark** *41* markieren, kennzeichnen
mark *80T* Note
marker *57V* Filzstift
market researcher *64* Marktforscher/in
maroon *5* kastanienbraun
married *34P* verheiratet
martial arts *pl* *28* Kampfsport
mascot *78* Maskottchen
to **match** *18D* zueinander passen; **~ sth** *25* zu etw passen; **~ sth to sth** *10* etw einer Sache zuordnen
maths *6* Mathe(matik)
to **matter: It doesn't ~.** *57V* Es ist egal.
May I ... *10* Darf ich ...
maybe *26* vielleicht, womöglich
meal *22* Essen, Mahlzeit
mealtime *23* Essenszeit
to **mean** *26* bedeuten, heißen; *46* meinen; **~ to do sth** *56* beabsichtigen, etw zu tun; etw tun wollen; **How do you ~?** *46* Wie meinst du das?
meaning 9V, *41* Bedeutung
mechanic *16* Mechaniker/in
media *pl*, social ~ *14* soziale Medien; **~ designer** *60T* Mediengestalter/in
medical *51* medizinisch; **~ equipment** *51* Medizingeräte
medicine *51* Medikament(e)
to **meet: ~ sth** *78* etw (Vorschrift usw.) erfüllen; **Pleased/Nice to ~ you.** *6* Schön, dich/Sie/euch kennenzulernen.
meeting, to hold a ~ *57* eine Versammlung abhalten
member *23* Mitglied; **~ of staff** *52* Mitarbeiter/in
to **mend a flat tyre** *49* eine Platten flicken
mental *62* mental, geistig
to **mention sth 20V,** *38* etw erwähnen

message, to take a ~ *10* eine Nachricht entgegennehmen, etw ausrichten; **text ~** *27* Textnachricht, SMS
messaging app *33T* Nachrichten-App
methodical, to be ~ *60T* systematisch vorgehen
middle, in the ~ of *19T* mitten in
might: You ~ as well be … *19T* Dann kannst du auch … sein.
milestone *24* Projektabschnitt, Meilenstein
to **mind** *34V* etw dagegen haben; **~ sth** *5* etw gegen etw haben
mind, to change one's ~ *6* es sich anders überlegen, seine Meinung; to **free up your ~** *69V* den Kopf freimachen; **~ map** *55* Mindmap
minded, technically ~ *21P* technisch interessiert/begabt
minority *34* Minderheit
to **miss: ~ sb** *19T* jdn vermissen; **~ sth** *44* etw verpassen
missing, to be ~ *11* fehlen
mistake, by ~ *27* aus Versehen
to **mix sth** *51* etw mischen
mobile (phone) BE *10T* Handy
model, role ~ *15* Vorbild
modest *34P* bescheiden
money, to raise ~ for charity *20V, 21* Spenden(gelder) sammeln; to **save ~** *22* Geld sparen
more, any ~ *16* weitere; **not any ~** *68P* nicht mehr
mostly *56* größtenteils, meistens
to **motivate** *55P* motivieren
motivated *19T* motiviert
to **move** *22* umziehen, (wohin) ziehen; **~ in with sb** *22* zu jdm ziehen, bei jdm einziehen
movement *40* Bewegung
moving image *39T* bewegtes Bild, Film
to **mow** *51T* mähen
mushroom *68* Pilz
musician *51* Musiker/in

N

nail *48* Nagel
name, first ~ *34* Vorname; **full ~** *13* vollständiger Name; **The clue is in the ~.** *9V* Wie der Name schon sagt.
national park *41* Nationalpark
nationality *20* Staatsangehörigkeit
native: ~ language 9V, *20* Muttersprache; **~ speaker** *8* Muttersprachler/in
natural *58* natürlich; **~ fibre** *70* Naturfaser
nearly *63* fast
necessary *47* nötig
need *60T* Bedürfnis
neighbour *40* Nachbar/in
neither … nor *68* weder … noch
nephew *15* Neffe
nervous *25* aufgeregt, nervös
network, train ~ *40T* Bahngesellschaft
news *pl* *33* Nachrichten, aktuelle Meldungen; **fake ~** *7* Falschmeldungen, verdrehte Fakten
next: What ~? *19T* Was kam danach? Und dann?; **~ door** *32T* nebenan
nickname *14* Spitzname, Nickname
niece *15* Nichte
nightmare *79* Albtraum
to **nod one's head** *34P* mit dem Kopf nicken
noisy *23* laut, voller Lärm
non-toxic *58* ungiftig
to **number** *15* nummerieren
numerical skill *64* Zahlenverständnis, Rechenkompetenz
nurse *16* Krankenschwester, Krankenpfleger
nursery assistant *79* Kinderbetreuer/in

O

object *60T* Gegenstand, Objekt
obviously *34V* natürlich, selbstverständlich
occasion *34V* Anlass, Gelegenheit
occasionally *60T* gelegentlich
to **offer: ~ sth** *54* etw anbieten, etw bieten; **~ an opinion** *34P* (s) eine Meinung äußern
office, ticket ~ *40T* Fahrkartenschalter
officer, fire ~ *64* Feuerwehrmann; **police ~** *51* Polizeibeamte/r; **security ~** *50* Sicherheitskraft
official language *8* Amtssprache
on, and so ~ *30* und so weiter
once *17* einmal
to **open sth carefully** *49* etw vorsichtig öffnen
to **operate sth** *40T* etw bedienen
operations *pl*, day-to-day ~ *40T* (operatives) Tagesgeschäft
operator, camera ~ *54* Kameramann/-frau; **forklift ~** *50* Gabelstaplerfahrer/in
opinion *31* Meinung, Ansicht; **in my ~** *56* meiner Meinung/Ansicht nach; to **offer an ~** *34P* (s) eine Meinung äußern; to **give a strong ~** *34P* (s)eine Meinung mit Nachdruck äußern; to **agree with sb's ~** *31* jds Meinung sein, jds Ansicht teilen
opportunity *36* Gelegenheit, Chance; **equal ~ies *pl*** *58* Chancengleichheit, Gleichstellung
opposite *39T* gegenüber (von); *79* Gegenteil, Gegensatz
optional *34P* fakultativ, optional
order *11* Bestellung; *48* Reihenfolge; to **take an ~** *51* eine Bestellung aufnehmen; **in ~ to** *8* um … zu
ordinary *80T* gewöhnlich, normal
organizational *20* organisatorisch, Organisations-
to **organize sth** *21* etw organisieren
organizer *60T* Organisator/in, Veranstalter/in
orientation, sexual ~ *58* sexuelle Orientierung
original *9V* ursprünglich; *57V* eigene/r/s
other, the ~ day *30* neulich; **~ than** *34P* ausgenommen, außer
Outback AusE *36* Hinterland, Busch
outdoor *50* im Freien
outdoors *51T* draußen
outgoing *38* kontaktfreudig
outside *46* (draußen) vor; *62* außerhalb von
over: ~ there *39T* da drüben; **~ to you** *71* jetzt bist du dran
to **overheat sth** *48* etw überhitzen
own, of one's ~ *59* eigene/r/s; **on one's ~** *81* alleine
owner *66* Besitzer/in

P

pack *38* Paket
to **pack sth up** *51* etw zusammenpacken
paint *58* Farbe; **coat of ~** *49* Farbschicht, Anstrich; **~ brush** *58* Pinsel; **~ roller** *58* Farbwalze, Streichrolle
to **paint sth** *41* etw (an)streichen
painting and decorating business *58* Malerei- und Dekorateurbetrieb
pair, in ~s *7* paarweise
panel *80* Gremium, (Experten-)Gruppe
to **panic** *20V* in Panik geraten; **Don't ~!** *20V* Keine Panik!
paramedic *50* Sanitäter
particular *59* bestimmte/r/s, speziell
particularly *62* insbesondere, besonders
part-time *46* Teilzeit(-)
to **pass: ~ sth on** *10T* etw weitergeben; **~ an exam** *47* eine Prüfung bestehen
pass, security ~ *50* Ausweis, (Backstage-)Pass
passenger *40* Fahrgast, Passagier
past *23* Vergangenheit; **~ sth** *68* an etw vorbei
pastry chef *18* Konditor/in
path *65* Weg, Pfad
patient *50* Patient/in

pay *58* Bezahlung, Lohn
to **pay cash** *32T* bar zahlen
payment *70* Bezahlung
pen *57V* Stift
pencil *57V* Bleistift
per year *58* pro Jahr
performance *63* Leistung, Abschneiden
performer *52* Künstler/in
permanent staff *78* festangestellte Mitarbeiter/innen
permission *29* Erlaubnis
permit, learner's ~ *AE* *51T* Lernführerschein
personal *6* privat, persönlich; **~ qualities *pl*** *20V, 81* persönliche Eigenschaften
personality *70* Persönlichkeit
perspective *69T* Blickwinkel, Sicht, Perspektive
to **persuade sb** *18* jdn überzeugen, jdn überreden
phone, mobile ~ *BE* *10T* Handy; to **answer the ~** *10* ans Telefon gehen; **~ call** *28* Anruf, Telefongespräch
phonetics *10* Phonetik
photographer *78* Fotograf/in
physical *34* körperlich; **~ ability** *58* körperliche Fähigkeiten
to **pick: ~ sth** *55* sich etw aussuchen, etw wählen; **~ sth up** *60T* etw abholen
pie chart *45* Tortendiagramm
pile *64* Stapel
pitch *34V* Fußballplatz, Spielfeld
placemat *44* Tischset
plain *32T* einfach, einfarbig, uni
planning *63* Planung, Vorbereitung
plant *51T* Pflanze
to **plant sth** *49* etw pflanzen
platform *40* Bahnsteig
to **please: to be tough to ~** *78* schwer zufriedenzustellen sein
plumber *68P* Installateur/in, Klempner/in
plumbing *61* Klempnerei, Gas-/Wasserinstallation; **~ company** *68P* Installateurbetrieb, Sanitärfirma
PO box *78* Postfach
to **point one's finger at sb** *34P* mit dem Finger auf jdn zeigen
point: Good ~. *19T* Da hast du recht.
police officer *51* Polizeibeamte/r
polite(ly) *21P* höflich
to **pop: ~ out** *69V* rauskommen; **~ into your head** *69V* in den Sinn kommen
popular *8* beliebt
porter *40* Fahrgastbetreuer/in auf dem Bahnsteig
position *20* Stelle, Position
possessions *pl* *28* Habseligkeiten, Sachen
possibility *69* Möglichkeit
post, temporary ~ *78* befristete Stelle
pot *49* Topf
PR manager *70* Pressechef/in
practical *15* praktisch; *54* geeignet, umsetzbar
practice *12* Training, Übung; **in ~** *54V* in der Praxis
to **practise sth** *11* etw trainieren, etw üben
precise *27* genau, präzise
to **predict sth** *65* etw vorhersagen
to **prefer: ~ sb/sth** *27* jdn/etw bevorzugen; **~ to do sth** *80T* etw lieber tun
pregnant *68* schwanger
to **prepare: ~ (for sth)** *77* sich (auf etw) vorbereiten; **~ sb for sth** *62* jdn auf etw vorbereiten; **~ sth** *76* etw vorbereiten
to **present sth to sb** *14* etw jdm vorstellen, etw jdm präsentieren
pressure *21P* Druck
primary school *19T* Grundschule
priority *15* Priorität, Vorrang
probably *8* wahrscheinlich
problem solver *21P* Problemlöser/in
producer *54* Produzent/in
product, finished ~ *60T* fertiges Produkt; **~ line** *70* Produktlinie
professional *53* Profi; *18* professionell; *20* beruflich, berufsbezogen
profile *14* Profil
proper(ly) *56* ordentlich, richtig, sachgerecht
props manager *54* Requisiteur/in
pros and cons *pl* *75* Für und Wider, Vor- und Nachteile
protection, ear ~ *48* Gehörschutz; **eye ~** *48* Schutzbrille
protective equipment *58* Schutzausrüstung
proud *19* stolz
to **provide: ~ sth** *40T* etw bieten, etw zur Verfügung stellen; **~ a service to sb** *56* jdm eine Dienstleistung erbringen
public *35* öffentlich; **~ relations *pl* (PR)** *70* Pressearbeit; **~ transport** *38* öffentliche Verkehrsmittel
purple *5* violett, lila, purpur
to **put: ~ sb through to sb** *10T* (Telefon:) jdn mit jdm verbinden; **~ oneself in danger** *80T* sich in Gefahr bringen

Q

qualification *20* Qualifikation, Abschluss, Ausbildung; **vocational ~** *67* Berufsabschluss, berufliche Qualifikation
qualified *59* qualifiziert, ausgebildet, mit Abschluss
quality *61* Qualität; personal **~ies *pl*** *20V, 81* persönliche Eigenschaften
queue *34V* Warteschlange
quiet *26* ruhig, still
quite *26* ziemlich, ganz; **not ~** *18* nicht ganz, irgendwie nicht; **It's not ~ that simple.** *53* Es ist nicht ganz so einfach.

R

rack *32T* (Kleider-)Ständer, Regal
railway *35* Eisenbahn, Bahn
to **raise money for charity** *20V, 21* Spenden(gelder) sammeln
range, a ~ of ... *41* eine Reihe (von) ...
rank, taxi ~ *35* Taxistand
rather than *78* eher/lieber ... als
raw materials *pl* *58* Rohstoffe
to **reach an agreement** *54* eine Einigung erzielen
to **react (strongly) to sth** *34P* (heftig) auf etw reagieren
reaction *68* Reaktion
ready, to be ~ to do sth *76* bereit sein, etw zu tun; to **get ~ (for sth)** *76* sich (für etw) bereit machen, sich (auf etw) vorbereiten
real *16* wirklich, echt; **a ~ character** *60T* ein Charakterkopf, ein Unikum
reality *53* Wirklichkeit
to **realize: sb ~es sth** *68* jdm wird etw klar, jd stellt etw fest
reason *70* Grund, Motiv; **for no ~** *34P* ohne Grund, einfach so; to **give ~s for sth** *21* etw begründen
receipt *32T* Quittung, Kassenbon
recent *62* aktuell
to **recommend sth** *39T* etw empfehlen
recording *10* Aufnahme
to **recruit sb** *78* jdn einstellen
regular *60T* Stammkunde/-in
to **reinvent oneself** *61* sich neu erfinden
relation, public ~s *pl* (PR) *70* Pressearbeit
relationship *15* Verwandtschaftsverhältnis; *68* Beziehung
relative *76* Verwandte/r
to **relax** *41* sich erholen, sich entspannen
relaxed *46* entspannt, locker
relevant, work-~ *20V* arbeitsbezogen, wichtig für die Arbeit
reliable *20* zuverlässig
to **relieve stress** *69V* Stress abbauen
to **remember** *19T* daran denken; **~ sth** *6* sich an etw erinnern; *31* etw nicht vergessen, an etw denken

to **remind sb about sth** *29* jdn an etw erinnern
to **repair sth** *51* etw reparieren
to **repeat sth** *19T* etw wiederholen
reply *71* Antwort
to **reply to sth 34V,** *71* auf etw antworten
to **report: ~ to sb** *40T* jdm unterstellt sein, jdm unterstehen; **~ back to sb** *9* jdm berichten, jdm Bericht erstatten
request *34P* Bitte, Anfrage
required *51* erforderlich, nötig
requirements *pl*, job ~ *80* Stellenanforderungen
research *53* Recherche, Forschung; to **do ~** *68* recherchieren
to **research sth** *76* etw recherchieren, Nachforschungen über etw anstellen
researcher *62* Forscher/in, Wissenschaftler/in; **market ~** *64* Marktforscher/in
resident *56* Bewohner/in
resort, ski ~ *36* Wintersportort
resources *pl* *54V* Mittel, Ressourcen
respect 34V, *55* Achtung, Respekt
to **respect sb/sth** 31D, *66* jdn/etw respektieren
response *12* Antwort, Reaktion
responsibility *19T* Aufgabe, Verantwortung
responsible *21P* verantwortungsbewusst; 20V, *40T* verantwortungsvoll, verantwortlich; to **be ~ for sth** *29T* für etw zuständig/verantwortlich sein
restoring *60T* Restaurierung
restriction *78* Beschränkung
result *53* Ergebnis, Resultat; **as a ~** *60T* demzufolge
retail *40T* Einzelhandel
review *70* Kritik, Rezension, Besprechung
to **review sth** *70* etw besprechen, etw rezensieren; *76* etw überprüfen, etw überarbeiten
reviewer *70* Kritiker/in, Rezensent/in
ride *78* Fahrgeschäft; **bike ~** *82* Fahrradtour
to **ride** *16* (Fahrrad, Motorrad) fahren; **~ a horse** *41* reiten
right, to get sth ~ *6* etw richtig machen, etw hinbekommen; **~ away** *80T* sofort
to **ring** *29D* läuten, klingeln
risk, security ~ *51* Sicherheitsrisiko
rock climbing *16* Klettern
role *19* Funktion, Aufgabe, Rolle; **~ card** *7* Rollenkarte, Rollenkärtchen; **~ model** *15* Vorbild
to **roll up one's sleeves** *48* die Ärmel hochkrempeln
roller, paint ~ *58* Farbwalze, Streichrolle
rollercoaster *79* Achterbahn
roof *22* Dach
routine *28* Routine
roving *78* mobil
rubbish 29D, *60T* Abfall, Müll; to **be ~** *33T* nichts taugen
rude *30* derb, unfreundlich, unhöflich
rule *28* Regel, Vorschrift; **set of ~s** *28* Regeln; **exception to a ~** *34* Ausnahme von einer Regel
run, charity ~ *80T* Benefizlauf
to **run sth** *54* etw leiten, etw durchführen; *57* (Firma usw.:) etw betreiben, etw führen
rural area *62* ländliches Gebiet

S

sadly *53* leider, bedauerlicherweise
safe(ly) *6* sicher
safety *38* Sicherheit; **~ conscious** *80T* sicherheitsbewusst
sale *50* Verkauf; to **be on ~** *32T* im Angebot sein
sales assistant *21P* Verkäufer/in
same, all the ~ *61* immerhin, dennoch
sample *70* Muster, Probe
sandwich bar *18* Imbiss
to **save: ~ up** *65* sparen; **~ money** *22* Geld sparen
to **scare sb** *36V* jdn erschrecken
scared *25* ängstlich, verängstigt; to **be ~ (of sb/sth)** *26* (vor jdm/etw) Angst haben
scene, behind the ~s *78* hinter den Kulissen
schedule *53* Zeitplan
school, primary ~ *19T* Grundschule; **secondary ~** *19T* weiterführende Schule; to **drop out of ~** *68* die Schule abbrechen; to **leave ~** *9* von der Schule abgehen, mit der Schule fertig sein, den Schulabschluss machen; **after-~ activities *pl*** *62* außerschulische Aktivitäten; **~ leaver** *40T* Schulabgänger/in; **~ leaving certificate** *20* Schulabschluss(zeugnis)
scooter *46* (Motor-)Roller
screen *52* Bildschirm
screw, to tighten a ~ *49* eine Schraube anziehen/festziehen
screwdriver *48* Schraubenzieher
script *54* Drehbuch
to **search for sth** *76* (nach) etw suchen
seat, to take a ~ *80T* Platz nehmen
secondary school *19T* weiterführende Schule
secondly *29T* zweitens
section *54* Abschnitt
security, job ~ *53* sicherer Arbeitsplatz; **~ guard** *79* Sicherheitskraft; **~ officer** *50* Sicherheitskraft; **~ pass** *50* Ausweis, (Backstage-)Pass; **~ risk** *51* Sicherheitsrisiko
to **see: ~ a doctor** *13* zum Arzt gehen; **you ~** *19T* weißt du / wissen Sie
seeds *pl* *49* Samen
to **seek sb/sth** *70* jdn/etw suchen
to **seem** *53* scheinen
to **select sth** *54* etw auswählen
self-confidence *62* Selbstvertrauen, Selbstbewusstsein
self-confident *21P* selbstbewusst
self-starter *55* jd mit Eigenitiative
to **sell sth** *47* etw verkaufen
senior *28* älter, erfahren
sensible *8* vernünftig
sensitive *27* sensibel
separate *40T* gesondert/e/s, eigene/r/s
to **separate sth** *54* etw unterteilen
series *5* Serie
serious *26* ernst
seriously *80V* im Ernst
to **serve: ~ sb** *20* jdn bedienen; **~ sth** *60T* etw servieren
server, food ~ *21* Bedienung, Servierkraft
service *71* Dienst; to provide **a ~ to sb** *56* jdm eine Dienstleistung erbringen
session *6* Veranstaltung; **briefing ~** *38* Einweisung; **training ~** *28* Trainingseinheit
set: ~ of instructions *21* Anleitung; **~ of rules** *28* Regeln
to **set: ~ sth** *53* etw festlegen; **~ sth up** *51* etw aufbauen
several *34* mehrere
sexual orientation *58* sexuelle Orientierung
to **shake hands** *34P* sich die Hand geben
share, to do one's ~ *55* seinen Beitrag leisten
to **share sth** *8* etw gemeinsam haben; *31D, 52* (sich) etw teilen; **~ sth with sb** *69T* jdm von etw erzählen, jdm etw anvertrauen
shared flat *48* Wohngemeinschaft
shark *36V* Hai
sheet (of paper) *20V, 24* Blatt (Papier)
shelter, animal ~ *67* Tierheim
to **shoot** *28* (Film) drehen
shoot *54* Dreh, Filmaufnahmen
shot *52* Aufnahme, Einstellung
to **shut sth** *29* etw schließen, etw zumachen

sick *13* krank, unwohl
side *39T* Seite
sight *36* Sehenswürdigkeit
sign *29* Schild, Hinweis
signaller *40* Fahrdienstleiter/in, Bahnwärter/in
silly *80T* albern, dumm
similar *60T* ähnlich
simple: It's not quite that ~. *53* Es ist nicht ganz so einfach.
since *77* seit
sincerely: Yours ~, *71* (Brief, E-Mail:) Mit freundlichen Grüßen
to **sink** *62* sinken
situation *18* Lage, Situation
size *32T* Größe
ski resort *36* Wintersportort
skiing *36* Skifahren
skill, manual ~ *64* handwerkliches Geschick; **numerical ~** *64* Zahlenverständnis, Rechenkompetenz; **~ level** *64* Kompetenzniveau, -stufe
skills *pl* *12* Kenntnisse, Fertigkeiten; **interpersonal ~** *66* soziale Kompetenz; **social ~** *62* Sozialkompetenz
skilled *61* qualifiziert
to **skim a text** *56* einen Text überfliegen
skin *58* Haut
sky *33T* Himmel
sleeve, to roll up one's ~s *48* die Ärmel hochkrempeln
slice of lemon *34V* Zitronenscheibe
to **slice sth** *49* etw in Scheiben schneiden
smart *76* (Kleidung:) schick, elegant, gepflegt
to **smash sth up** *48* etw zertrümmern
smile *34P* Lächeln
to **smile** *34P* lächeln
smooth(ly) *68* reibungslos, glatt
to **snack on sb** *36V* jdn verspeisen
snake *41* Schlange
snapshot *14* Schnappschuss
so *18* daher, deshalb; **and ~ on** *30* und so weiter
soccer *19T* Fußball
sociable *80T* gesellig, kontaktfreudig
social *45* sozial, gesellig, gesellschaftlich; **~ media *pl*** *14* soziale Medien; μ **skills *pl*** *62* Sozialkompetenz
solution *48* Lösung
to **solve a problem** *56* ein Problem lösen
solver, problem ~ *21P* Problemlöser/in
soon, as ~ as *80T* sobald
sort *40T* Art
to **sound** *36* klingen
sound *51* Klang, Ton; **~ equipment** *50* Beschallungsanlage; **~ engineer** *50* Tontechniker/in
southeast *36* Südosten
space *36* Platz, Raum, Fläche; space *60T* Ort
to **spare sth** *38* etw erübrigen
spare time *45* Freizeit
to **speak: ... ~ing.** *12* (Telefon:) Sie sprechen mit ...
speaker, English ~ *9* Englischsprachige/r; **native ~** *8* Muttersprachler/in
special *16* besondere/r/s
specific *34V* bestimmt, speziell
to **spell** *10T* buchstabieren
spelling *10* Schreibweise, Rechtschreibung
to **spend** *23* (Zeit) verbringen; *57* (Geld) ausgeben; **~ time on sth** *45* Zeit in etw investieren, Zeit für etw aufwenden
spicy *37D* pikant, würzig, scharf
spider *36V* Spinne
to **split up** *68* sich trennen
spoilt *75* (Kind:) verwöhnt, ungezogen
spoken, widely ~ *8* (Sprache:) weit verbreitet
sponsorship *53* finanzielle Unterstützung, Sponsoring
spreadsheet *21* Tabelle, Tabellenkalkulation
spring *82* Frühling
staff *pl* *40T* Personal, Mitarbeiter; **permanent ~** *78* festangestellte Mitarbeiter/innen; **member of ~** *52* Mitarbeiter/in; **~ meeting** *57* Personalversammlung
stage *57V* Phase
to **stand: ~ sth** *5* etw ertragen, etw aushalten; **~ out from the crowd** *55P* sich von der Masse abheben, auffallen; **~ close to sb** *34P* dicht bei jdm stehen
standard *20V* genormt, Standard-
to **start: ~ a business** *16* ein Unternehmen gründen; **~ a family** *65* eine Familie gründen
state *22* Staat, (USA:) Bundesstaat
statement *9* Aussage
station: ~ hand *AusE* *41* landwirtschaftliche/r Hilfsarbeiter/in; **~ manager** *40T* Bahnhofsvorsteher/in; **~ supervisor** *40* Bahnhofs-Chef/in
status *55* Ansehen, Prestige, (soziale) Stellung
to **stay** *12* bleiben, übernachten; **~ up** *46* aufbleiben, wach bleiben; **~ calm** *51* die Ruhe bewahren, ruhig bleiben
steady, to hold sth ~ *48* etw festhalten
to **steal** *46* stehlen, rauben
step *48* Schritt
steward *BE* *79* Oberkellner/in
still *8* nach wie vor, immer noch
store *39* Laden, Geschäft
straight *16* direkt, geradewegs; **~ on** *39T* geradeaus
strange *26* seltsam, komisch
strategy *68* Strategie
strength *80* Stärke
stressed *47* erschöpft, gestresst
strict *61* streng
strong *27* stark, kräftig; *34P* (Händedruck:) fest; (Reaktion:) deutlich
study *63* Studie; **~ group** *6* Arbeitsgruppe
style *29T* Art, Stil
subject *19T* (Schul-)Fach; *34* Thema; **~ line** *70* Betreff(zeile)
suburban area *62* Vorstadt, Stadtrand
to **succeed** *67* erfolgreich sein, Erfolg haben
success *68P* Erfolg
suddenly *7* plötzlich
to **suggest** *36* vorschlagen
suggestion *81* Vorschlag
to **suit sth** *71* zu etw passen, sich für etw eignen
suitable *21* geeignet, passend
summary *20* Zusammenfassung, Kurzdarstellung, Resümee
summer: ~ camp *75* Ferienlager; **~ job** *75* Ferienjob
to **sunbathe** *36* sonnenbaden
to **supervise sb** *40T* jdn (Personal, Mitarbeiter) führen; *56* jdn beaufsichtigen, jdn (als Vorgesetze/r) betreuen
supervisor *38* Betreuer/in, Vorgesetzte/r; **station ~** *40* Bahnhofs-Chef/in
supplier *58* Lieferant/in, Zulieferer
to **support sb/sth** *58* jdn/etw unterstützen
to **suppose** *33T* vermuten, glauben, annehmen
supposed, to be ~ to be *48* etw sein sollen
sure, to make ~ *28* dafür sorgen (, dass ...), sicherstellen(, dass ...)
surf *36V* Brandung
to **surf the internet for information** *45* im Internet nach Informationen suchen
surgery *13* (Arzt-)Praxis
surname *10T* Nachname
to **surprise** *29T* überraschen, erstaunen
surprise *32T* Überraschung
surprised *25* erstaunt, überrascht
surprising *62* überraschend, erstaunlich
survey *35* Umfrage
to **swap** *11* tauschen

sweatshop *70* Ausbeuterbetrieb, Sweatshop
to **sweep** *28* kehren, (aus)fegen
swim, to go for a ~ *41* schwimmen gehen

T

tailor *64* Schneider/in
to **take: ~ sth off** *28* etw (Kleidung usw.) ausziehen; **~ part in sth** *62* an etw teilnehmen
talented *53* begabt, talentiert
to **talk sb/sth up** *80V* jdn/etw anpreisen
to **tap the card** *32T* die Karte kurz auflegen (aufs Lesegerät)
target funding *58* Finanzierungsziel
task, to complete a ~ *10* eine Aufgabe ausführen
tasty *36V* lecker
taxi rank *35* Taxistand
to **teach sb sth** *18* jdm etw beibringen
team leader *20* Teamleiter/in
technically minded *21P* technisch interessiert/begabt
technician, event ~ *60T* Veranstaltungstechniker/in
to **tell sb sth** *10* jdm etw sagen
temper, with a bad ~ *66* jähzornig, aufbrausend
temporary post *78* befristete Stelle
term *6* Trimester
tester *70* Prüfer/in
text (message) *27* Textnachricht, SMS
theme park *78* Freizeitpark, Themenpark
theory *54V* Theorie
there, over ~ *39T* da drüben
thief, thieves *46* Dieb, Diebe; Räuber
though *48* allerdings, jedoch, aber; **even ~** *30* obwohl
thought *57V* Gedanke, Idee
three-year course *20* dreijährige Ausbildung
through *60T* durch, über
to **throw sth away** *68* etw wegwerfen
ticket: ~ attendant *79* Kartenabreißer/in, Kartenverkäufer/in; **~ clerk** *40* Schalterbedienstete/r, Fahrkartenverkäufer/in; **~ office** *40T* Fahrkartenschalter
tidy *28* ordentlich, aufgeräumt
to **tidy up** *28* aufräumen
to **tighten a screw** *49* eine Schraube anziehen/festziehen
timeline *18* Zeitachse, Chronik
time, free ~ *45* Freizeit; **spare ~** *45* Freizeit; **on ~** *30* pünktlich; **part-~** *46* Teilzeit(-); **amount of ~** *62* Zeit, Dauer, Zeitaufwand; **waste of ~** *47* Zeitverschwendung; to **have the ~ of one's life** *78* sich großartig amüsieren; to **spend ~ on sth** *45* Zeit in etw investieren, Zeit für etw aufwenden
timer *49* (Küchen-)Wecker
tired *30* müde, erschöpft
tiring *47* anstrengend, ermüdend
title *16* Titel
tool *49* Werkzeug
topic *34* Thema
touch, to be in ~ *80T* sich melden; **to keep in ~ with sth** *33T* auf dem Laufenden über etw bleiben
to **touch** *34P* berühren
tough, to be ~ to please *78* schwer zufriedenzustellen sein
tourist attraction *38* Sehenswürdigkeit
toxic *58* giftig; **non-~** *58* ungiftig
track *40T* Gleis
trail, walking ~ *41* Wanderweg
train: ~ driver *40T* Lokführer/in, Zugführer/in; **~ guard** *40* Zugbegleiter/in; **~ network** *40T* Bahngesellschaft
to **train sb** *61* jdn schulen, jdn ausbilden
trainee *56* Auszubildende/r
training *20* Ausbildung; **vocational ~** *61* Berufsausbildung; **~ session** *28* Trainingseinheit
to **transmit** *33T* übertragen, senden
transport, public ~ *38* öffentliche Verkehrsmittel
travel *43* Reisen
to **travel** *43* reisen
to **treat** *28* behandeln
treatment *59* Behandlung
tree, family ~ *15* Stammbaum
trip *32T* Reise
trouble *30* Schwierigkeit(en), Problem(e), Ärger; to **get into ~ with sb** *69* Schwierigkeiten mit jdm bekommen
true *7* wahr, zutreffend, richtig
truly *53* wirklich
trust *53* Vertrauen
to **trust sb** *66* jdm vertrauen
to **try** *20V, 30* versuchen; **~ sth** *54* etw ausprobieren; **~ sth on** *32T* etw anprobieren; **~ hard** *68P* sich (sehr) anstrengen; **~ harder** *30* sich mehr bemühen/anstrengen
turn, to be one's ~ *51* an der Reihe sein
to **turn** *48* sich drehen; **~ into sth** *68* (zu) etw werden, sich in etw verwandeln; **~ out sth** *48* sich als etw herausstellen, am Ende etw sein; **~ out to be sth** *67* sich als etw erweisen, sich als etw herausstellen; **~ sth into sth** *60T* etw zu etw machen; **~ sth off** *29T* etw ausschalten, etw ausmachen; **~ left/right** *39T* links/rechts abbiegen; **~ one's life around** *69T* sein Leben umkrempeln
type *26* Art, Typ
typical *18* typisch
tyre *49* Reifen; to **mend a flat ~** *49* einen Platten flicken

U

ugly *66* hässlich
unbiased *70* unvoreingenommen, neutral
unclear *80* undeutlich, vage
underdog *69* Außenseiter/in, Underdog
to **underline** *9* unterstreichen
unexpected *68* unerwartet, überraschend
unfortunately *7* leider, unglücklicherweise
unhappy *19* unzufrieden, unglücklich
uniform *28* (Sport-)Anzug
to **unload sth** *40T* etw abladen, etw entladen
unsafe *58* unsicher, gefährlich
unskilled *61* ungelernt, nicht ausgebildet
until, not … ~ *16* erst
unusual *6* ungewöhnlich, außergewöhnlich
unwell, to be ~ *28* sich nicht wohl fühlen, krank sein
up: It's ~ to you. *57V* Es liegt ganz an dir.
to **upcycle** *60T* aufwerten, veredeln, upcyceln
to **upload sth** *53* etw hochladen
upright *80V* aufrecht
upset *30* aufgebracht, verärgert
urgent *28* dringend
use *8* Verwendung, Gebrauch, Nutzen
to **use one's initiative** *41* Eigeninitiative zeigen
used, sb/sth ~ to be sth *22* jd/etw war früher etw
useful *8* nützlich
usual *26* üblich, normal; **as ~** *30* wie üblich

V

vacancy *76* freie/offene Stelle
valuable items ***pl*** *29T* Wertgegenstände
valuables ***pl*** *28* Wertsachen
van *58* Lieferwagen
variation *34* Abweichung
varied *78* abwechslungsreich
variety *60* Abwechslung

venue *50* Veranstaltungsort
vet *66* Tierarzt/-ärztin; **at the ~'s** *66* in der Tierarztpraxis, beim Tierarzt
veterinary assistant *64* tiermedizinische/r Fachangestellte/r
video frame *49* Videobild
viewer *54* Zuschauer/in
vision *58* Vision
visitor *38* Besucher/in, Gast
visual *54* anschaulich, visuell
vocational: ~ college *20* Berufsschule; **~ qualification** *67* Berufsabschluss, berufliche Qualifikation; **~ training** *61* Berufsausbildung
voicemail *38* Sprachnachricht
voluntary *20* ehrenamtlich; **~ work** *19T* Freiwilligendienst, ehrenamtliche Tätigkeit
volunteer *38* ehrenamtliche/r Helfer/in
to **volunteer** *45* ehrenamtlich tätig sein; ~ to **do sth** *29T* sich bereiterklären, etw zu tun; sich freiwillig melden, etw zu tun
to **vote: ~ for sb** *80* für jd stimmen; **~ on sth** *79* über etw abstimmen

W

wage *58* Lohn
waiter *79* Kellner
waitress *79* Kellnerin
walk *66* Spaziergang; to **go for a ~** *33T* spazieren gehen
walking trail *41* Wanderweg
wall, to hang sth on a ~ *49* etw an die Wand hängen
wanted *38* gesucht
to **warm up** *5* sich aufwärmen
to **wash the dishes** *78* Geschirr spülen
waste *68* Abfall; **~ of time** *47* Zeitverschwendung
to **watch out for sth** *36V* nach etw Ausschau halten, auf etw achten
water, fresh ~ *41* Süßwasser, frisches Wasser
to **wave around one's arms** *34P* mit den Armen fuchteln
way *18* Art (und Weise); **by the ~** *6* übrigens; **out of the ~** *29T* nicht im Weg; to **go along ~ with sth** *9V* mit etw weit kommen
weak *80* schwach
weakness *80* Schwäche
weather *19T* Wetter
welcome: You're ~. *12* Gern geschehen.; **~ to ...** *7* willkommen bei/im/in/zu ...
well: You might as ~ be ... *19T* Dann kannst du auch ... sein.; to **do ~** *55P* erfolgreich sein, gut abschneiden
whether *6* ob
while *22* Weile; *10* während; **for a ~** *56* eine Zeitlang, eine Weile
whole *20V* ganze/r/s; **the ~ of ...** *36* ganz ...
widely spoken *8* (Sprache:) weit verbreitet
wife *10T* (Ehe-)Frau
to **win** *25* siegen, gewinnen
with sb *12* bei jdm
without *22* ohne
to **wonder** *51T* sich fragen, sich Gedanken machen
to **work: ~ on sth** *14* an etw arbeiten; *53* sich mit etw beschäftigen; **~ out** *45* trainieren; *69T* klappen, gut laufen; **~ sth out** *55* etw herausfinden, etw erledigen; *59* etw herausarbeiten; *66* etw erstellen
work, voluntary ~ *19T* Freiwilligendienst, ehrenamtliche Tätigkeit; **All in a day's ~.** *60* Das gehört zum (Arbeits-)Alltag.; **world of ~** *62* Arbeitswelt; **~ experience** *18* Praktikum; *20* Berufserfahrung; **~-relevant** *20V* arbeitsbezogen, wichtig für die Arbeit
worker *30* Arbeiter/in; **hard ~** *51* fleißige/r Arbeiter/in; **food and beverage ~** *78* Gastronomie-Mitarbeiter/in
working conditions ***pl*** *56* Arbeitsbedingungen
working holiday *18* Arbeitsurlaub
working hours ***pl*** *19T* Arbeitszeiten
workplace *58* Arbeitsplatz, Arbeitsstätte
workshop *60T* Werkstatt
world: ~ of work *62* Arbeitswelt; **around the ~** *8* auf der ganzen Welt
worried, to be ~ *18* besorgt sein, sich Sorgen machen
worry *60T* Sorge
worse, to get ~ *69T* sich verschlimmern, sich verschlechtern
wristband *51* Armband
writing *21* (Hand-)Schrift
wrong, to get sth ~ *34* etw falsch verstehen; to **go ~** *68P* schieflaufen

Y

year, per ~ *58* pro Jahr
yet, not ... ~ *36* noch nicht
Yours faithfully/sincerely, *71* (Brief, E-Mail:) Mit freundlichen Grüßen
youth *58* Jugend, Jugendliche

Z

zone *52* Bereich

Irregular verbs

be	was/were	been	*sein*
break	broke	broken	*brechen, kaputt machen*
bring	brought	brought	*bringen*
buy	bought	bought	*kaufen*
choose	chose	chosen	*wählen*
come	came	come	*kommen*
cost	cost	cost	*kosten*
cut	cut	cut	*schneiden*
do	did	done	*tun, machen*
draw	drew	drawn	*zeichen*
drink	drank	drunk	*trinken*
drive	drove	driven	*fahren*
eat	ate	eaten	*essen*
feel	felt	felt	*fühlen*
fight	fought	fought	*(be)kämpfen*
find	found	found	*finden*
forget	forgot	forgotten	*vergessen*
get	got	got	*bekommen*
give	gave	given	*geben*
go	went	gone	*gehen*
hurt	hurt	hurt	*(sich) verletzen*
know	knew	known	*wissen, kennen*
leave	left	left	*(ver)lassen*
lose	lost	lost	*verlieren*
make	made	made	*machen, tun*
meet	met	met	*treffen*
put	put	put	*legen, stellen, setzen*
read	read	read	*lesen*
ride	rode	ridden	*fahren*
run	ran	run	*laufen, rennen*
say	said	said	*sagen*
see	saw	seen	*sehen*
send	sent	sent	*senden*
show	showed	shown	*zeigen*
sing	sang	sung	*singen*
speak	spoke	spoken	*sprechen*
spend	spent	spent	*ausgeben, verbringen*
steal	stole	stolen	*stehlen*
sweep	swept	swept	*fegen*
take	took	taken	*nehmen*
tell	told	told	*erzählen*
think	thought	thought	*denken*
understand	understood	understood	*verstehen*
wake up	woke up	woken up	*aufwachen*
win	won	won	*gewinnen*
write	wrote	written	*schreiben*

Quellenverzeichnis

Cover: Shutterstock.com / FS Stock; **S. 5:** (people) Shutterstock.com / Rawpixel.com; (runner) Shutterstock.com / Panomphon Damri; Cornelsen / D'Avila Illustration Agency; **S. 6:** Shutterstock.com / Prostock-studio; **S. 8:** Shutterstock.com / AJR_photo; **S. 9:** Cornelsen / D'Avila Illustration Agency; **S. 10:** Shutterstock.com / Olena Yakobchuk; **S. 12:** Shutterstock.com / TMA Harding; **S. 13:** Shutterstock.com / Dean Drobot; **S. 15:** (family) Shutterstock.com / Monkey Business Images; (girl) Shutterstock.com / 4 PM production; Cornelsen / D'Avila Illustration Agency; **S. 16:** (1) Shutterstock.com / Olena Yakobchuk; (2) Shutterstock.com / altanaka; (3) Shutterstock.com / loreanto; (4) Shutterstock.com / Nejron Photo; **S. 19:** Cornelsen / D'Avila Illustration Agency; **S. 21:** Cornelsen / D'Avila Illustration Agency; **S. 22:** Shutterstock.com / NeonShot; **S. 24:** Cornelsen / D'Avila Illustration Agency; **S. 25:** (woman) Shutterstock.com / Dean Drobot; (emojis) Shutterstock.com / Magnos Weber; (man) Shutterstock.com / Luis Molinero; Cornelsen / D'Avila Illustration Agency; **S. 26:** Shutterstock.com / Magnos Weber; **S. 28:** Shutterstock.com / Fotokvadrat; **S. 29:** Cornelsen / D'Avila Illustration Agency; **S. 30:** Shutterstock.com / Rawpixel.com; **S. 31:** Cornelsen / D'Avila Illustration Agency; **S. 32:** (1) Shutterstock.com / Iasha; (2) Shutterstock.com / Magdalena Wielobob; (3) Shutterstock.com / Magdalena Wielobob; (St. Patrick's Day) Shutterstock.com / Netkoff; (magnets) Shutterstock.com / gabriel12; **S. 33:** Shutterstock.com / ra2 studio; **S. 35:** (bicycle) Shutterstock.com / Valeriy Velikov; (pool) Shutterstock.com / StockLite; Cornelsen / D'Avila Illustration Agency; **S. 36:** (Didgeridoo) Shutterstock.com / ChameleonsEye; (map) Shutterstock.com / Tupungato; (Koala) Shutterstock.com / Yatra; (Uluru) Shutterstock.com / structuresxx; (Sydney) Shutterstock.com / siwawut; **S. 38:** ©Steve Williams 20190704; **S. 39:** Cornelsen / D'Avila Illustration Agency; **S. 40:** Shutterstock.com / Taras Vyshnya; **S. 41:** (ranger) Shutterstock.com / Sandy Morelli; (island) Shutterstock.com / Melissa Carne; (farm) Shutterstock.com / Leah Kennedy; **S. 42:** Shutterstock.com / TierneyMJ; **S. 43:** (B) Shutterstock.com / JaySi; (C) Shutterstock.com / motive56; (D) Shutterstock.com / Rawpixel.com; **S. 44:** Cornelsen / D'Avila Illustration Agency; **S. 45:** (woman) Shutterstock.com / Milles Studio; (social) Shutterstock.com / america365; (creative) Shutterstock.com / Alona_S; (entertaining) Shutterstock.com / Chinch; (sporty) Shutterstock.com / Roman Borodaev; (educational) Shutterstock.com / VLADGRIN; (what else?) Shutterstock.com / file404; (boy) Shutterstock.com / Take A Pix Media; **S. 46:** Shutterstock.com / James Steidl; **S. 48:** Shutterstock.com / Luca Santilli; **S. 49:** (box) Shutterstock.com / DUO Studio; (screws) Shutterstock.com / Melinda Nagy; (instructions) Shutterstock.com / Gajus; (screwdriver) Shutterstock.com / Stenko Vlad; (painting) Shutterstock.com / Africa Studio; (planting) Shutterstock.com / Ramil Gibadullin; (dyeing) Shutterstock.com / ID stock photography; (burger) Shutterstock.com / MaraZe; **S. 50:** Cornelsen / D'Avila Illustration Agency; **S. 51:** Shutterstock.com / simplerdesign; **S. 52:** Shutterstock.com / Radovancev Zarko; **S. 53:** Shutterstock.com / TuiPhotoEngineer; **S. 55:** (measuring) Shutterstock.com / Dusan Petkovic; (1) Shutterstock.com / fizkes; (2) Shutterstock.com / kamui29; (3) Shutterstock.com / VGstockstudio; (4) Shutterstock.com / Lestertair; (5) Shutterstock.com / Monkey Business Images; (nurse) Shutterstock.com / LightField Studios; **S. 56:** Cornelsen / D'Avila Illustration Agency; **S. 58:** (tools) Shutterstock.com / eelnosiva; (Oz & Simon) Shutterstock.com / loreanto; **S. 60:** (1) Shutterstock.com / Nejron Photo; (2) Shutterstock.com / Mr Twister; (3) Shutterstock.com / Monkey Business Images; (Emily) Shutterstock.com / WAYHOME studio; (Amira) Shutterstock.com / WAYHOME studio; (Luke) Shutterstock.com / Cookie Studio; **S. 62:** (dance) Shutterstock.com / Pressmaster; (basketball) Shutterstock.com / Vasyl Shulga; **S. 64:** Cornelsen / D'Avila Illustration Agency; **S. 65:** (family) Shutterstock.com / Luna Vandoorne; Cornelsen / D'Avila Illustration Agency; (backpacker) Shutterstock.com / Marmolejos; **S. 66:** (dogs) Shutterstock.com / adadem; (woman) Shutterstock.com / Monkey Business Images; (training) Shutterstock.com / Eudyptula; **S. 67:** Shutterstock.com / James Kirkikis; **S. 69:** (Lily) Shutterstock.com / Kseniia Perminova; (Charlie) Shutterstock.com / Chaay_Tee; (Sameen) Shutterstock.com / WAYHOME studio; (Dylan) Shutterstock.com / Dean Drobot; **S. 70:** Shutterstock.com / fizkes; **S. 72:** Shutterstock.com / Iryna Inshyna; **S. 73:** Shutterstock.com; **S. 74:** (travel) Shutterstock.com / Lucky-photographer; (film) Shutterstock.com / kuzmaphoto; (free) Shutterstock.com / HstrongART; (adventure) Shutterstock.com / Duet PandG; (crowd) Shutterstock.com / amasterphotographer; **S. 75:** (hothouse) Shutterstock.com / Iakov Filimonov; (manufacturing) Shutterstock.com / Photographee.eu; Cornelsen / D'Avila Illustration Agency; **S. 77:** (1) Shutterstock.com / addkm; (2) Shutterstock.com / SpeedKingz; (3) Shutterstock.com / Robert Kneschke; **S. 78:** (theme park) Shutterstock.com / Racheal Grazias; (Otmoor Castle) Shutterstock.com / ArtMari; **S. 79:** (Samira) shutterstock.com / Monkey Business Images; (Lars) Shutterstock.com / Rawpixel.com; (rollercoaster) Shutterstock.com / Suz7; **S. 80:** Shutterstock.com / Rawpixel.com; **S. 81:** Shutterstock.com / Antonio Guillem; **S. 82:** Shutterstock.com / matimix; **S. 83:** Shutterstock.com / Susan Montgomery; **S. 84:** (Unit 1) Shutterstock.com / Prostock-studio; (Unit 2) Shutterstock.com / Nejron Photo; (Unit 3) Shutterstock.com / AJR_photo; (Unit 4) Shutterstock.com / Tupungato; (Unit 8) Shutterstock.com / ArtMari; Cornelsen / D'Avila Illustration Agency; **S. 85:** Shutterstock.com / Sapihens; **S. 87:** (1) Shutterstock.com / Ramon Carretero; (2) Shutterstock.com / Ken Griffiths; (3) Shutterstock.com / TheHighestQualityImages; (4) Shutterstock.com / Gekko Gallery; (5) Shutterstock.com/Tap10; (6) Shutterstock.com / simon berenyi; **S. 88:** (1) Shutterstock.com / OSTILL is Franck Camhi; (2) Shutterstock.com / Morakot Kawinchan; (3) Shutterstock.com / Shirstok; **S. 89:** Cornelsen / D'Avila Illustration Agency; **S. 90:** Cornelsen / D'Avila Illustration Agency; **S. 91:** Cornelsen / D'Avila Illustration Agency; **S. 92:** Cornelsen / D'Avila Illustration Agency

INDONESIA
EAST TIMOR
INDONESIA
PAPUA NEW GUINEA
Darwin
Cairns
NORTHERN TERRITORY
QUEENSLAND
Alice Springs
Uluru
WESTERN AUSTRALIA
SOUTH AUSTRALIA
Brisbane
NEW SOUTH WALES
Perth
Adelaide
Sydney
Canberra
VICTORIA
Melbourne
TASMANIA
Hobart